Microcomputer Design

MICROCOMPUTER DESIGN

CAROL ANNE OGDIN

Software Techniques, Inc.
Alexandria, Virginia

Prentice-Hall, Inc., Englewood Cliffs, N.J. 07632

Library of Congress Cataloging in Publication Data

OGDIN, CAROL ANNE, *(date)*
Microcomputer design.

"About two-thirds of this manuscript originally appeared in EDN magazine's third annual microprocessor reference issue, November 20, 1976."

Includes index.

1. Microcomputers—Design and construction.
I. EDN. II. Title.
TK7888.3.033 621.3819'58'2 78-2766
ISBN 0-13-580977-0
ISBN 0-13-580985-1 pbk.

Printed in the United States of America

10 9 8 7 6

PRENTICE-HALL INTERNATIONAL, INC., *London*
PRENTICE-HALL OF AUSTRALIA PTY. LIMITED, *Sydney*
PRENTICE-HALL OF CANADA, LTD., *Toronto*
PRENTICE-HALL OF INDIA PRIVATE LIMITED, *New Delhi*
PRENTICE-HALL OF JAPAN, INC., *Tokyo*
PRENTICE-HALL OF SOUTHEAST ASIA PTE. LTD., *Singapore*
WHITEHALL BOOKS LIMITED, *Wellington, New Zealand*

To Elisabeth—
Celebrated ...

Contents

Preface

This book is different. It assumes that you are about to design a microcomputer, and anticipates your questions. It shows how other designers have successfully applied microcomputers and microprocessors in the past, and how their experience can be used in your daily work. There is little theory here, only practical techniques and guidance. And the emphasis is on how to *use* microprocessors, not on the details of how they work or are made.

The electronics and computer press have already produced many books on micros—do we need another one? Few of the books published to date have been based on actual experience of real designers—this book is a definite exception. Furthermore, this book has already been "field tested" in part. About two-thirds of this manuscript originally appeared in *EDN* magazine's "Third Annual Microprocessor Reference Issue," November 20, 1976. Several hundred readers responded with comments on the course contents—all of them favorable. This original publication was submitted as a candidate for the coveted Jesse Neale award of the business press.

The real purpose of this book, however, is not to merely reprint a highly successful series of articles, but to add to the constructive literature of this dynamic field. I have as my intent to show the designer who is already comfortable with the design of conventional digital logic systems how to use micros for better design results. Most readers will have already learned TTL or CMOS well, but have never been exposed to computers or programming. In this book, I have endeavored to show that the very principles that competent designers used with digital logic are still applicable in the new age of micros to solve more interesting and difficult problems. Furthermore, it is my conviction that software is merely another digital design discipline, albeit wrapped up in a new set of symbols and a novel vocabulary.

The book is arranged into a logical progression of eleven chapters, from fundamentals to sophisticated detail.

Chapter 1 reviews the basic notion of computers to establish a rationale for what follows. By starting with basic principles, the reader will find that the design details that follow in subsequent chapters will be easier to place in perspective. Computers are nothing more than digital logic systems without an intrinsic application. By applying the principles that all competent digital designers already know, we establish a known departure point for the rest of the book.

Chapter 2 shows how the basic elements of a microcomputer are tied together. The data, address and control buses are the heart of any computer design, and are explained in overall generalities. The timing of events on the buses is important, too, and is discussed along with clockery.

The use of a microcomputer usually requires some hands-on experience; *Chapter 3* points out some of the features to look for in a learning tool the designer might acquire to gain the essential experience.

From *Chapter 4* onward, chapters alternate between hardware or circuit-related issues and software or programming topics. The first topic in software must be how instructions actually work inside the computer, and that is the topic of Chapter 4. This chapter explains how all common micros operate and how to evaluate and understand new microprocessors that are bound to be introduced after this book goes to press. The usage of the hardware resources of instructions in the construction of small programs is the key application topic discussed here.

Computers need memory, and memories are discussed in *Chapter 5.* Only those memory devices used in practical designs are considered for discussion, rather than a general treatment of all possible memories. Again, the emphasis in this chapter is on how to use available inexpensive memory parts to store data and programs, along with the practical problems of buffering and address decoding.

The *use* of memory is a software and programming topic, and is the subject of *Chapter 6.* After programming for nearly two decades, I've come to the conclusion that most good designs are characterized by well-designed memory usage patterns *before* programming. In this chapter, I show you how it can be done effectively. The solution of some novel design problems are explained in sufficient detail to allow the reader to duplicate the concepts in other application areas.

Chapter 7 discusses the ins and outs of input/output design. Whereas microcomputers make a lot of the digital circuit designers skills obsolete, input/output circuitry challenges even the most creative designer. A summary of all possible ways to perform input/output data transfers between a microcomputer and some external equipment is followed by some specific design solutions for difficult problems.

The input/output hardware needs software to make it function, and that software is described in *Chapter 8.* The software required to manage a complex computer configuration with multiple input/output devices, all of which impose real-time demands, can be designed logically, as this material shows. Specifically, the handling of interrupts and the controlling of time-critical events is treated as just another set of engineering options.

With both hardware and software as critical required components of microcomputer systems, tradeoff between the two becomes important; that is the subject of *Chapter 9.* By seeing several examples of hardware-oriented versus software-oriented designs to accomplish the same function, the reader can gain some insight into how other designers have solved some of these problems.

Chapter 10 addresses the features of the tools used in software development, including assemblers, compilers, editors and their respective languages.

Finally, microcomputer projects—like all projects—need to be managed, and those management issues are raised in *Chapter 11.* The text ''walks through'' a typical project, illustrating the resources required, the potential problems and their cures at each stage of progress.

All of these chapters describe techniques that designers like me use every day. I hope you, too, will find them useful and practical. Once you've grasped the concepts laid out in this book, I'm certain that you will find the joy and pleasure that can come from producing well-structured designs without undue complexity.

CAROL ANNE OGDIN
Alexandria, Virginia

Microcomputer Design

1

Processor Prelude

All too often novice microprocessor users leap directly to the manufacturer's manual to learn all about how a microprocessor works. And, sadly, all too often they become terribly confused.

It is important to establish a "matrix" of understanding into which you can cast each new processor. Before embarking upon our detailed education course on microprocessors, then, it is important to lay the groundwork.

Nothing that is presented in this section is new. However, it is an approach to understanding computers that is seldom taught. Since you, the reader, are expected to understand the elements of digital systems design, a brief review of basic principles should make it easy for you to absorb the rest of this book.

The Basic Element

The most elementary component of any digital system, whether general-purpose computer or special-purpose circuitry, is the *register.* A register is a physical device that can hold a *value,* usually expressed as a number. In its simplest form, a register may be no more than a single wire; that register is capable of representing one bit of information. A more common kind of register is made up of a rank of parallel latches (Figure 1.1); it is capable of representing a number in the range from 0 to $2^N - 1$, where N is the number of latches in parallel. A *clock* signals when the register should record the input; the last-latched data always appears at the output.

It has been proven in the technical literature that all digital systems can be designed as a set of interconnected registers. The required behavior of the system

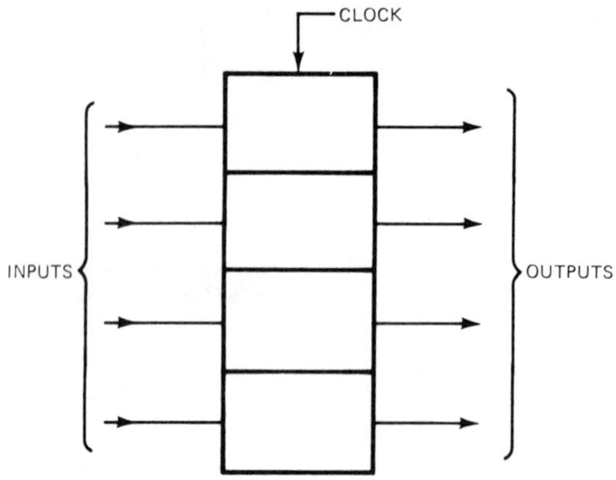

Figure 1.1 A four-bit register composed of latches.

is then created by selectively transferring the contents of one register to another, step by step. In fact, the DEC PDP–15 is based on this concept. Using modules called Register Transfer Modules, the designer can create almost any kind of digital system.

Data can be transformed through some kinds of registers. In the simplest case, in Figure 1.2, consider the parallel shift register. It may be made up of a complex group of multiplexers or just a few wires, but data placed into the register is modified before it can be read back out. This is the means by which data can be manipulated and changed from one form into another. This simple example also points up another property of register transfers: The details of the operation may vary from application to application. When the data placed into a register is shifted "left" one place, what happens to the most-significant bit? And what is inserted into the vacated least-significant bit? If it is fed back around into the least-significant bit position, that is called the *rotation* operation. In other designs the most-significant bit is shifted out and lost. In still different designs the least-significant bit position is cleared to zero or left at its original input value. Note that for this simple example of a register there are many, many subtle variations

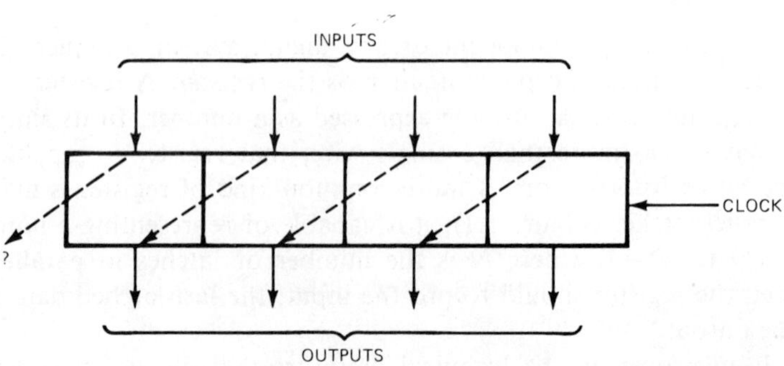

Figure 1.2 A simple shift-register.

on the basic theme. It is just these kinds of subtleties that make different microprocessors so radically different.

Computer Structure

Every computer is made up of five basic elements (Figure 1.3). It is essential that all five elements be present. However, it should be noted that not all systems that have all of these elements are known as computers; a calculator has all five of them, but it is not a computer. The reason will appear obvious shortly.

The Arithmetic Logic Unit (ALU) is the data-transforming part of the computer. Data presented at its inputs is changed according to some specified plan. The Storage facility provides a means for saving intermediate values for later use; it may be thought of as a gigantic scratch pad. The Input and Output components provide a way to accept data for processing and to present processed data for use. Without Output, the computer is utterly worthless. Without Input, the computer

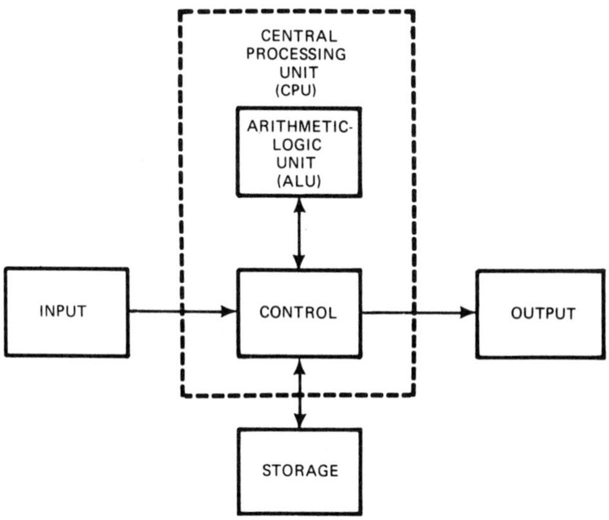

Figure 1.3 All computers are organized with these five elements.

is doomed to repeat some single sequence over and over again; that may prove useful in some sequential control applications. Finally, all four of these elements operate under the aegis of the Control section of the computer. It is the Control section that determines which register transfers to perform in the computer, and in which order. Therefore, the overall behavior (and therefore the *architecture*) of the computer is determined by the Control section's behavior.

In operation, external stimuli in the form of data are accepted from some Input registers and placed into Storage under command of the Control section.

When data modification is necessary, data is retrieved from Storage and supplied to the registers of the ALU; the results are accepted from an ALU register and placed back into Storage. Eventually, as appropriate to the application, the data in Storage is presented to the Output registers for external use.

Of what use is all this sequential generality? Well, it has been proven (in 1936) that the proper sequence of transfers between registers can solve any problem that has a convergent solution, given enough time. What this means is that a computer can solve any problem that has a definite solution that can be achieved in a finite number of distinct steps. A special hardware design of a collection of registers doesn't have to be created for each and every new application. This is the power and the promise of the digital computer: It is the everything machine and it is capable of being used to solve many problems that would be too expensive to solve if special hardware had to be constructed.

The first applications of computers (during World War II) were for mathematical computation (classic examples of problems that can be solved in a finite number of steps).

Later, computer users discovered that computers need not work solely with numbers. Those numbers can represent non-numeric data. For example, we might assign the number 41 to stand for the letter "A," 42 for "B," and so on. Now, each register holds some data that may be interpreted as a number (41) or a symbol ("A"). This explains the essential difference between *data* and *information.* The number 41 is data. It might represent the number of times some operation is to be performed, or it might stand for the value of a resistor, or it could represent the letter "A." When meaning is attached to the pure number (for example, to say that this register holds the number that stands for the letter "A"), the data becomes information.

Information is data that has an associated meaning. Computers process data; humans process information. Many of the problems with understanding what computers can and cannot do rest on this one principle. It also explains why computers will not replace humans (at least in our lifetimes).

Computer Operations

All computers, even microprocessors, operate under the same basic ground rules. Once the basic operational simplicity is understood, the experienced digital designer will be able to adapt to a new microprocessor (or any other kind of computer) quickly and effortlessly.

Computers are made up of registers. The architecture of the computer is characterized by the different kinds of transfers that can be performed between registers. In turn, each of the subsystems of the computer is made up of registers. Storage is the classical example (Figure 1.4). Storage is made up of a collection of several (typically identical) registers, each of which may be individually selected. For all intents and purposes, storage can be treated as a selectable group of registers. But how are those registers selected? By using another register (Figure 1.5).

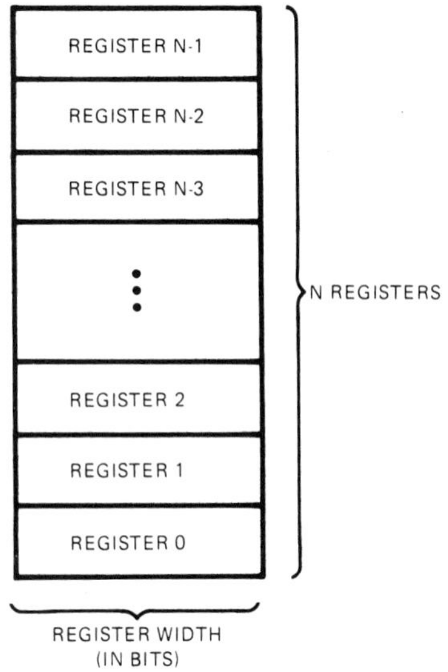

Figure 1.4 Storage is arranged as a collection of registers.

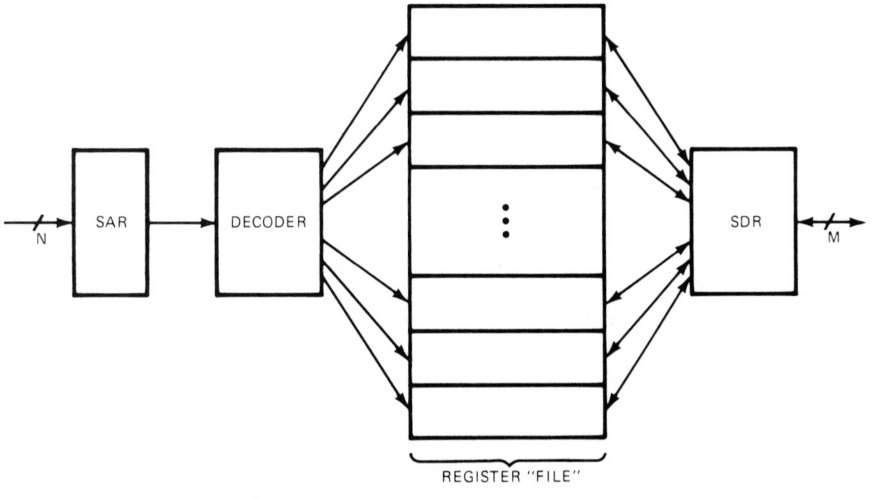

Figure 1.5 Basic structure of any randomly-addressable storage medium.

When a specific register of a Storage module is to be accessed, the numeric address that will select that one register is placed into a Storage Address Register (SAR). This register typically has an N-bit input capacity from which it generates one of 2^N outputs; this decoding function is just a complex register. If the Storage module is being read from, the data in the selected register is transferred into the Storage Data Register (SDR).

In a general sense, the Storage module of a computer is made up of an array of registers (called *storage cells*) and a pair of interface registers (SAR and SDR). The width of the SDR is called the *word size* of the Storage module.

Both Input and Output may be considered extensions of the Storage structure, the major difference being that the selected registers are accessible to the outside world. Using Input as an example (Figure 1.6), it is apparent that some kind of

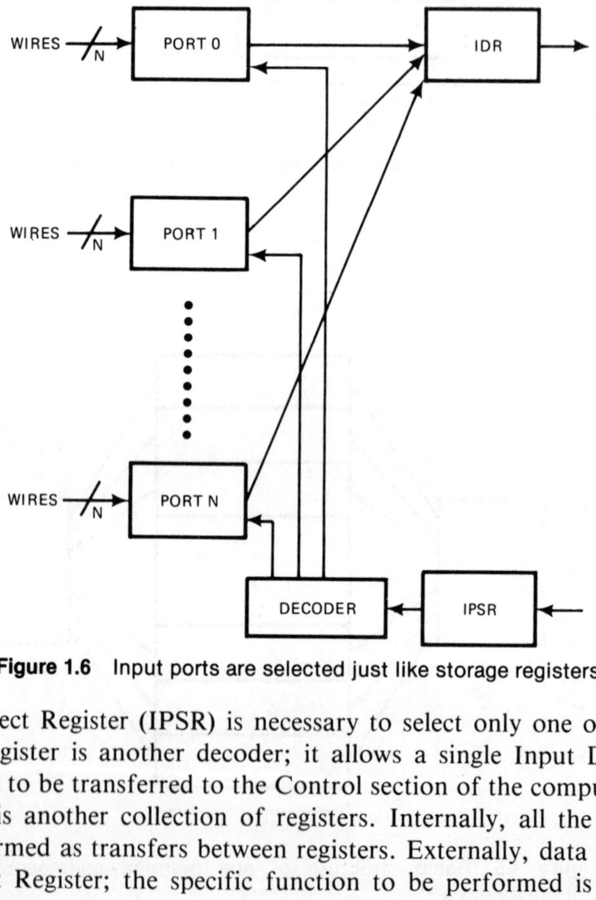

Figure 1.6 Input ports are selected just like storage registers.

Input Port Select Register (IPSR) is necessary to select only one of the registers. This Select Register is another decoder; it allows a single Input Data Register's (IDR) contents to be transferred to the Control section of the computer.

The ALU is another collection of registers. Internally, all the operations on data are performed as transfers between registers. Externally, data is presented to an ALU Input Register; the specific function to be performed is usually represented as a binary number and it is placed into the ALU's Function Register (Figure 1.7). The ALU typically operates on pairs of register contents; to add one number to another requires the two data values to be accessible at the same time.

The ALU often has associated with it a single register called the *Accumulator;* it is one of the two operands in each operation and it is the register into which results are stored. The size of the Accumulator is the *word size* of the computer. Eight-bit microprocessors have eight-bit wide Accumulators. Generally, the ALU processes the Accumulator contents in parallel, but not always.

The Control section of the computer links all of the diverse registers together over time to perform some required set of tasks. Since all possible register transfers that can take place are under the control of this central section of the computer, some way of specifying which transfers are to take place is necessary. These specifications are called *instructions,* and the list of all possible instructions the computer can accept is called the *instruction set.*

A typical instruction might be one that selects a particular Input Register and then transfers its contents to some specified Storage register. This register transfer is, in turn, made up of a sequence of other smaller register transfers that are not directly under the control of the programmer. These internal register transfers, called *microinstructions,* are governed by the Control section of the computer. In

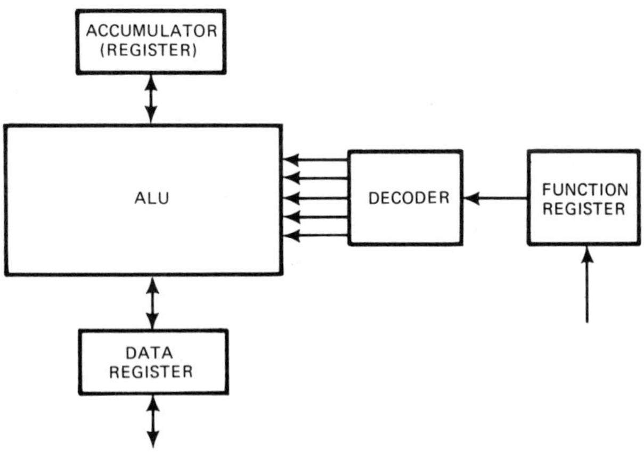

Figure 1.7 Arithmetic-Logic Unit is another register array.

most of today's computers the Control section has a small read-only memory of its own that contains one or more words for each instruction in the instruction set. These words contain the specific internal control signals necessary to microscopically control the individual internal register transfers required to effect the instruction. If this read-only memory can be modified, the computer has the property of being *microprogrammable.* Most microprocessors can only be microprogrammed at the factory.

The instructions for the computer carry the details about how to solve the specified problem. Each set of instructions is unique and must be created for each application. These instructions are kept in some Storage medium. In most of today's microprocessors instructions are stored in the same Storage module as

Microprocessors vs. Microprocessors

Computers that can be microprogrammed are often called microprocessors (from a contraction of "microprogrammable processor"). But what most people mean by the term microprocessor is a one-chip CPU (contracted "microelectronic processor"). A one-chip CPU may or may not be microprogrammable. If it is, should it be called a microprocessor[1]?

Generally, microprogrammable processors are being designed on a much larger scale than today's one-chip CPU's, so there is little confusion. However, technology is forcing the one-chip CPU's up into larger configurations while the designers of microprogrammable processors are growing downward to take advantage of economics.

Take care in using the term microprocessor. It may or may not mean what you want it to mean. When we talk of microprocessors in this book, we will mean the one-chip variety. Microprogrammable microprocessors also exist.

data. The specific instruction to be fetched from Storage and executed is selected by a simple Program Counter Register (PC; see Figure 1.8). Each time an instruction is to be fetched, the contents of the PC are placed into the Storage Address Register. While the physical action of register selection (known as *access time*) is taking place, the Program Counter is incremented by one so that it will be ready to fetch the very next instruction upon completion of this one. After the Storage produces the contents of the selected register, the Control section transfers the contents of the Storage Data Register into the Instruction Register.

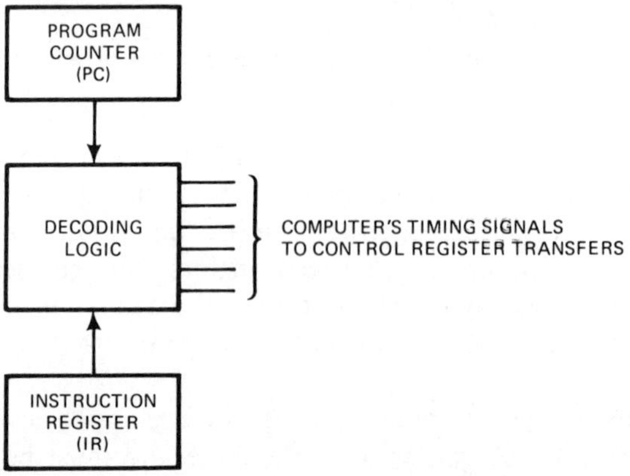

Figure 1.8 Basis of the control section of a computer.

The Instruction Register may be either a complex register that has a significant amount of "random" logic or it may be the Storage Address Register of a read-only storage facility that serves to decode the instruction. In either event, the result is the same: a sequence of control signals that selectively transfers the contents of some registers into other registers. At the end of the instruction the fetch-and-execute operation is repeated.

Tying all of the various elements together, Figure 1.9 shows the overall structure of one hypothetical computer. To be sure, we have oversimplified. For example, there are numerous control signals that have to be generated in synchronism with some master clock. However, these control signals can be treated as one-bit wide registers, and transfers to and from them are handled just like any other register transfer. On the other hand, it is possible to add many more registers with special functions to the computer. The Control, for example, may have a small suite of "local" registers that can be used to store intermediate data without referring tc Storage. The advantages of such registers include speed (since the Storage access time need not be involved) and efficiency (since the local registers can be selected with a few bits in the instruction instead of an address that is as wide as the Storage Address Register).

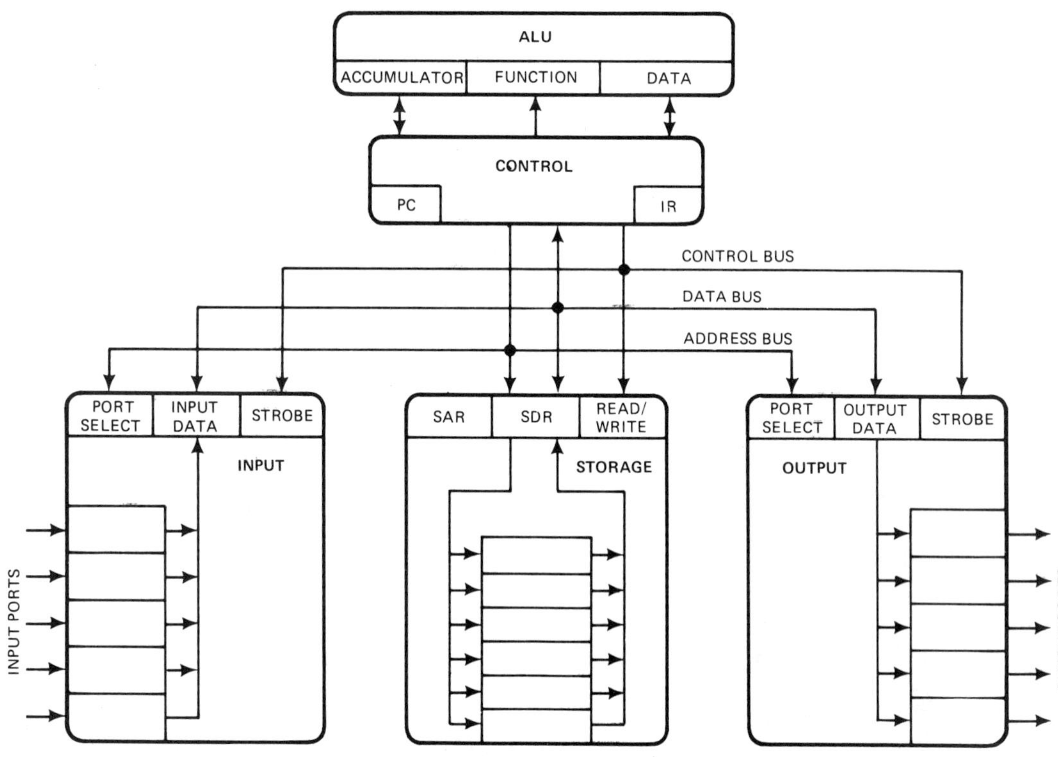

Figure 1.9 A simple computer is a collection of registers.

The interconnection of the elements of a computer nearly always takes advantage of the concept of a *bus.* In effect, a bus is an abstract register that has a single agreed upon format for all of the connected elements. Most microprocessors have three buses: Address, Data, and Control. Most often, the Address and Control buses are generated by the CPU and are used by the other system elements. So that data can be exchanged between the CPU and other elements, the data bus is always bidirectional. It is possible, of course, to organize the bidirectional data bus as two unidirectional buses; a single bidirectional bus is most often used to minimize the number of pins required for data transfer into and out of the microprocessor.

The word size of a computer may refer to the width of addressable units in storage, to the width of the accumulator, or to the width of the data bus. Because of the importance attached to intercommunication among computer elements, if these three definitions of word size differ, the width of the data bus generally rules.

The differences among computers are best understood by analyzing what registers have been provided and what means are available for transferring data from one register to another. The smaller the repertoire of registers, the easier it is to understand the computer. But, at the same time, if only a few possible register transfers are available, an easy to understand computer may be relatively inefficient. Conversely, the complex computers with wide varieties of different kinds of registers with special applications will often be hard to comprehend. But, once comprehended, these computers may be very efficient because they require fewer instructions to accomplish the equivalent amount of work.

A very small sample of instructions from a larger program can be used to illustrate all of these principles. The *program* (i.e., the collection of instructions that specifies what to do) is simple; "Add 17 to the contents of the register addressed as 61 in Storage; store the results in the Storage location 70." This program segment consists of three instructions; on another computer it might be more or less. The instructions and the required internal register transfers are illustrated in Figure 1.10.

The Central Processing Unit

The Arithmetic Logic Unit and the Control section of a computer have traditionally been constructed together. In earlier days the one large central cabinet that housed these two major computer elements was called the Central Processing Unit. Input, Output, and Storage were considered appendages.

The term has stuck. It is conventional to refer to the one-chip microprocessor as a "CPU." Some writers prefer to distinguish the large Central Processing Units from microprocessors by calling the latter MPU, which stands for Micro Processing Unit.

USER INSTRUCTION	MICROINSTRUCTION OPERATIONS (REGISTER TRANSFERS)	COMMENT
LOAD "17" INTO ACCUMULATOR	SAR ← PC	ADDRESS THE INSTRUCTION
	PC ← PC + 1	INCREMENT PROGRAM COUNTER
	IR ← SDR	FETCH THE INSTRUCTION
	SAR ← PC	FETCH THE SECOND WORD OF THE INSTRUCTION (CONTAINS "17")
	PC ← PC + 1	
	ACC ← SDR	PUT DATUM INTO ACCUMULATOR
ADD CONTENTS OF LOCATION 61 TO ACCUMULATOR	SAR ← PC	ADDRESS THE INSTRUCTION
	PC ← PC + 1	INCREMENT PROGRAM COUNTER
	IR ← SDR	FETCH THE INSTRUCTION
	SAR ← PC	FETCH THE SECOND WORD OF THE INSTRUCTION (CONTAINS "61")
	PC ← PC + 1	
	SAR ← SDR	ADDRESS THE LOCATION HOLDING THE DATA
	ALU ← SDR	GET THE DATA
	FUNCTION ← ADD	START THE ALU IN OPERATION
STORE THE RESULTS NOW IN ACCUMULATOR INTO LOCATION 70	SAR ← PC	ADDRESS THE INSTRUCTION
	PC ← PC + 1	INCREMENT PROGRAM COUNTER
	IR ← SDR	FETCH THE INSTRUCTION
	SAR ← PC	FETCH THE SECOND WORD OF THE INSTRUCTION (CONTAINS "70")
	SAR ← SDR	ADDRESS THE LOCATION TO RECEIVE THE RESULT
	SDR ← ACC	PUT DATA INTO STORAGE

NOTE:
Y ← X MEANS PLACE CONTENTS OF REGISTER X INTO REGISTER Y

SAR: STORAGE ADDRESS REGISTER
SDR: STORAGE DATA REGISTER
ACC: ACCUMULATOR REGISTER
ALU: ALU OPERAND INPUT REGISTER
FUNCTION: ALU FUNCTION REGISTER
PC: PROGRAM COUNTER OF CONTROL SECTION
IR: INSTRUCTION REGISTER OF CONTROL SECTION

Figure 1.10 Detailed execution sequence of three successive instructions.

Addressing Modes

As this example has shown, there is a persistent need for programs to refer to various data values stored in different registers. Most of the data references from instructions are accomplished by addressing some single location in Storage. This is called *direct addressing.* The address part of the instruction, which may be in the first word or in a successive word of the instruction, is placed into the Storage Address Register, and the Storage Data Register receives the data (for a read from Storage).

Direct addressing is simple but it is somewhat expensive in many applications. If Storage is made up of as many as 65,536 registers (as is true of many of the eight-bit microprocessors), the Storage Address Register must be 16 bits wide. Therefore, each instruction that refers to Storage must supply a full 16-bit address. In many small applications actual Storage may be only 256 registers long; that requires only 8 bits worth of address. Therefore, in these cases, every instruction that refers to Storage contains 8 worthless bits.

This inefficiency can be overcome by introducing the concept of *abbreviated addressing.* An abbreviated address is one in which only the significant bits are presented from the instruction; the rest of the Storage Address Register bits are either preset (usually to zero) or come from yet another register. If abbreviated addressing is provided, it is usually an adjunct to normal direct addressing. One or more bits in the instruction will specify which addressing *mode* is being used so that the Control section can cause the appropriate register transfers to take place.

Another form of abbreviated addressing is used to refer to a local set of registers that are designed as part of the Control section. This is called *register addressing.* If there are eight special registers provided in the Control section, for example, then only three bits are necessary to select one of them for use in an ALU operation. This means that more bits are left in the instruction for specifying what operation is to be performed. It is not uncommon to see a computer designed so that only local registers can be operands to ALU operations; full direct addressing may then be used to fetch Storage register contents into these local storage registers of the Control section.

When dealing with constants, such as the "17" in the example of Figure 1.10, it is often useful to have the data directly available in the instruction rather than in an addressable register in Storage. This eliminates one additional Storage access cycle over direct addressing. This incorporation of the data in the instruction is called *immediate addressing.*

Another popular form of addressing is called *indirect addressing.* In order of complexity, immediate addressing involves only one reference to Storage to gain access to data, direct addressing uses one reference to obtain the address to be used by a second reference, and indirect addressing uses three such references. That is, the instruction specifies the address at which the address of the required data will be found. This is useful when creating "pointers" in Storage to other data items. One particular variant of this addressing mode is *register indirect addressing;* in this form, the instruction refers to a register of the Control section in which a Storage address appears. The instruction thus indirectly refers to Storage via the Control section's special register.

Indexing is the most complex of the addressing schemes and may be combined with any of the other addressing modes. In *indexed addressing,* the contents of a special register (called an *index register*) are automatically added to another address (given as part of the instruction), yielding a new "effective" address. Indexing is powerful because it allows instructions to remain unmodified yet refer to various parts of Storage at different times. If indexing is not present in the instruction set of the computer, it can be synthesized at some cost in execution time by performing address computations and then referring to the data indirectly via the computed address.

All these addressing modes are summarized in Figure 1.11. Note that not all microprocessors have all of these modes and that some have other slight variations on the basic themes. However, all of the modes are designed to provide an efficient alternative to simple direct addressing. The lack of a breadth of addressing modes in a computer means that more instructions will have to be executed to perform tasks that would otherwise be very simple and brief.

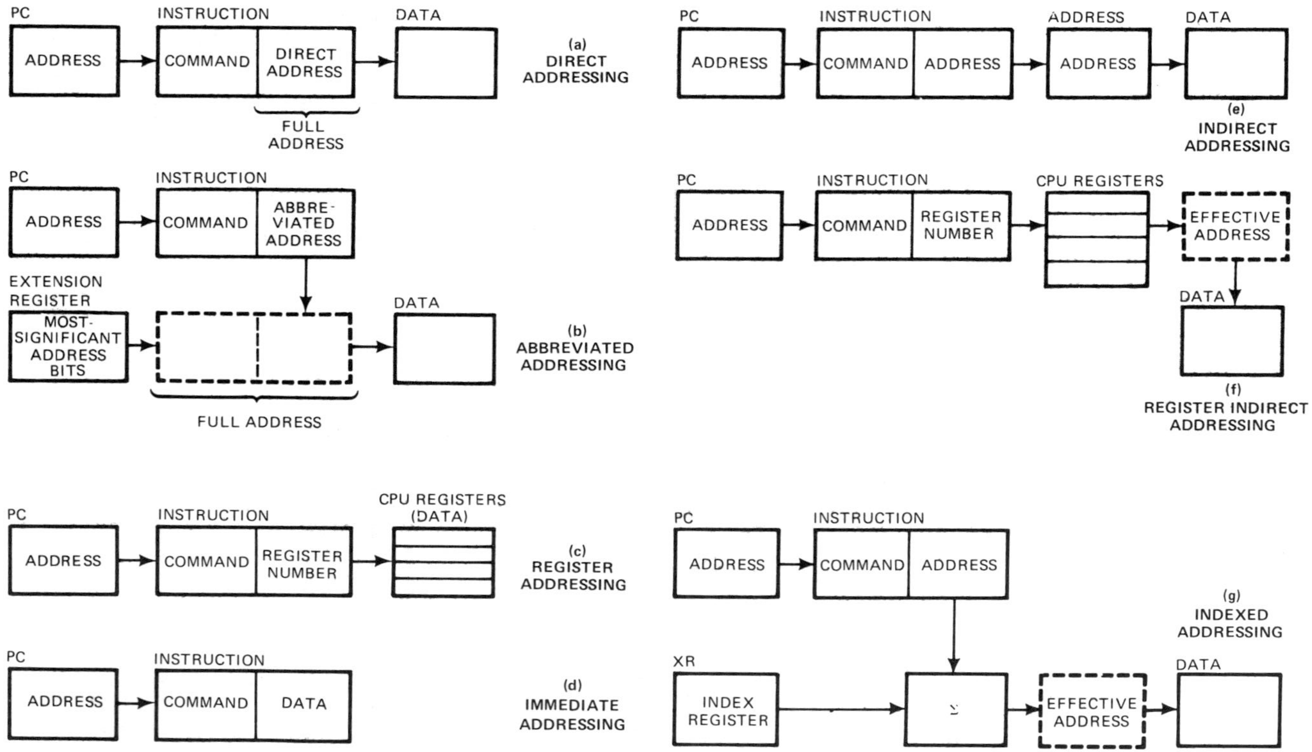

Figure 1.11 Several common addressing modes.

What Is a Microprocessor?

Today's *microprocessors* are the ALU and Control sections of a computer implemented in one IC package (or a very small number of such packages). Note that microprocessors are generally not whole computers (Input, Output, and Storage are absent), although there are some notable exceptions. The one-chip processors with Input, Output, and Storage should more properly be called *microcomputers.*

Generally, microcomputers are computers (therefore, they have all five basic elements) based on microprocessors. Every product that incorporates a microprocessor is, in fact, a microcomputer. But when it is suitably programmed and becomes a constituent part of the product into which it is designed, this microcomputer tends to lose its own individual identity.

There are many approaches to microprocessor implementation. The most active part of the market is in the one-chip variety, generally based on NMOS or PMOS. However, there are also some "slice" architectures that provide for even more flexibility in design (see Figure 1.12). In a "slice" model the various regis-

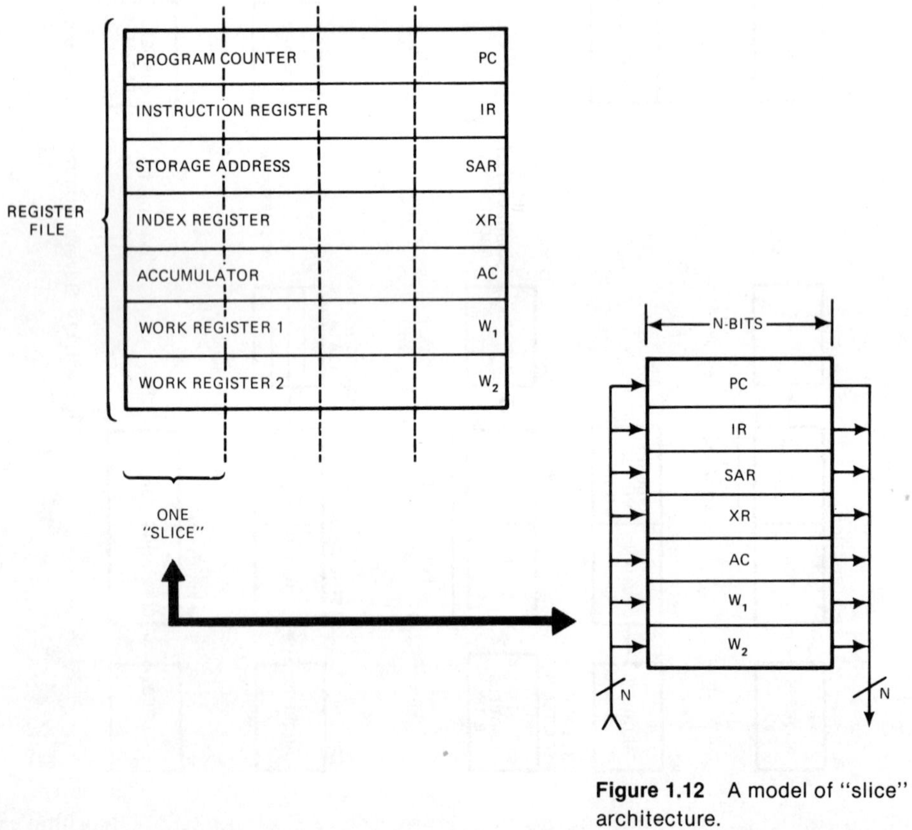

Figure 1.12 A model of "slice" architecture.

ters of the CPU are arranged as a Storage array and each IC holds a few bits (typically two or four) for each register. Several IC's can be cascaded together to create wide register widths. These devices are generally more powerful than the one-chip varieties, but at a significantly higher engineering and a slightly higher manufacturing cost.

What Is Software?

The contents of registers are numbers, even when these numbers are instructions for the computer itself. The abstract intangible part of a computer system, the instructions themselves, is called the *program.* It is the program that makes this particular combination of hardware perform some specific task. By changing the program, the same hardware can be made to perform a different task.

There is much to microprocessor-based product design that is intangible. The program (in its various forms, from written specifications down to bits stored in a chip somewhere), the documentation (both electronics and program), and other support objects are all considered part and parcel of the software for a computer.

A separate family of software also exists. The programs that the microprocessor vendor supplies for the customer's convenience are called *systems software.* The debug monitors, assemblers, compilers, and their associated documentation all qualify as examples of systems software. Generally, systems software is used to generate applications software.

What Is Programming?

Programming is a complex task, not unlike engineering, that requires a disciplined approach to the translation of requirements into unambiguous instructions for a suitable computer. Programming, however, is more—much, much more—than merely transcribing cryptic symbols onto a punched paper tape.

Programming involves at least five major steps:

1. Design
2. Coding
3. Translation
4. Testing
5. Debugging

In general, if design is slighted, testing and debugging will take an inordinately long time to complete. In that way, programming is precisely like other forms of engineering. However, the design of a computer program requires more analysis than many engineers are used to doing. Not only must the problem to be solved be firmly understood, the complex issues of suitable algorithm selection must be resolved. The first part of the problem understanding process may determine the need to multiply two numbers together. However, the second part (algorithm selection) requires even more detail so that any of the hundreds of different algorithms for numeric representation and multiplication can be selected.

Once a program has been designed (which usually results in some document that embodies that design), it can be coded. When a program is coded, each component of the design is manually converted into some suitable sequence of instructions for the microcomputer selected for the job. Although many errors are made in this part of the process, these errors are generally easy to find and correct.

After the program has been coded, it must be transalted from the letters and numbers meaningful to the author into the one's and zero's that the computer can operate upon. Fortunately, computer programs that will perform this translation automatically already exist; they are called *assemblers* and *compilers.* The difference between them and the reasons for selecting each will be discussed in Chapter 10.

Once the translated program is placed into the microcomputer's memory, the program must be tested. Depending on how well the author has modularized the program, this testing may be either simple or complex. Testing must have as its end goal the intent of finding all potential faults in the program before it is released for use or for production. All too often testing has the goal of "proving" the programmer's assertion that the program operates correctly. The former approach requires tough-minded test case selection; the latter permits the simplest possible test cases to be used as demonstrations.

Once testing reveals an error, the process of debugging (tracking down the error) begins. Approximately two-thirds of all errors that must be tracked down are design errors and are the most difficult errors to test for. The remainder tend to be coding errors and are usually easy to catch and repair.

Once a bug has been isolated, some redesign, recoding, retranslation, and retesting must be applied. These five steps of programming tend to be used over and over until the program achieves some acceptable behavior.

2

Connecting to External Registers

Before getting too deeply involved in the internal structure of microprocessors, it is imperative that the prospective designer understand the environment in which these processors operate. As we showed in Chapter 1, all computers consist of five basic elements: The Control and ALU are combined in the microprocessor chip, and the computer must include Storage, Input, and Output capabilities. A complete microcomputer system is shown in Figure 2.1.

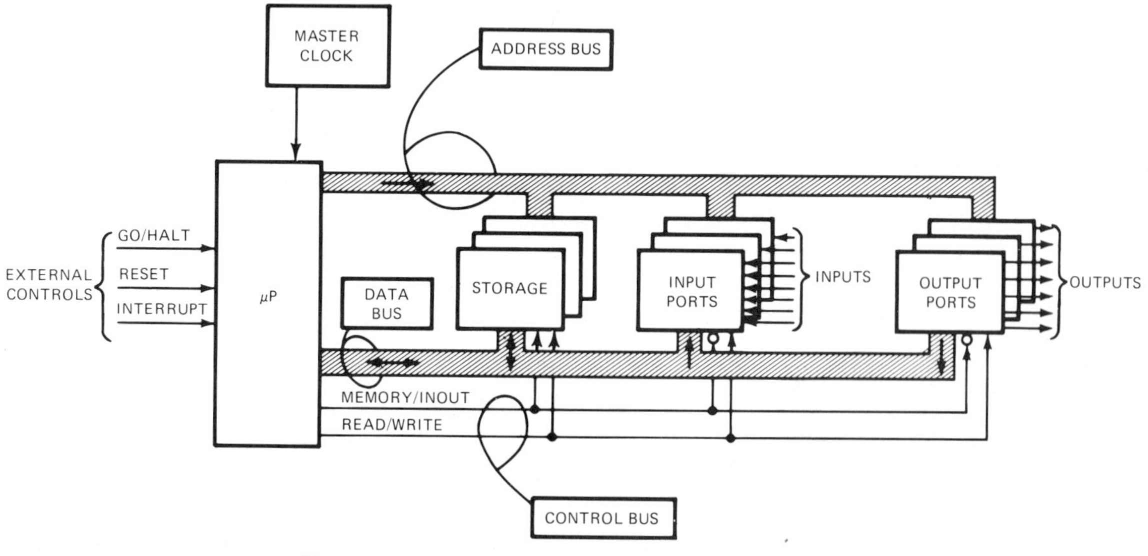

Figure 2.1 A typical microcomputer arrangement.

Communication between elements of the computer takes place over the standard buses, one each for address, data, and control lines. The microprocessor reads from memory, for example, by placing the address of the required location in the storage array onto the address bus and establishing the proper signals on the control bus (e.g., READ and MEMORY both high). After a suitable delay for storage access time and settling, the data can be assumed to be present on the bidirectional data bus; since the microprocessor initiated a read operation, the bidirectional data bus is being driven by the memory and the microprocessor is the data destination.

All microprocessors have these three buses, although in a wide diversity of forms. Sometimes you have to look closely to find all of these signals. The address bus is almost as wide as necessary for complete storage addressing. However, there are microprocessors (particularly earlier generations) that multiplex the address bus out of the chip into external latches. These multiplexing processors must have an additional set of control signals to control the multiplexing operation, but they save on the number of pins used to actually present the address out to the bus. Of course, these multiplexing systems require additional hardware external to the processor itself to latch the storage addresses; the microcomputer's address bus is considered to be that part of the system beyond those demultiplexing latches.

The system data bus is usually arranged for bidirectional operation, although two unidirectional buses can be created instead. Some processors are capable of interfacing a considerable amount of storage and input/output capacity without additional buffering. However, in large systems or in microprocessors that have limited drive capability, some additional buffering may be required. It is in the organization of this buffering where the unidirectional or bidirectional bus arrangement is decided. Additional buffering considerations will be found in Chapter 5 (Storage Organization).

The control bus shown in Figure 2.1 is about the most primitive that can be imagined. Most systems have many more control signals to synchronize all the activities of the separated elements of the microcomputer. However, in this simple example only two basic signals are provided. The READ/WRITE signal is high (in this example) for transmission of data on the data bus toward the microprocessor and it is low for outbound data. The MEMORY/INOUT signal selects whether memory or input/output devices are to be involved in the data transfer. The width of these pulses and the timing between them may make microcomputer design easy or difficult.

Synchronous Machines

Microprocessors, like most digital computers, are operated in a synchronous fashion. Data transfers between internal registers and between registers of different elements of the computer are synchronized by master clock signals and control signals derived from the master clock. Therefore, in a well-designed system there will be no cases in which two different registers or other components of the computer are driving the same bus at the same time. If the Control section of the computer is considered as the orchestra's conductor, then the timing diagrams must be considered the score.

The interrelationships among the three major buses of a microcomputer can be most easily represented in a timing diagram. In fact, the timing diagram is so important to understanding the operation of a microcomputer that every specification sheet for processors includes one, although it is often needlessly complex. Basically, the timing diagram specifies when data is transferred between registers. A simple example for reading and writing storage is shown in Figure 2.2.

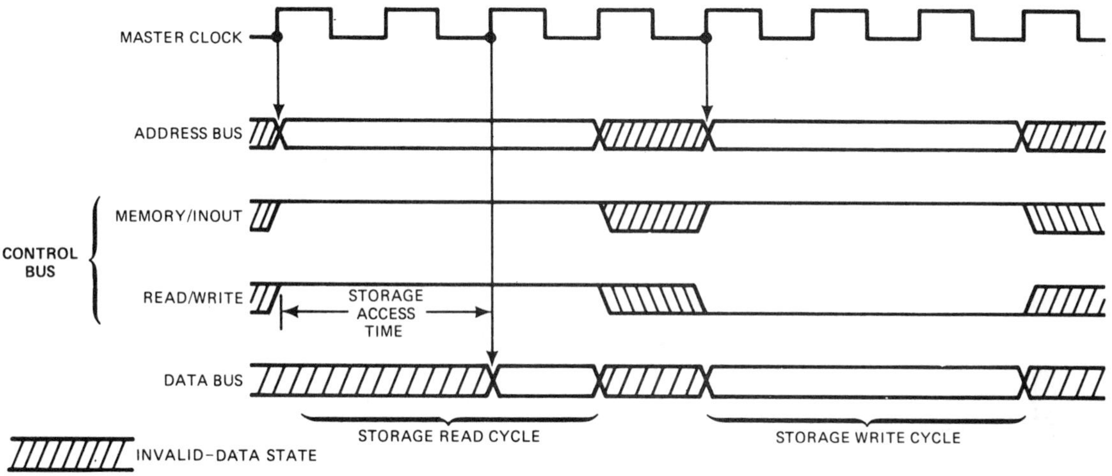

Figure 2.2 Master timing for storage accessing.

Typically, all of the edges of the bus signals are synchonized to some part of the master clock pulse(s). Although most microprocessors have multiphase clocks, in this simple example we opt for a single symmetrical phase. In this hypothetical computer all memory operations take place in three successive master clock periods. At some point in time (shown here as the rising edge of the master clock) the address and control buses are set up by the microprocessor. The desired storage location is specified by the address bus, but input/output ports and storage media ignore the bus until specifically commanded to accept the address. In this case, memory is selected (MEMORY/INOUT is high during address bus time). Furthermore, the direction of the data transfer is established on the READ/WRITE line.

For reading from storage, the time between the presentation of the address and READ and MEMORY signals and the instant at which the processor expects the data to be available on the data bus (the rising edge of the third clock pulse in Figure 2.2) is called the required storage access time. The entire storage subsystem, including all buffering, decoding, and control internal to that computer element, must be able to complete a reading cycle within the specified time. If the storage medium is too slow, the master clock may have to be slowed down to suit.

In real systems (and real timing diagrams), matters are more complex than

Logic Naming Conventions

In this book a single convention for naming electrical signals has been adopted. A signal name is made up of any combination of letters and digits, and spaces may freely appear within names. The negative-logic convention is indicated by preceding the signal name with the "/" symbol.

Complementary signals are written juxtaposed with the positive-logic name first. Thus, if the signal names READ and /WRITE are, in fact, different names for the same wire, then we write that as READ/WRITE.

shown here. The various control and address bus signals may be presented at different times as a result of the internal time delays in the microprocessor itself. Furthermore, the control signals may not be completely compatible with the memory devices designed into the microcomputer. Therefore, some external control logic that can convert the signals available from the microprocessor into signals compatible with the storage media may be required.

Input/output ports are treated almost identically with storage selection, except I/O ports are generally faster since large arrays and address decoding are not involved. However, the timing principles remain the same.

Alternative Control Buses

In the example we have been using the microcomputer is assumed to generate two primary signals, READ/WRITE and MEMORY/INOUT. In practice, different microcomputers generate different kinds of signals. However, after a lot of experience with a lot of different microprocessor design, many designers have nearly always adopted a four-wire system. The four signals are:

/MEMW (active-low Memory Write)
/IOW (active-low Input/Output Write)
/MEMR (active-low Memory Read)
/IOR (active-low Input/Output Read)

The reasons for these signals and their logic sense are derived from the pragmatic assessment of commonly available chips. Typically, memory and input/output parts have active-low chip select signals; therefore, we choose to make these four signals active-low. Similarly, buffers for the data bus need different kinds of controls to ensure proper data transfer direction and most often these are negative logic inputs. Since buffers for each direction are usually separated on the bidirectional data bus, it serves a useful purpose to have the read and write control signals as separate wires.

Even in computers in which these four signals do not naturally appear, they have been found most efficient. In the 8080A, for example, these four signals are easy to derive (and, in fact, are derived for the engineer with one of Intel's support parts). However, in the Motorola 6800 the RD/WRT and associated signals are used. We have found that by using the available control signals to create the four signals we consider standard, the total amount of support logic for control steering is dramatically reduced.

Clockery

Different microprocessors require different kinds of clocks. In some systems, like the Intersil 6100, RCA COSMAC, and Fairchild F8, no external clock is required. A crystal or R-C network is used to set the operating frequency within specified limits. In other cases (certainly the most common), a two-phase clock system with nonoverlapping pulses is required; since in the 8080A the two-phase clock is asymmetrical, the two phases cannot be simply created by a division by two. In other processors a single phase may be required. In the National GPC/P (and IMP–16 series) and in the Texas Instruments TMS9900, four phases are necessary. All the elements of common external clocks are illustrated in Figure 2.3.

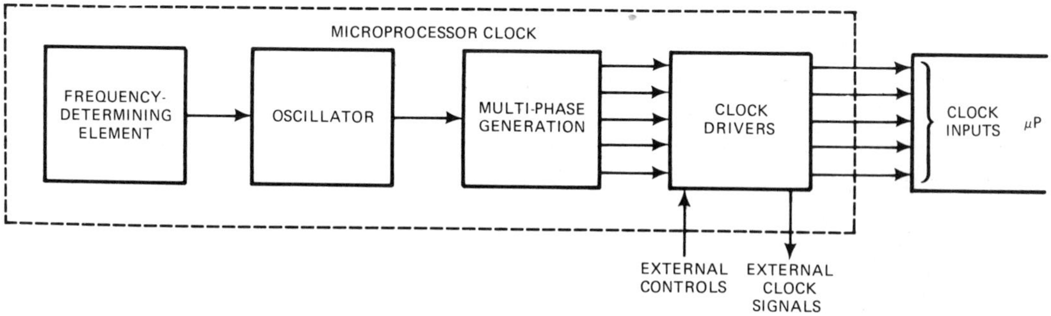

Figure 2.3 Elements of a master clock.

Most designers look at the upper frequency limit of operation for the microprocessor. However, the lower limit should also be examined. Some processors (such as the CMOS systems) are static and can be operated at any low clock frequency, even DC. This is useful during system debugging because the computer can be slowed down to a point where individual machine cycles can be monitored. However, most microprocessors are dynamic and require a fast enough clock to be certain to cause the processor's registers to be refreshed often enough to avoid loss of data. This ratio between highest and lowest operating frequency may be important in production if you use a simple clock that is not crystal controlled. Drift of the master clock frequency may cause either the upper or lower limit to be exceeded which, in turn, may cause some production devices to fail sporadically.

Crystal control of microprocessors is used in most designs. The specific operating frequency may not be exact (crystals are often "pulled" off frequency by the odd oscillators based on digital IC's some designers adopt), but the stability is what is important. If any timing is to be done in software, crystal control is imperative. However, if all timing is to be done under the control of some external hardware that can maintain a stable reference, crystal control is not critically important.

After the basic oscillator design has been set, the designer must select the appropriate operating frequency and then derive the required interrelated phases for the processor. In very simple and inexpensive designs these phases may be generated by different oscillators all "tweaked" to the proper frequency and pulse widths. However, these designs based on one-shots are not considered useful for production purposes because of the highly interactive nature of the "tweaking" process. Any money saved in parts (since RC-controlled oscillators *are* inexpensive) will be more than wasted in production-line adjustments. In most designs the master oscillator frequency is divided down to some common denominator and then some combination of the signals is used to create the asymmetrical pulses.

The Intel 8080A, for example, operates with a master clock period of 500 ns and two phases. The required clock specifications to operate at this frequency are shown in Figure 2.4. The easiest way to generate these two pulses is to start with an 18-MHz oscillator and divide by nine to achieve the 500-ns period (2 MHz). Then combinational logic (also shown in Figure 2.4) can be used to create the clock phases. Clever designers can always find some higher operating frequency that can be divided down to create clock signals of the required proportions.

The microprocessor presents a large dynamic and static load on the clock inputs. Virtually every part of the internal circuitry is synchronized to one or another of the clock phases. To ensure proper clean data transfers, it is important that the clock pulse waveforms be carefully controlled. To ensure against on-chip clock degradation, some relatively high-power and high-voltage levels are required. Nearly every major semiconductor manufacturer makes a family of clock driver IC's (very often little more than power transistors in a package). The 8080A clock, for example, must be able to swing 12 V, drive up to 25 pF of capacitive load, and still maintain rise and fall times of 50 ns.

Fortunately, all this design of clock circuitry is now mostly academic. Necessary clock driver circuitry is available from many of the microprocessor manufacturers as well as from other sources. The Intel 8224 Clock Generator and Driver for the 8080A CPU is an example of a single sixteen-pin IC that accepts a crystal (18 MHz) on one side and generates all of the important clock signals on the other. Alternatively, the designer may select the Motorola K1117 clock series for the 8080A; this device is a hybrid package that includes the crystal and is packaged in a twenty-four-pin DIP-like container. The Motorola MC6870 clock series is a similar design intended for 6800 users.

Whether the clock generator circuitry is home grown, purchased from the semiconductor company, or is from some third source, it is important to know what other signals may be required or accepted to that clock. It is often necessary

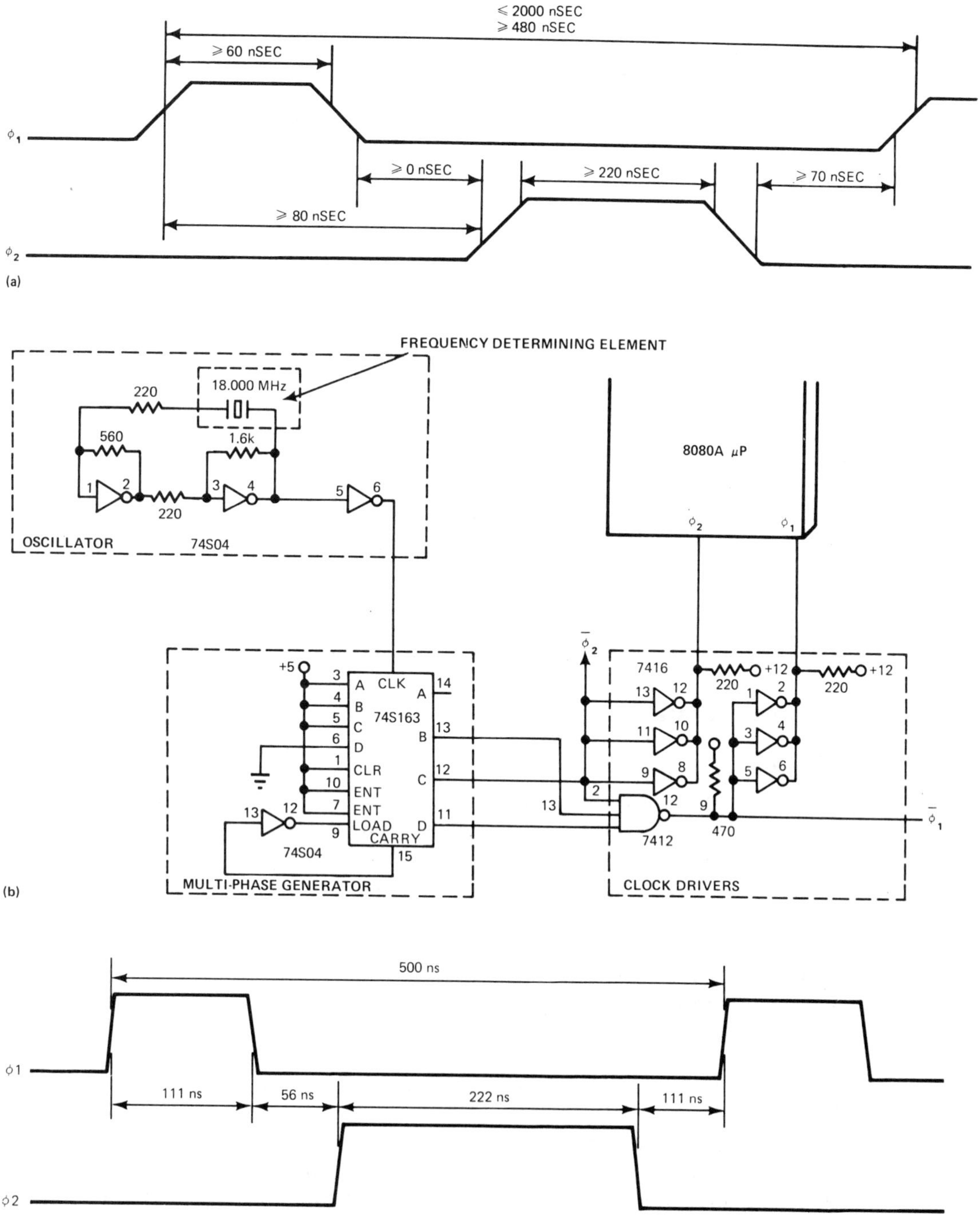

Figure 2.4 A typical clock circuit.

to have TTL-level clock signals to create signals for the control bus of a microcomputer; the clock generator should be able to produce those signals. Some additional circuitry may be required to properly delay these TTL-level clock pulses to synchronize them with the high-energy pulses presented to the microprocessor clock inputs.

Whenever common functions must be synchronized with the clock, it is often best to insert these functions into the clockery. When you select a clock generator chip, consider how much external circuitry will be needed for simple synchronization chores. Most clocks intended for use with a particular microprocessor will have inputs and outputs for these common synchronization problems already included.

Another feature of many clock circuits is the "stretching" capability. Usually, there is a pin that can be activated to cause one of the clock pulses to be lengthened beyond the normal period. This is useful in dynamic microprocessor systems in which the microprocessor cannot be slowed down for special storage chips. With clock stretching, whenever the slow memory is selected the appropriate clock phase is stretched out in time to add sufficient delay to permit proper storage accessing. When that memory module is not selected, the clock operates at the higher operating frequency. You must be careful, of course, to avoid holding down the "stretch" control to the clock circuitry so long that the CPU looses its mind (i.e., register contents) because of the dynamic RAM's on-chip.

System Data Transfers

All of the general discussion about the three basic buses can be applied to all of the popular microprocessors. However, each micro is unique and has its own set of signals and timing rules. You must carefully study each processor's reference manual to determine precisely how to interface the signals provided. There are generally a few major areas you should concentrate on, for example, on the following:

1. Reading from storage
2. Writing to storage
3. Reading from input ports
4. Writing to output ports
5. Synchronizing important control signals to the processor.

Of course, if you address input/output ports like storage locations, you need not look at input/output timing separately from storage timing.

Reading from storage is generally accomplished by presenting an address on the address bus and then raising (or lowering) some control signal to act as a read-from-storage strobe. This control signal may also establish the direction of data transfer (toward the processor) so that buffers may be controlled; alternatively, a separate direction control line may be used.

Writing to storage is similar, but the timing of the write strobe may be different from the read in order to accommodate the unique characteristics of some popular RAM's.

Usually, input/output instructions cause timing and control signals that are similar (if not identical) to those used with storage. However, since ports are usually simple latches or buffers, some processors generate different timing for input/output from storage in order to avoid unnecessary waiting for nonexistent cycle time.

Many microprocessors have control inputs that must be synchronized with parts of the various clock phases. In some popular processors, for example, it is imperative that the RESET signal to the CPU be synchronized to one of the clock phases and be held for some minimum number of those clock cycles. Not investigating these requirements can lead to designs that fail sporadically and nonrepeatedly.

Media Selection

The medium that you use to implement the microprocessor-based product depends on your goals. In general, you have three major alternatives:

1. Use one of the available sets of prefabricated microcomputer card sets.
2. Use a prototyping system.
3. Start from scratch and build your own microcomputer out of available parts.

There is a natural inclination among engineers to start out with the intent to design a complete microcomputer from the chips up. For certain applications that is the best possible choice, but never at the outset. Certainly, if production volume is expected to be high enough to warrant a customized microcomputer design, there is value in building and proving a prototype first. To start from scratch means that a large amount of effort has to be spent designing and building CPU and memory and clock and bus interfaces before anything can be tested. Software is severely delayed because there's nothing to check it out on until all the hardware has been fabricated and checked out.

One of the necessary tools of the microprocessor user is the prototyping system. The system concists of microcomputers, usually sold by the semiconductor vendors, specifically designed to support software and hardware development efforts. Prototyping systems, like Intel's Intellec series, Motorola's EXORciser, National's IMP-16, and Rockwell's Assemulators, are microcomputers made up of stock printed circuit cards with a front panel and some way to connect external input/output devices. With these, instead of investing lots of effort in making the basic computer go, the engineer can spend time worrying about the truly unique parts of the application: input/output and software. The prototyping systems range in cost from $2,500 to about $6,000, exclusive of the cost of a teletypewriter. The prototyping system has three features that make it different from other microcomputer card systems:

1. A front panel that allows the user to debug programs more easily
2. A software monitor that uses a teletypewriter terminal for man–machine dialogue
3. An input/output bus scheme that the user must live with

The front panel switches and lights allow the user/engineer to monitor and control the operation of programs in the microcomputer's memory. This is especially important when the programs are unique to the intended application and interface with the special input/output equipment. The software monitor and teletypewriter allow the software to be debugged more easily. When the application program goes into a permanent loop, for example, the front panel controls can be used to return control back to the software monitor. The software allows the user to dump selected memory locations to the terminal so that the problem can be isolated. It can also be used to insert changes to the program into memory. The alternative to using a terminal is to use the switches and lights of the front panel, but it is a time-consuming and error-prone activity. The teletypewriter terminal is the software analog of an oscilloscope. It allows the implementer to look inside to see what's happening.

The greatest feature (and largest headache) of a prototyping system is its input/output bus. Because the bus and appropriate connectors already exist, it seems easy to use them to connect prototype input/output equipment to the system for debugging both hardware and software. However, some compromises are inevitable. The bus system used in the prototyping system may not be at all appropriate for your final product; some redesigning may be required later. Some careful forethought will minimize the problems. For example, the device selection logic may be overkill for your particular needs. However, each input/output circuit can be designed with a one-bit select line; that line can then be connected to one place in the prototyping system and to a different place in the final production design. This compromise should cost little, and it should impact software and hardware design only trivially.

In between the home-brew microcomputer and the prototyping system lies the domain of the prepackaged microcomputer. These card systems are available from the semiconductor companies (often the very same cards used in their prototyping systems), minicomputer companies, and a new group of companies that builds special microcomputer systems from available MSI logic or microprocessors. A whole secondary industry of small companies that makes these microcomputer systems is growing up. The advantage of using a card system is that you buy subsystems that work. You don't have to spend time designing, fabricating, testing, and debugging your own CPU and memory cards.

The microcomputers available from the semiconductor vendors provide a good option between your own design and a whole prototyping system. However, these cards have been designed for uses other than production. Some of the logic used is awkward and the shapes and sizes of the cards tend to be odd. For a prototype, don't hesitate to use the microcomputer cards from the semiconductor companies. If you expect to buy dozens of cards, consider some of the alternate sources. The microcomputers sold by the independent companies tend to be more complete. Usually the family of cards includes those you'll need for implementation of specialized input/output facilities. Some of the independent makers' equipment is intrinsically safe, too; that is important to many industrial users.

When you buy a prototyping system you are stuck with the speed of the memory chips that the vendor selected. Many of these systems cannot operate at the highest microprocessor speeds. This can be a real problem if your ultimate goal is a product that will run at that highest attainable speed. Although some vendors slow the system down by incorporating slow RAM's, PROM's tend to be the more common culprit. Most of those handy ultraviolet erasable ROM's cannot keep up with a 2-μs processor cycle. Therefore, if you're counting on speed, it will probably be necessary to build special memory cards. You may even have to purchase them from a different supplier. Since the actual speed of the prototyping system when using its various memories is frequently not clearly specified, you have to ask about it.

Microcomputers are commonly available in two kinds of packages: one-card systems and multicard systems. *One-card systems* are often designed to displace minicomputers in dedicated applications. The CPU, memory, and input/output facilities are all on one board; unfortunately, that makes for a relatively large board. These one-card systems all seem to be in one size: the wrong one. In order to use a one-card system you have to be able to mount it and connect to it. If the card size isn't consistent with your application, you have to adapt. Also, because all input/output interfaces (at a bus level) are done for you, you are constrained to matching that interface. One-card systems usually cost just under $500 in small quantities (including some memory).

Multicard systems are usually partitioned into families of printed circuit cards along computer architecture lines. There is usually a card for the CPU and clock, there are commonly several different kinds of storage cards, and a complement of different input/output cards usually rounds out the set. Because of the variety of potential I/O cards, interfacing is often easier than with one-card systems. The engineer's own special sensing and control hardware is interfaced to the lines available on the input/output cards. Individual cards may cost from $100 to $500; a whole system usually costs about $1,000.

Some of the one-card microcomputers come with complete families of peripheral devices; this is especially true of micros made by minicomputer companies. In these cases, the designers have been careful to create input/output interfaces that are identical to other minicomputer models; you'll have to adapt to these.

If you are going to design one and only one product for production in quantities of less than ten, you can probably do the whole job by using microcomputer cards. In this situation, consider the minicomputer companies products. You'll be able to use the rest of that company's product line to do much of the hardware and software work. However, since few microprocessor users have one-time applications with small volumes, a prototyping system is almost mandatory.

If your needs call for many one-of-a-kind systems, the prototyping system can be used to support the development of special input/output and software for each application. If the end products are to be fabricated out of somebody's stock card family, the prototyping system should use the same cards and bus structure. All reputable makers of card systems offer a prototyping configuration.

If your needs call for the development of a high-volume production item and you intend to design your own CPU, memory, and input/output hardware, you ought to create a software development system around a prototyping system first. Later, after software and hardware concepts have been proven, you can implement the repackaged configuration for production's use. This means that most of the hardware and software development efforts can proceed in parallel. If all the custom hardware must be built before the software can be tried out, the project may take twice as long to complete.

3

The Computer As Learning Tool

Computer programming may be difficult to learn, but it is even more difficult to teach. Because the field is only a couple decades old, we don't yet know very much about how to teach it well. In fact, most programming courses in colleges and universities don't teach programming so much as they teach coding, a significantly simpler skill.

The only way to learn programming is by doing it. In years gone by the cost of a couple of minutes of computer time was so precious that programmers got experience in small increments, much like pilots of airplanes. Now, however, that computers are inexpensive it is practical for each new budding programmer to have one all to himself. The announcement of dozens of different microprocessor-based learning tools in the past couple of years has lent support to this conclusion. To learn programming, you should acquire one of the microcomputers and actually *do* programming.

There are several different classes of instruments you can acquire for learning purposes. You may have used elementary logic trainers to learn about digital logic; some of the computer learning tools are of the same level of complexity. Certainly, as a primitive learning device, the Texas Instruments LCM-1001 Microprogrammer Learning Module is in this class. You may find it useful to establish the concepts of register transfers (see Chapter 1) in your mind. However, you will *not* learn programming from that equipment.

For learning you should use a small microcomputer that has sufficient software already in place. A too primitive learning tool will cause you to waste time on unessential details. A too advanced system may prevent you from understanding the internal details. In this chapter we will outline the important features of a good learning tool and how to use it.

Basic Environment

Each learning tool presents a learning environment. You should try to determine which elements of that environment you will need and which elements are not important. For example, to enter programs into your microcomputer, you will need some kind of keyboard (or other medium). Similarly, to see the results of your program, you will need some way of displaying data from memory under program control. Some of the kits and complete microcomputers come with a keyboard but others demand the use of a teletypewriter or other kind of computer terminal. It seems unbalanced to have a $250 microcomputer connected to a $1,500 terminal, but that may be necessary.

If you are making a large commitment to microprocessors, you will need the terminal during software development anyway; it is essential as a good digital 'scope. Since you will need the terminal, you may as well learn with it too. Therefore, for those of you who are certain you will need the capability, the acquisition of a good computer terminal is a good first step. Whether you use a printing terminal or a CRT depends on personal preference. If your terminal will be used solely with your microcomputer, you should choose a printing terminal. Since you will eventually have to acquire and use an assembler program on your microcomputer, you will need that hard-copy capability. Of course, you will also need some data recording and playback means. If, however, you intend to assemble your programs on another computer and then transport the final object program to the microcomputer, you may find the CRT more attractive. A CRT terminal is quiet, it allows rapid change of displayed data, and it prevents unnecessary paper consumption. However, here you will still have to have some program storage medium.

If you are not too sure whether or not you will be using micros in your future jobs, you may wish to rent a terminal from any one of the equipment rental firms. In major metropolitan areas you should be able to get a thirty-day rental agreement with overnight delivery.

If you are operating on a more restricted budget (or doing it at home on your own money), you may wish to limit your microcomputer choices to those that include some elementary keyboard and display capability. Devices like the Cramerkits, the MOS Technology KIM-1, and the EPA Micro-68, which include seven-segment LED's for output and keyboards or switches for input, are slow and painful to use, but they have the advantage of avoiding the necessity of acquiring an expensive terminal.

The microcomputer you choose is relatively unimportant. Remember, what you are trying to learn is not the specific idiosyncracies of some particular microprocessor (although you will certainly learn those, too). Instead, you are trying to grasp the fundamentals of sequential program execution so that you can easily write programs for any computer you may have in the future. Because of the trend in microprocessors, it seems more practical to select one of the eight- or sixteen-bit machines. The Intersil 6100, modeled on the DEC PDP-8, may be a good choice because of the wealth of educational material and the good books that are available on the PDP–8. The four-bit microprocessors are so strongly idiosyncratic that they are probably not good learning models. Since the de facto emerging standard of microprocessors (the 709 of micros, if you will) is the 8080A, you might want to learn on that one first.

Program Storage Media

Regardless of the computer you choose and regardless of the terminal configuration, you should have some way of saving and retrieving programs externally. If you have access to a teletypewriter, your problem is solved: use the paper tape punch/reader designed into that terminal. If you are fortunate enough to have one of the computer terminals that has magnetic tape cassettes (especially if the cassettes can be controlled from the microprocessor under software control), you have the best possible medium for program storage. Even if you don't have a terminal, you can still record programs by using a common audio cassette recorder. One possible interface circuit is described in Chapter 7.

Microcomputer Features

A microcomputer that is designed to be used as a major OEM component will tend to be designed with different features from a microcomputer that is designed as a learning tool. Fortunately, most of the OEM products can also double as learning devices. There are some basic features that you should look for, however. There are important kinds of controls that most microcomputers should have for learning use, and there are displays you should have so that you can monitor the progress of your programs.

Certainly, the address, data, and control buses should be displayed on LED's. In the simplest systems the bus lines drive buffers for single LED's. In more elaborate systems groups of four bus bits are fed into a seven-segment decoder to drive a hexadecimal display. In the most elaborate systems a device like the Burroughs' Self-Scan is interfaced to display the system buses at all times.

The address and data buses are easily displayed. However, the control bus must also be displayed. Knowing what address and data bus contents are may be useful, but only if you know whether memory is being read or written; the control bus signals /MEMW and /MEMR (see Chapter 2) are good candidates for display. You may also want to see that important CPU control and response signals (like RESET, INTERRUPT, and ACKNOWLEDGE) are also displayed.

A microcomputer that does not have these displays is limited as a learning tool. Many semiconductor companies, on the advice of their software designers, claim that you don't need these displays to learn with or during system debugging. Nevertheless, experienced microcomputer designers nearly always put them into prototype systems. Some complex hardware/software interface problems are very difficult to debug without these displays. If your microcomputer doesn't have these displays, it is easy to add them. The appropriate signals can be tapped with either inverting or noninverting buffers to drive external LED's. You must be sure to account for the load these buffers present to the buses.

The controls on the microprocessor are as important as the displays. In fact, the displays are virtually useless unless you have a control that can manually halt the microprocessor. Otherwise, the data will be changing in the displays at a rate faster than you can comprehend. As a minimum, you must have some kind of control that will RESET the processor to the equivalent of a power-up condition. This control is used whenever you have to regain control of an errant program. If you do not have this control, you have no way of recovering a program that enters an endless loop.

Connecting to Logic State Analyzers

The new logic state analyzers are powerful debugging tools, but connecting thirty-two probes to the address, data, and control buses is often a chore that is deferred much too long. Besides, that task is error-prone and may lead to analysis of non-existant problems caught by faulty connections.

Experienced microcomputer designers always make up a set of sixteen-pin DIP plugs with connections directly to the logic state analyzer and then they arrange the buses on sixteen-pin socket patterns on the board under test. Thirty-two connections can then be made by plugging in two DIP plugs. For eight-bit processors, one plug is usually allocated to the sixteen-bit address bus and the other plug carries the eight-bit data bus and eight of the important control signals.

When you lay out a printed-circuit card, you should arrange to leave space for these two sockets so that you can debug the product on the production line.

A HALT or WAIT switch that can suspend program execution under manual control is also useful. This switch enables you to stop the processor and examine the address and data buses for valid values.

Another powerful capability, usually combined with the HALT or WAIT ability, is the SINGLE-STEP function. This push button allows the execution of one instruction at a time. After halting the processor, you can depress SINGLE-STEP several times and observe the changes in the bus displays until you reach a point of particular interest in your program. You will use this feature many times in your initial learning days.

If your computer does not have HALT or SINGLE-STEP capabilities, you can usually add them. If there is any way at all to halt the processor, you can insert the appropriate switching and (if necessary) decoding logic. If the processor is static, inhibiting the clock is enough to halt the processor. In dynamic processors, which represent most of today's offerings, special synchronization circuitry may be required. If you scout around, you will probably find someone who has already added this circuitry to one or another of the configurations of your selected micro.

If your microprocessor permits, you may also want to have a switch that selects between single-step instructions or memory cycles. In the instruction mode, each depression of the SINGLE-STEP switch will cause the complete execution of one instruction. In the memory cycle mode, use of this push button will cause advancing by a single memory cycle. This is particularly important when you debug interfaces that have external equipment; you can single-step by instruction up to the point you are about to execute an input or output instruction and then you can revert to the memory cycle mode. If it is an output instruction, you can single-step by memory cycle until the data is present on the data bus and the address bus holds the output port address. When your processor is in this static condition you can follow the signal from the processor all the way out to the external equipment to ensure proper circuitry and control.

In addition to these controls and displays, a separate set that can be used under software control should be included. You may have to wire this set up to an input/output port yourself. A rank of switches and a seven-segment LED may be all that you need, but they can be used as simulated input/output devices while you learn to program. If you have (or wire) a seven-segment LED on an output port, for example, one of your initial experiments in learning can be writing a program to count on that digit, say, once per second. Similarly, some switches on an input port enable you to write programs to read in some data and then produce more elaborate displays. Of course, if you have a computer terminal connected to your microcomputer, you won't need these simple devices (although, if they are already designed in, you can certainly exploit them).

A complete learning system (Figure 3.1) should include all these hardware features. External peripherals, such as teletypewriter interfaces, may also be included in the design. Finally, some spare input/output port capacity should be provided. Ideally, this capacity should be provided in the form of chips, although sockets for chips that you supply are acceptable. The lack of additional input/output capacity means that you will have to disconnect your own special equipment each time you want to use debugging facilities, an unnecessary and time-consuming chore.

Monitor Software

A microprocessor is a naked animal if it doesn't have some resident software. In most computer kits or learning tools some kind of small utility program called a *monitor* is usually provided. The monitor provides you with the following:

1. An example of programming on the computer you have
2. An aid in loading, executing, and debugging your own programs
3. A source of additional software resources

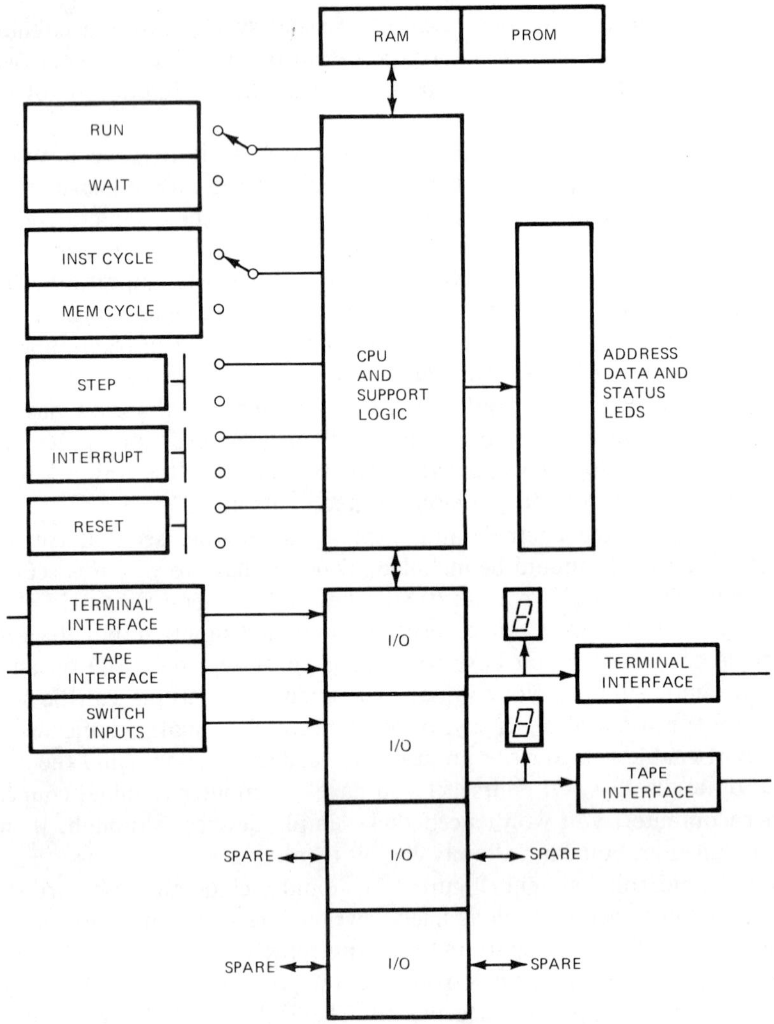

Figure 3.1 Typical learning tool configuration.

The monitor is generally not a very large program, usually on the order of 512 to 2,048 bytes. Since it is easily understood, it should be read, but you should definitely *not* assume that because the manufacturer wrote it the monitor represents good progrmming practice. Some of the worst code in the industry has been published from monitors produced by reputable semiconductor firms. Nevertheless, the monitor program should be read because it is better than nothing at all. Where you read the program, assume that it all works (which may be a rash assumption). If you don't understand how some particular bit of code works, study the reference manual for the monitor and for the microprocessor; if you still cannot understand it, consult you semi maker's technical representative.

The basic purpose of a monitor program is to give your microcomputer elementary power. A minimal monitor should have the following features for:

1. Controlling your terminal and/or other input/output media
2. Accepting hexadecimal or octal code representing your desired program and depositing it into successive bytes of memory
3. Displaying selected (and successive) bytes of memory so that you can verify your program and examine intermediate data values
4. Loading the program counter so that you can transfer control to your own program

In addition, you will find numerous other features in most monitors, some of which will be described later in this chapter.

Since the monitor is a program that resides in memory (usually in a ROM or a PROM so that it is ready for execution when power is applied), you can use components of the monitor as subroutines. If your monitor can effectively control your terminal or other input/output device, for example, you won't have to write your own programs for that function ("Immature artists imitate, mature artists steal," to paraphrase Robert Blake). Depending on your needs, you can either copy that software into your own program or you can use the subroutine calling instructions from your program to invoke the monitor's facilities.

Monitor Commands

Most monitors are written to operate from a terminal like a teletypewriter. There are exceptions, such as the KIM-1, which rely solely on their own keyboards and displays. However, the basic operational concepts of the monitor are essentially identical regardless of the specific form of your communications with the microcomputer. In this discussion of the monitor we will assume that a terminal with printing capability exists.

A monitor is nothing more than a computer program for your microprocessor that allows you to maintain a dialogue. The monitor requests information and you provide it. The monitor acts upon that information and then requests more. Usually, during power-up sequence the monitor will print out a "prompt" character to let you know that it is in control and ready for you to "speak." The usual prompt character is a question mark, although the period is also frequently used.

In response to a prompt character, you have a selection of characters you may type; each letter you type specifies a different feature of the monitor that you wish to use. Since each monitor assigns these characters differently, you have to learn each one anew. For example, to be able to insert data into memory, one monitor may require that you type "A" (for ALTER), another may require an "M" (for enter-to-MEMORY), and a third may call for you to type "S" (for SUBSTITUTE). You will notice, however, a mnemonic significance to the letters chosen.

In the following examples we will use the assignments listed below:

"A" (ALTER) Used to alter the contents of RAM
"D" (DISPLAY) Used to display the contents of memory
"G" (GO) Used to go to your program in memory

Each command may have (zero or more) *operands,* also known as *arguments.* These operands are usually supplied as hexadecimal numbers. In a computer that has sixteen-bit addressing the addresses may be of up to four hexadecimal digits. Bytes are represented as one or two hex digits.

Good monitors can be separated from poor monitors by the way in which they handle errors. Humans are error-prone; good software acknowledges this fact by providing some method of correcting errors. If you make a typing error and the monitor requires that you retype your command entirely, the monitor is a poor one. If you make a typing error and the monitor provides you with no "out," that is a terrible monitor. If you can correct your mistakes without affecting the software, you have a good monitor. In most microprocessor monitors errors are easily corrected in one of two ways:

Octal vs. Hex

Computers talk binary, but humans find binary representation very error-prone, especially when talking about the thousands of bits in a typical computer program. Therefore, for the benefit of humans, a shorthand is used.

Octal represents digits in three-bit groups with symbols in the range 0 ... 7; hexadecimal (called hex for short) represents binary quantities in four-bit groups with symbols in the range 0 ... 9 and A, B, C, D, E, F. There is nothing magical about the choice of the six letters of the alphabet. They could have been chosen as any arbitrary six symbols, but letters are easy to remember.

Because most microprocessors have words and bytes in increments of four bits (i.e., 8, 12, and 16), most people use hex for representing data and programs in the machine language form. Some people prefer octal. The choice is arbitrary, although those who cling to octal because they are afraid of hex will just have to learn the hex as more and more software becomes available that assumes the hexadecimal character set.

There is no such thing as an "octal" computer or a "hex" computer. Some computers have instructions with subfields that are made up of three or four bits. These computers are sometimes claimed to be octal or hex machines; but this is misleading terminology.

Use what you feel comfortable with.

1. Some "escape" is provided that aborts the current command and restarts the monitor. You will see a new prompt character printed.
2. Operands may be typed in at length. If an address is expected, only the *last* four hexadecimal digits you type will be accepted.

Another way to judge the quality of the monitor is by examining its handling of optional operands. Some commands might meaningfully have one or two operands. If the monitor always requires two (regardless of your needs), the monitor has not been very well designed with you in mind.

When more than one operand is supplied for a particular command, those operands must be separated from one another. A space or a comma is usually typed to separate the operands. In monitors typing *any* character except a hexadecimal digit will cause the successive digits to be taken as a new operand. This can cause problems if you make a typing mistake like "123X4."

Finally, each command is terminated by some unique character or set of symbols. In most microcomputer monitors a command is terminated by typing the carriage return (CR) key on the terminal.

Some basic command sequences are shown for the simple three-command monitor in Figure 3.2. In this illustration each character typed by the user is underscored; other characters are typed by the monitor. The symbol CR stands for the carriage return key on the terminal.

```
?A2000 00-C3 00- 00- (CR)
?D2000,2002 (CR)
2000: C3 00 00
?G2000 (CR)
?
```

Figure 3.2 An extremely simple monitor use example.

After the first prompt character, the user typed in a request for the ALTER capability ("A"). The first operand (2000) is the address at which memory is to be altered; that address is terminated by a space character. Since only one operand is required on an ALTER (the address at which to begin changing RAM contents), the monitor proceeds to display the actual contents of the byte at location 2000; in this example, the memory contains zero. Any hexadecimal content can be inserted into that memory location by typing it. The monitor accepts all of the hexadecimal characters (C3) and keeps the last two typed (in case of typing error). When a nonhex character (the space) is detected, the new value alters storage and the next storage location is printed out (00). Since nothing is typed in by the user except the space, nothing is changed in memory, but the third byte is printed out. Typing carriage return causes the monitor to terminate the ALTER function. A new prompt character is printed.

The user can now have the three bytes just entered printed back out for verification. The "D" command is used to DISPLAY the contents of locations 2000 through 2002. The monitor first prints out the address of the first byte and then prints out up to sixteen bytes on a line. Each line starts with the address of the first byte on that line. At the end of the printing of all the specified data, a new prompt character is printed.

To execute this program, the user uses the "G" command to GO to the entry point. Upon sensing the carriage return, the monitor causes the new program at location 2000 to be executed. In this particular example the program will return control to the monitor (a good practice during debugging), which responds with a new prompt character.

If your program has a bug, you can either insert or delete code with the ALTER command, take periodic checks of actual storage contents with the DISPLAY command, and enter the program at different points with the GO command. If your program captures control of the processor, you may regain control by using the RESET push button on the physical hardware. Normal program termination should cause a jump back to the starting point of the monitor; printing of the prompt character tells you that your program has completed execution.

Other Monitor Functions

There are many more capabilities that can be operated under a monitor. Certainly, the cassette tape reading and writing routines can be invoked as monitor commands to make it easier to save and reload programs. Additional peripheral equipment, such as PROM programmers, can be controlled so that debugged programs can be copied into ROM form directly from RAM. Diagnostic capabilities, designed to test memory for example, can also be placed in the monitor.

Some features found in most monitors include the following:

1. Breakpoint
2. Register display
3. Data conversion

When you are debugging a program, it is often useful to "plant" a "trap." When the "trap" is executed, control automatically reverts to the monitor. This trap is usually called a *breakpoint.* It can be planted by command at a specified address; whenever a breakpoint is set, the prior breakpoint is removed and the original code is replaced.

A breakpoint works by removing some of your code from the specified address and inserting a reference to the monitor instead; the removed code is saved for future restoration. When the monitor gains control, all of the processor's registers are saved so that the program can be resumed at a later time. While the monitor is in control, all of the monitor's capability can be used to display the interrupted program's registers as well as memory contents. If a bug is detected, the ALTER capability can be used to insert a "patch" into the program.

During the initiation of a breakpoint the processor's registers are saved somewhere in memory. Instead of requiring the user to display that memory, it is useful to have a monitor command that will print out an annotated set of registers. Each register is identified by name and content so that there is little confusion.

Another useful capability is numeric conversion. These commands enable you to type in a decimal number and see it displayed in binary, octal, and hex. Given a number in any one of these bases, the other three equivalent values are printed out.

4

Manipulating Internal Registers

Programming is easy to learn, especially for anyone who has had some digital design experience. The skills necessary for programming are few, but they must be conscientiously applied. Since we've already treated the microprocessors and microcomputers as little more than bunches of registers, you can readily see that programming is little more than causing data to move from one register to another. That is all that instructions do; they cause data to move from one register to another.

This part of programming, however, is not the whole subject. Even after you know to manipulate the internal registers of the computer, you'll have to acquire the skills needed to convert vague English-language specifications into instructions that will satisfy the need. That part of programming will be the subject of another chapter (see Chapter 6).

Classes of Registers

There are different kinds of registers in different computers, but some registers are nearly always provided. A good example is the Program Counter. The Program Counter (called the *PC* or *P-register*) appears in some form in every microprocessor. As we discovered in Chapter 2, it is the Program Counter that allows us to select which of all of the possible instructions to execute next.

One absolute requirement for a computer is the ability to change the contents of the PC. An instruction always included in the computer is the capability to permit the programmer to specify the contents of the Program Counter (Figure 4.1). These are called *Jump instructions* (also known as *Branch* or sometimes

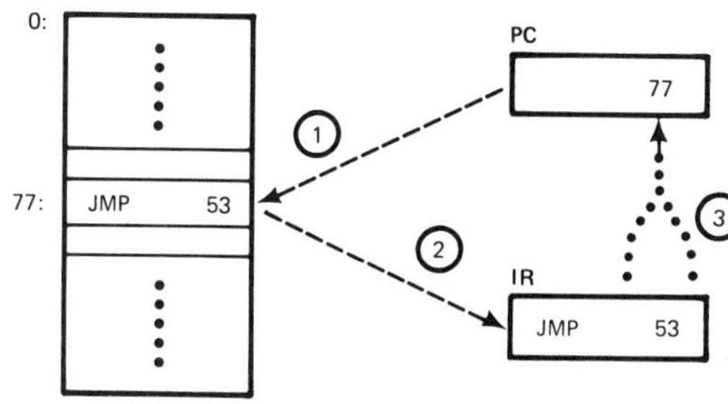

Figure 4.1 Execution of a jump instruction.

Transfer instructions). Jump instructions specify where the next instruction is to be fetched from. In other words, the control of the computer's instruction fetch cycle is sent off to the specified address. A simple *unconditional jump* contains the desired PC contents as an immediate address in the instruction itself. Remember, any of the addressing modes introduced in Chapter 2 may be incorporated into the design of the jump instruction. Various microprocessors have absolute, indirect, indexed, relative, or even more complex jump addresses. No matter what addressing scheme is used, somehow the entire Program Counter is loaded with a completely new value so that the next instruction can be fetched.

A very important class of instructions derived from the simple jump set is the set of *conditional jumps.* These instructions usually offer the possibility of causing the PC to be loaded, depending on the setting of some one-bit register. If the one-bit register holds a "1," then the PC will be loaded from the instruction; if "0," the PC will remain unchanged and so the next instruction in sequence will be executed.

Notice that the jump instructions don't do any data processing but they provide a powerful tool to implement the ability to execute some specified code over and over again. For example, in Figure 4.2 we have written a small program for the 8080. It reads some input port, selects the least-significant bit, and then returns to the top of that program segment until the input port's least-significant bit is a "1." After the intervening code (not shown) is executed, the control eventually reverts to the top of the input loop.

The program segment in Figure 4.2 is shown in three different but equivalent forms. First is the flow chart, a graphic representation of what is to be done, albeit in a form not yet acceptable to the computer. The second example is in symbolic form in which the operations of the computer (the instructions) are individually specified by name; these names are chosen by the designer of the computer to remind the reader of the function that the instruction is to perform. The IN instruction, for example, causes data to be read into the computer from a specified input port. The ANI (AND immediate) symbol specifies an instruction that will AND the immediate operand with the contents of the accumulator (which was initialized by the IN instruction). As a side effect of this particular computer's execution of that instruction, a one-bit register is set or cleared to tell the pro-

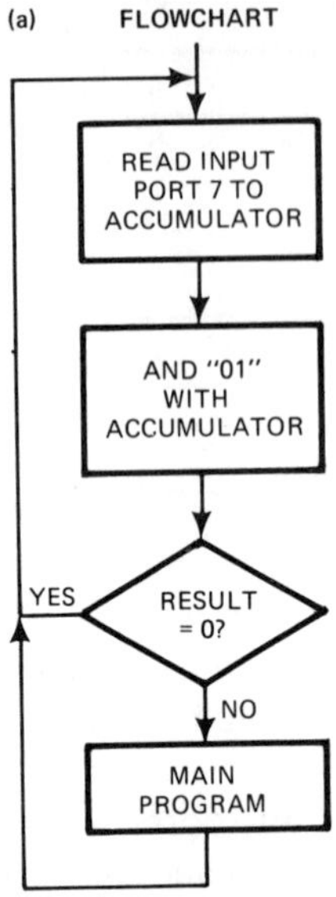

(b) SYMBOLIC CODE

LOCATION	OPERATOR	OPERAND
	⋮	
53	IN	7
55	ANI	1
57	JZ	53
	⋮	
	JMP	53

(c) OBJECT (HEX) CODE

LOCATION	CODE
53	DB07
55	E601
57	CA5300
	C35300

Figure 4.2 A small program with jumps.

grammer whether the result was zero or nonzero. In this program segment we take advantage of that register by using the conditional jump instruction JZ that will cause the program counter to be loaded with 53 only if the last instruction (the ANI) causes a zero result. If the result of the last instruction was nonzero (i.e., the least-significant bit of input port 7 was "1"), then execution will proceed from the instruction immediately following the JZ.

The last instruction in a program segment is often an unconditional jump (JMP in Figure 4.2). That causes the computer to repeat the execution of the important instructions all over again.

Another important class of registers contains the (one or more) accumulators of a computer. These registers are referenced by a rich set of instructions and can usually be involved in operations involving the Arithmetic Logic Unit (ALU) of that computer. Some accumulators are very powerful, but others have limited capability. Remember, the accumulator itself is only a register and the power comes from the instructions that may refer to that register. A related set of registers may be limited in power; these registers are called the *general-purpose registers* of the computer. All these registers that can be used to hold data to be manipulated by the program are usually combined together conceptually and called the computer's *register file.*

The register files of different computers are of different sizes. The popular 6800, for example, has two accumulators and no general-purpose registers. The 8080 has one accumulator and six general-purpose registers. The 9900 has sixteen general-purpose registers, most of which may also be used as accumulators.

An accumulator is distinguished from a general-purpose register by its ability to receive the results of an ALU operation. In a computer like the 9900 the destination address of an add instruction, say, can be specified in the instruction. In the 6800, however, a single bit specifies which of the two accumulators is to receive the result. The 8080, with only one accumulator, always places the results of an ALU operation into that register. Thus we can say that the accumulator is implicitly referenced in that computer.

Operation on Accumulators

The typical instruction sets of common microprocessors include instructions to add, subtract, perform logical operations like AND, OR, and Exclusive-OR, and to shift data left and right in a word. Nearly all computers produce "side-effect" changes in one-bit wide registers called *ALU flags;* these are of tremendous utility (and occasional inconvenience) to the programmer.

Microcontrol of the CPU

The architectural features of the instructions in a particular CPU are usually embodied in a ROM or PLA (Programmed Logic Array). Even when a ROM is used, it is usually treated as a PLA, an example of which is shown in Figure A.

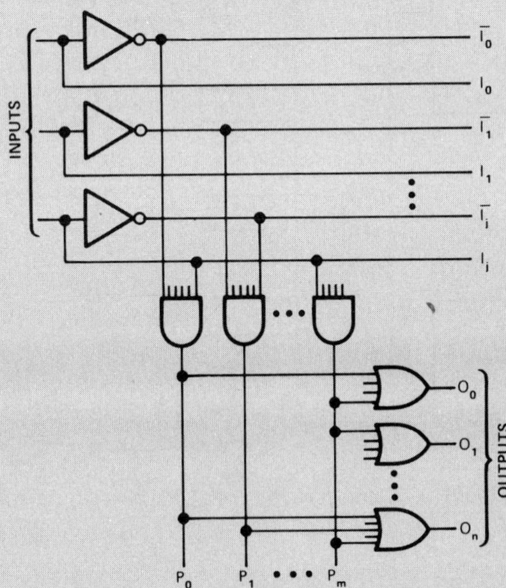

Figure A Basic PLA structure.

A PLA is a way to implement AND-OR-INVERT combinational logic in an orderly way. Each PLA consists of inputs (both normal and inverted), a rank of AND-gates so that various combinations of inputs can be combined together into what are called *product terms,* and a rank of OR-gates so that various product terms can be combined into output signals. These devices are usually very fast and simple to design. Since they are easy to change, variants of the basic design (or correction of errors) are relatively easy to accomplish.

Inside the CPU the PLA is used (Figure B) to combine the specific Instruction Register contents with various derived timing signals to create signals to the registers. Literally, each register transfer is individually controlled. At one instant in time, for example, a particular register may be enabled onto the internal data transfer bus inside the CPU, while another register is strobed to cause the contents of the data bus to be latched. All these register transfers occur inside the chip out of sight of the programmer and engineer.

Changing the PLA contents makes it easy to change the subtle architecture of the computer.

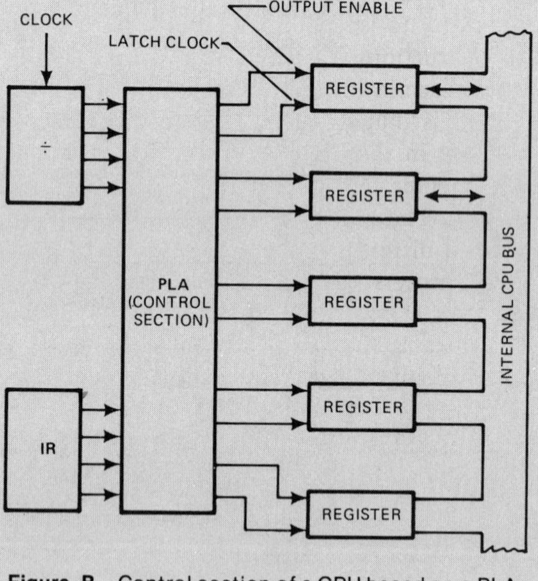

Figure B Control section of a CPU based on a PLA.

Like all other instructions, the ALU instruction set may include simple and/or complex addressing opportunities. In the simplest microprocessors the ALU operations may only involve the register file. If operands are to be fetched from memory, they must be copied from memory into a general register before the ALU operation can proceed. In other computers memory locations can be specified for these operations. In a few microcomputers storage can be used as both the source and the destination of operands (that is, the results can be placed right back into memory instead of into an accumulator).

Operations on data may involve one or two operands. Instructions that require only one operand include the shifts, logical inversions, and increment or decrement instructions. Shift instructions typically move data one bit to the right or left in some specified register. Logical inversions usually complement every bit in the specified register. The increment and decrement instructions are one-operand types, but this is because the second operand is implied (a "1"). Most of the important ALU instructions require two operands, one of which may be implied (the sole accumulator). If the accumulator is implied in the instruction, the accumulator is used as a source for one of the operands and as the destination of the result; the second operand is specified as part of the instruction.

The uses of the common ALU instructions should be fairly obvious, but some uses are clever. Since all data is processed inside the computer in word-sized increments, it is often necessary to isolate one or more bits of interest out of a larger register. The logical instructions (AND, OR, Exclusive-OR) are used to do just that, as we have already seen in Figure 4.2.

Since each computer is unique in its rules of processing data, a generalized treatment is not relevant in this book. However, you should try to group the instructions of the computer into classes in order to help you understand the power at your disposal. The ALU operations of the 8080 are summarized in Figure 4.3. If you use a different computer, you should create a similar chart. Users of the 6800 microprocessor will find that all of the literature that summarizes the instruction set is arranged this way. However, as a learning tool, you should create your own table because it will help you learn what resources you have with this particular computer.

PARTIAL LIST OF 8080 ALU INSTRUCTIONS:

INSTRUCTION	ADDRESSING SCHEME			
	IMPLIED ACCUMULATOR	REGISTER FILE	STORAGE	IMMEDIATE
ADD	–	ADD r	ADD M	ADI d
SUBTRACT	–	SUB r	SUB M	SUI d
AND	–	ANA r	ANA M	ANI d
OR	–	ORA r	ORA M	ORI d
EXCLUSIVE-OR	–	XPA r	XRA M	SRI d
COMPARE	–	CMP r	CPM M	CPI d
ADD WITH CARRY	–	ADC r	ADC M	ACI d
SUBTRACT WITH BORROW	–	SBB r	SBB M	SBI d
ROTATE ACCUMULATOR LEFT	RAL	–	–	–
ROTATE ACCUMULATOR RIGHT	RAR	–	–	–

Figure 4.3 A partial list of 8080 ALU instructions.

ALU Side Effects

The conditional instructions and the basic power of the ALU go hand-in-hand. For example, the ALU instructions are often used to count some event. To count N events, we establish a register initially with N and then decrement that register by one each time the expected event occurs. When the register attains zero, we know that we are done. A flow chart for this instruction sequence is shown in Figure 4.4(a). This program has the following three major sections:

1. Look for the event
2. Decrement the count
3. See if the count is yet at zero

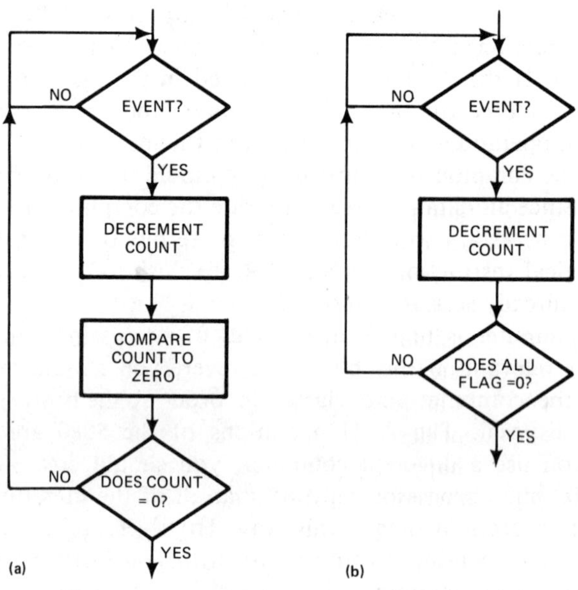

Figure 4.4 Alternative ways to count events.

Some computers have special instructions that can set up some one-bit registers with comparison results so that conditional jump instructions have something to refer to, as in Figure 4.4(a). After the count is decremented, it must be explicitly compared with zero to see if the task is finished.

If the computer's ALU has "side effects," the extraneous comparison with zero can be eliminated, provided that the ALU automatically sets a "zero/nonzero" flip-flop after each operation is performed [Figure 4.4(b)]. Whenever the ALU is used, the ALU flag (flip-flop) specifies whether the result was zero or nonzero, regardless of whether that information is of importance to this particular program or not.

Provisions for different ALU side-effect flags are made in different computers. It is common to have a "zero/nonzero" flag. Another common flag is the *carry* flag;

computers that do not have the carry flag make programming difficult. Another flag (not exactly the same as a carry) is the *overflow* flag. This flag specifies that the result is too large to be contained in the destination register. Overflow and carry flags may mean the same or different things at different times.

Computers sometimes provide for external signals as ALU flags. In these designs the same conditional jump instructions that can refer to ALU flags can be used to make decisions based on the logic state of some pin of the microprocessor itself. These flags are useful for limited data volumes of a high-priority nature.

To illustrate that the flags are part of the ALU and not the accumulator, the flags are usually drawn to show that they are connected to the ALU itself. In some microprocessors every operation involving the accumulator is forced through the ALU. In these designs the ALU flags are always representative of the accumulator's contents. In other architectures specific ALU instructions must be used to set those flags. In the latter processors the flags are often set by executing an OR instruction specifying the accumulator as both of the operands; this forces the data through the ALU without changing the accumulator's contents.

Miscellaneous Instructions

In addition to the basic jump and ALU operation instructions, which all computers have in some form or other, there are miscellaneous instructions. This is the largest set, by far, of all of the instruction groups, and it is unique to the computer's architecture. It is the designer's choice that makes some computers powerful and others incomprehensible. Each computer must be analyzed on its own merits, not by how the register transfers provided match some other computer's miscellaneous instructions. Careful use of the individual instructions may lead to nonobvious and very efficient designs. Slavish devotion to some subset of the miscellaneous instructions that happens to be similar to some other computer is a sure way to waste many of the inherent resources of the computer.

Many of the miscellaneous instructions are used for house keeping chores. In an eight-bit computer, for example, it is common to have several instructions that can move word *pairs* from register to register; this can make your program run faster. A special set of registers, may be provided by the computer designer. One good example is the Stack. See Figure 4.5.

Instructions must be provided in the computer to prime the Stack Pointer, to push data onto the Stack, and to pop data off the Stack. Usually, during the housekeeping instructions that are executed whenever power is first applied to the CPU, the Stack Pointer is initialized to some known address. Thereafter, a properly debugged program will keep all push-pop operations executing in pairs to ensure that only validly "pushed" data is ever "popped." Without push-pop parity, a program might "pop" some unexpected data with unpredictable results.

When data is pushed onto the Stack, the Stack Pointer (SP) is decremented (or incremented, depending on the designer's whim). The SP is used as an address to storage so that the data can be put away. Any number of push operations can be

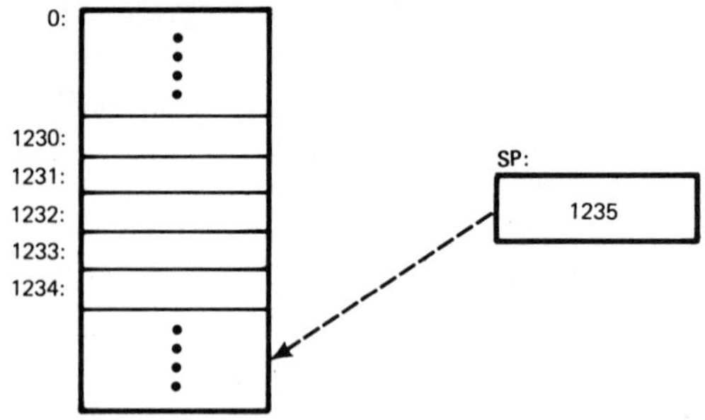

Figure 4.5 Organization of a stack.

performed, but each one consumes one more word in storage. Data is retrieved from the Stack by using the SP as an address to read from; after the data has been retrieved, the SP is incremented. Notice that data is always retrieved in a Last-In, First-Out order. Without special manipulation of the Stack Pointer, this order is rigidly maintained. Therefore, data will be retrieved in exactly the reverse order of original entry. This is both a bane and a boon, depending on what you're programming at the time. Obviously, to avoid unnecessary usage of RAM space, data should be removed from the Stack just as soon as practical.

Whenever data must be stored temporarily, it can be pushed onto the Stack. Some computers permit ALU instructions to refer to operands in the Stack, but other computers prevent it. Some computers don't provide a Stack at all.

Subroutines

Most computer programs are too large to comprehend everything at once. Even programs of just a few instructions may require hours of study to completely understand. In the early days of computers, programmers learned to break down large programs into manageable pieces called *subroutines.*

Originally thought to be ways to make programs smaller, subroutines have been found to be even more important than that. A subroutine is a piece of program that has some kind of behavior that we can depend on, based on supplied data of a known kind and resulting in data (or actions) of a predictable kind. For example, subroutines can be specified to compute the square root of a number, or to convert hexadecimal code into ASCII for a teletypewriter, or to print out on a computer terminal, or to convert analog data into digital form.

Subroutines help preserve a programmer's sanity. By creating subroutines, a programmer can break a whole task into individually manageable pieces.

A subroutine consists of an identifiable piece of computer program that has known entry and exit conditions. The entry conditions are the required register contents that must prevail for this subroutine to operate correctly. The exit conditions are the register contents that will prevail (assuming the proper entry conditions and a bug-free subroutine). Some subroutines are executed by "falling into" them from some other code; these are called *in-line subroutines.* Other subroutines are isolated from the main body of the program and are invoked by using Jump instructions to get to the subroutine and back out again; these are called *out-of-line subroutines.*

In-line subroutines are useful in helping to break the program into manageable pieces. Out-of-line subroutines have the additional advantage that they can be used from many points in the main program without having to have more than one copy of the subroutine occupying space in storage. Most often we will concern ourselves with out-of-line subroutines, since these are complete and unique program segments that can be designed, written, tested, and debugged independently of all others. Out-of-line subroutines can be kept in a personal library of programs so that they don't have to be written and debugged over again.

Out-of-line subroutines gain control by using special jumps known as CALL instructions. A CALL acts like a jump instruction, but the computer "remembers" where the control came from; at the end of the subroutine, control can be returned to that point. The method of invoking a subroutine is represented graphically in Figure 4.6; in this example we assume the existence of a special "return address" register (R). When the CALL is executed, the address of the instruction after the CALL is recorded in R, the PC is loaded with the subroutine's starting address, and the subroutine executes a RETURN instruction that restores the original PC from the temporary R-register.

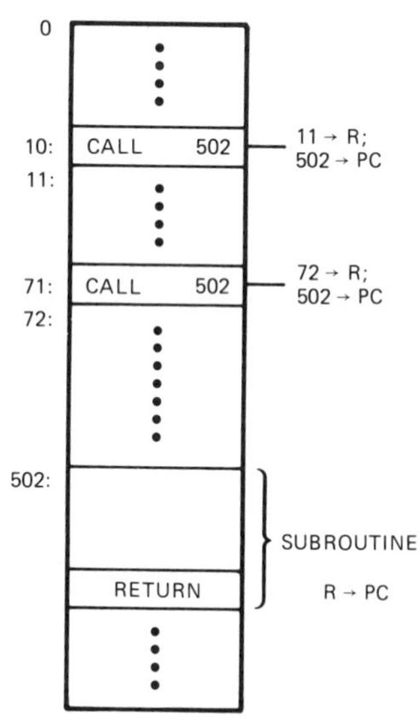

Figure 4.6 Invocation of an out-of-line subroutine.

Although some microprocessors have this primitive subroutine linkage/return mechanism, others use more elaborate schemes. In particular, with a single return address register, only one subroutine may be active at a time. What happens if our subroutine must, in turn, use another subroutine? Some way of preserving the R-register is imperative. If the R-register can be manipulated, it can be preserved elsewhere, but at considerable expense in terms of instructions that must be executed prior to each CALL instruction. Most microprocessors use a return address Stack (Figure 4.7).

With a return Stack, the Stack Pointer is used to define where the return address will be stored (and where it will be retrieved from upon execution of a RETURN. When the CALL is executed, the address of the location following the CALL is pushed onto the stack; upon RETURN, the topmost item is popped off the Stack and into the Program Counter. Now, the number of partially completed subroutines is limited only by the maximum Stack depth. In some microprocessors the Stack is a small register file on the CPU chip (the Signetics 2650 and Intel's 8008 are good examples); this is fast, but it places a fixed limit on the number of subroutines that may be pending at one time. The most popular micros, however, use the Stack Pointer to RAM for subroutine return address storage. This means a somewhat longer time for CALL and RETURN, but the depth of the Stack is limited only by the amount of available storage that can be reserved for this one use.

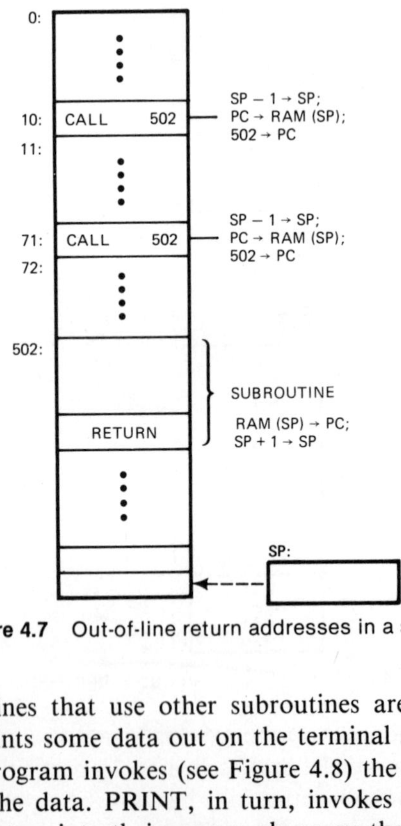

Figure 4.7 Out-of-line return addresses in a stack.

Chains of subroutines that use other subroutines are not uncommon. In a small program that prints some data out on the terminal several subroutines may be active. The main program invokes (see Figure 4.8) the PRINT subroutine that fetches and prepares the data. PRINT, in turn, invokes BUFFER, a subroutine that formats the characters into their proper places on the line to be produced on the terminal; BUFFER uses an area of RAM that holds one character for each

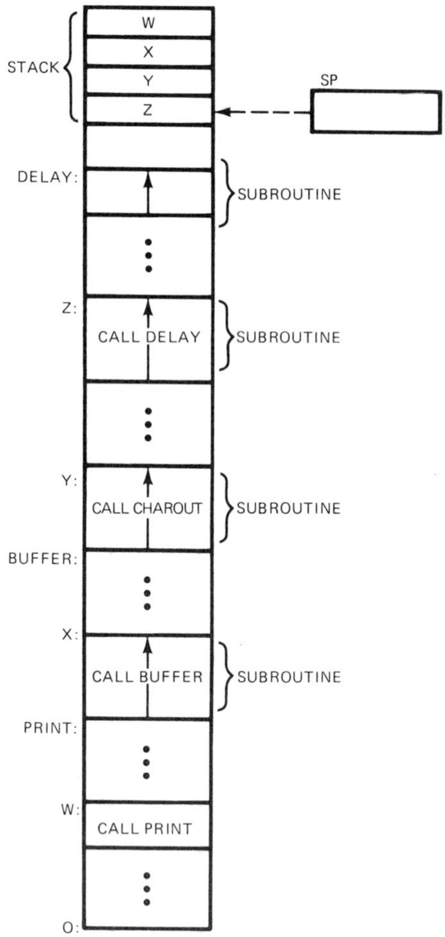

Figure 4.8 Several "nested" subroutines.

print position on the destination terminal. BUFFER, in turn, uses the CHAROUT subroutine to print a single character on the terminal. CHAROUT, in turn, uses the subroutine DELAY to wait after sending one character to the terminal. At the deepest point (once for each and every character printed on that terminal), there are four return addresses in the push-down Stack (one each to the locations following CALL's on PRINT, BUFFER, CHAROUT, and DELAY).

Analyzing the Processor

When you approach a new microprocessor for the first time, it is important to remember that all computers are fundamentally alike. What is unique about this particular microprocessor instruction set is what may make it most attractive for your set of tasks. What you seek is an understanding of which resources are *avail-*

able, not which resources are lacking. Almost any lack can be remedied with suitable software by using the instructions that *do* exist.

One of the first things to look for in a microprocessor is the set of ALU instructions. What operations can you perform, and on what kind of operands? In addition to these instructions, you should carefully study the various addressing modes. Ask how you can refer to the data to be operated on by these instructions.

See if there are any especially unusual instructions, for example, double-word addition or subtraction. For any instruction that may be new to you, try to imagine an application that would take advantage of it. If several instructions appear to do the same (or nearly the same) thing, try to determine how they differ. For example, if you can add the accumulator's contents to itself and if an instruction to shift the accumulator contents left one bit exists, how do these instructions differ and how are they alike? Do both of them treat the carry or overflow bit the same way under all conditions? You will discover subtle differences that will prove handy when you actually begin programming.

Once you understand the data manipulation instructions, you should concentrate on the instructions that provide for program control. Specifically, look at the conditional jumps, subroutine call, and return mechanisms and the registers used or affected by each. Now is a good time to tie the ALU instructions and control instructions together by examining the ALU flags. How are they set and cleared, and how may they be used? If the conditional jump instructions allow only one condition to be specified, how will you program jumps that depend on several simultaneous conditions? If complex jumps that depend on several flag-bit states are provided, how can you exploit this capability?

Once you understand the basic instructions, you should study the register complement. What registers exist in this microprocessor? How can you access them? You may safely ignore the registers over which you have no direct control. You might want to make up a table that relates the various registers to the instructions that may set or use them.

One very powerful way to learn all about a new computer is to create a register transfer table, a small portion of which may look like Figure 4.9. In this case, we have elected to show 8080's register transfers. However, this table can be constructed for any digital computer. Generally, the larger the complexity, the larger the table will be. The rows and columns are labeled with all of the registers of the CPU; at each intersection is written the instruction (or sequence of instructions) that will transfer data between these registers. Intersections on the diagonal, of course, are meaningless. Sometimes you will discover that no single instruction will accomplish what you want to do. In the 8080, for example, there are a couple of instructions provided for getting data *into* the Stack Pointer, but there is no single instruction for getting the Stack Pointer's contents into other registers for processing. Although the need to manipulate the Stack Pointer is rare, it is sometimes necessary. Note that in the intersection of the table we have outlined a two-instruction sequence that *can* transfer the Stack Pointer's contents into a register known as the HL. You may never need to perform this register transfer in all your

DESTINATION REGISTER

SOURCE REGISTER	A	B	C	D	DE	HL	SP	PC
A		MOV B, A	MOV C,A	MOV D, A	–	–	–	–
B	MOV A, B		MOV C, B	MOV D, B	–	–	–	–
C	MOV A, C	MOV B, C		MOV D, C	–	–	–	–
D	MOV A, D	MOV B, D	MOV C, D		–	–	–	–
DE	–	–	–	–		XCHG	XCHG SPHL XCHG	XCHG PCHL SCHG
HL	–	–	–	–	XCHG		SPHL	PCHL
SP	–	–	–	–	XCHG LXI H, 0 DAD SP XCHG	LXI H, 0 DAD SP		LXI H, 0 DAD SP PCHL
PC	–	–	–	–	CALL $ + 3 POP D	CALL $ + 3 POP H	CALL $ + 3 POP H SPHL	

Figure 4.9 A register transfer table for the 8080.

programming days, but the experience of constructing this table will provide you with an insight into the computer's architecture that no amount of manual reading will ever accomplish.

Whenever registers are totally incompatible, as, for example, when they have different sizes, that fact is noted by means of a dash.

What is important is this: Your goal is not to fill in the table but to prove to yourself that you *can* fill in the table. You can nearly always find a way to transfer one register's contents to another, although you may have to be clever or use another intermediate register. Whenever possible, you should choose examples that (although they may use other registers) do not modify contents of registers essentially involved in the transaction.

Selecting a Processor

Several factors must be considered before you can choose the right processor for a job. If, for example, you already have lots of a particular model on the shelf, the question is reduced to a simpler one: Can I do it with that processor or not? At the other extreme, if you are about to design a system to go into volume production, you will probably want to spend a lot of time making sure that you make the right decision.

The first question asked of a microprocessor is simple: Is it fast enough? How fast the CPU can perform an addition is only a rough guide. The addition time is only a gross approximation of the processor's speed. A better measure is application-dependent and requires that a *benchmark program* be written. The bench mark program assures you that you know enough about the processor or computer to justify making decisions about it.

A microprocessor benchmark should consist of from 100 to 200 instructions. The problem selected for the comparisons should be representative of the class of problems you will be facing. It is not a good idea to choose as the benchmark a simple algorithm like multiplication, unless the multiply function is a significant part of the intended application. At least part of the benchmark program should perform some input or output so that you can gain an appreciation of how much effort will be required in that area. It is not unreasonable to expect to spend two or three days on each microprocessor candidate. As a general rule, a cursory glance at a microprocessor summary will usually isolate one or more likely candidates. Once you have found several processors that will run at your (estimated) required speed, select one as an arbitrary choice. Then select one that is slower and one that is faster than the first one. A benchmark program should be written for each processor. The results of this exercise will probably yield a good appreciation of the most appropriate speed for your class of applications.

In addition to speed, your benchmark effort is supposed to uncover the inherently difficult idiosyncrasies of the instruction set. Even though you have never programmed a computer like this one before, you should be able to understand the manual, find the necessary instructions, and write them down. Although your intention should be to write error-free benchmark code, there is no way for you to assure correctness; your best efforts are necessary. As you write the benchmark programs, you will gain a feel for the things that are easy and the things that are difficult in this particular microprocessor; these are useful subjective inputs to the selection process.

Start with the benchmark program for the processor in the middle-speed range first. Write the benchmark program and then manually step through each instruction with test data to verify accuracy. Next, for each of the three test cases, compute the execution time; the three test cases should be made up of trivial, typical, and worst-case examples. A trivial test case requires the absolute minimum execution time through the benchmark program. The worst case, of course, should be selected to tax the software to the limit.

Computing execution time is relatively simple. First, divide the program into *basic blocks* (Figure 4.10); each block is made up of a sequence of code that has one entry point and one exit point. Each labeled instruction usually begins a basic block. The instructions just before a conditional jump instruction are a basic block. Each conditional jump instruction is a basic block. Now estimate the amount of time it will take for each basic block to execute. The estimates are made by summing up the execution times of the instructions. Be very careful to obtain the actual execution time for the manufacturer's literature; some of the manuals are deceptive and cite mythical numbers that ignore, for example, the instruction fetch time.

Once the basic blocks are identified and each block has an execution time determined, work through the benchmark program with the three test cases. For each test case, determine how many times each basic block will be executed; multiply each basic block's execution time by the execution frequency and sum them all up. You will obtain an estimate for the minimum, typical, and worst-case execution times. Some of these numbers may surprise you, for they may be significantly higher or lower than you expected.

The estimates you have derived from the benchmark examples will probably be

TYPICAL TIME(μSEC)	TYPICAL FREQUENCY	BASIC BLOCKS	INSTRUCTION TIME(μSEC)	PROGRAM		
				; 1-DIGIT BCD MULTIPLY		
			10.8	BCDMPY:	LD	5
32.4	1		10.8		CMA	
			10.8		XCH	5
129.6	6		21.6	LOOP1:	ISZ	5, BCDRET
			10.8		LD	7
			10.8		XCH	15
378.0	5		10.8		LD	3
			10.8		XCH	14
			10.8		LDM	–4
			10.8		XCH	13
			10.8		CLC	
			10.8	LOOP2:	SRC	1
			10.8		RDM	
			10.8		SRC	3
1728.0	20		10.8		ADM	
			10.8		DAA	
			10.8		WRM	
			10.8		INC	7
			10.8		INC	3
540.0	25		21.6		ISZ	13,LOOP2
			10.8	LOOP3:	SRC	3
			10.8		LDM	0
324.0	5		10.8		ADM	
			10.8		DAA	
			10.8		WRM	
			10.8		INC	7
108.0	5		21.6		JC	LOOP3
			10.8		LD	15
			10.8		XCH	7
324.0	5		10.8		LD	14
			10.8		XCH	3
			21.6		JUN	LOOP1
10.8	1		10.8	BCDRET:	BBL	0

3574.8 μSEC (TYP.)

Figure 4.10 A typical execution time computation.

lower than they would be in reality. In designing your benchmark program you have almost certainly not considered all of the necessary special-case processing that will be required. If you have never programmed the particular microprocessor before, you may have assumed some attributes about it that you will later find do not exist. Therefore, it is a good idea to double your estimated times before attempting to see whether or not the processor is fast enough to do the job. The additional factor of time will leave you a margin for cumulative errors; you will probably consume that margin thoroughly before the project is over.

Now that the benchmark program has been calibrated and measured, it is time to see whether or not the processor is fast enough. The benchmark program will be invoked with some frequency; this frequency is a function of the actual application, but it can be determined or estimated. If the benchmark program represents the processing of an event that occurs 5 times a second and the benchmark program requires more than 200 ms, then the processor is clearly too slow. If the benchmark program requires more than 100 ms, the processor will have 50% of its time available for executing all of the rest of the software. Since the benchmark tends to be the real-time critical portion of the software, this performance is usually satisfactory. In practice, a small amount of the code accounts for the majority of the time. Studies have shown that about 10% of the code may account for as much as 90% of the execution time.

If the benchmark program is too slow, you have two options:

1. Choose a faster processor at higher prices
2. Redesign to make the benchmark program faster

The first option is obvious. With the second option the engineer earns his keep. When the benchmark program was conceived, it assumed some complement of external hardware or other resources. The benchmark program may be made to operate faster by redistributing these resources. An essentially algorithmic process, for example, might be turned into a table look-up operation (mathematical procedures are often done this way). A benchmark that depends on a primitive input/output facility might be redesigned to take advantage of additional external hardware (provided, of course, that the new hardware doesn't drive prices into the infeasible region).

Similarly, if the processor is too fast, resources like memory or input/output hardware can perhaps be removed to make the program do more of the work. That can reduce the hardware costs.

Generally, speed costs money. Faster processors require faster memories and the associated control logic. They are also more difficult to debug because more critical timing relationships must be maintained. For economy, use only as much speed as necessary. Adopting a microprocessor just because it is faster than you think you will ever need it to be is an invitation to waste money.

Once the required speed range has been pinpointed, all of the processors that have similar or slightly faster addition times should be examined. Compare addition times by dividing the given register-to-register add time by the data word size to obtain addition time per bit. It will probably not be necessary to rewrite the benchmark programs for each and every one of the potential processors. However, after making the final selection, confirm it by wiring the benchmark program one more time.

Programming Steps

Once you know your microprocessor, you are no better equipped to program than a novice who has memorized the TTL Data Book is to design circuits. What is essential to programming is understanding the application and what has to be done. Once that is accomplished, you can draw on your understanding of your microprocessor's available resources to fulfill those application objectives.

Most successful programs go through the following steps on the road to implementation:

1. Problem specification
2. Formal definition and program design

3. Coding
4. Translating
5. Testing and debugging

The hardware and software specifications for a microprocessor system need to grow simultaneously and be compared with each other as they mature. Ideally, they mature together simultaneously. Practically, since digital design engineers usually size and specify the hardware of the system to fit the application, a reasonable estimate of the hardware requirements to perform the application is usually reached before any major consideration is given to software requirements. Unfortunately, at this point the software is often relegated to the back burner to be done later. Meanwhile, the digital designers start ordering parts and designing logic to implement this first hardware design. This common procedure nearly always leads to disaster.

When a reasonable hardware size and functional block diagram level of design is reached, design activities should be turned toward the software requirements in order to produce an equivalent documentation of the software size at the functional block diagram level of the software needed. The software designers will use the hardware specifications and their knowledge of the system application to specify the software design. While the software is being designed, the designers must be able to consult with knowledgeable digital designers in order to learn about any hardware changes that might be made that would result in a better overall system.

Make no mistake about it, software is just as difficult (and as easy) to design as hardware. Writing code down on paper is easier than wrapping wire or soldering. The same design and debugging steps still have to be taken. If you habitually read the specs and then go directly to the bench and wire up some circuitry, you are one of those rare people who can write correct code "on-the-fly." If, however, you are like the rest of us and have to spend time consulting books and trying alternatives on paper before you produce a schematic, you will find that the same methods also work best with software.

Many engineering-dominated companies relegate programmers to support and technician-level roles. Such organizations are easily identifiable. Their programmers produce programs that solve "flaps," are "transient" instead of "steady-state" (a programmer would say "real") programs, are devoid of documentation, can only be run by the programmer who wrote them, and are not saved as part of the company software resources library. When the programmer leaves the company, any attempt to use his program again or to extend it results in paying another programmer to rewrite the program, often with the same undesirable results just described. Experienced programmers know that there are no "quick-and-dirty" programs... not quick, anyway.

Of prime importance in any development project is the need to achieve the implementation of something that fulfills a need. The need is embodied in some specifications. Whether your job specifications are scribbled notes on an envelope or reams of formal documentation, you still must ferret out all the information

Assemblers and Compilers

Years ago all programming was done with decimal or binary numbers. Programmers—like most other people—are basically interested in minimizing unnecessary work. Therefore, they designed programs that would accept some legible input written by a programmer and automatically translate it into a computer-readable form. When the programmer submits typed inputs (on cards or tape) that looks like this:

```
STAB:     LHLD     MEMEND
          LXI      D,-SIZW
LOOP:     MOV      A,M
          ORA      A
          JZ       TABEND
          CMP      B
```

the automatic translation program produces code that looks like this:

```
2A5219
11F9FF
7E
B7
CA720C
B8
```

Those symbols can be read into the computer very easily and can be placed directly into memory as instructions to be executed.

Assemblers are computer programs that accept the symbolic form and produce an object program that the computer can accept. Another form of language translator is called the *compiler.* Compilers are more elaborate and allow an even nicer way of writing programs like:

LET A = B + (C/D)

but the program produced by a compiler might not be as efficient as a program produced by a competent programmer working in the assembler's symbolic language.

More details on assemblers and compilers will be found in Chapter 10.

you need. The English language is so powerful, but it is so ambiguous. Those well-meant words written into a formal specification may be misread by a reader who has a different set of experiences from the one who wrote the words. Therefore, it is absolutely essential that some form of intermediate documentation be produced that allows the designer to feed some description of the eventual system back to the end-user or the user's representative, for example, the marketing department.

Once the specifications have been reduced to an unambiguous form, the design of the program can begin. The specific needs of the application are studied and reduced to a detailed document that describes precisely how to implement each function that is required. This crucial step is so often ignored that we are going to harp on it in this book. Every software failure we have witnessed has been the result of inadequate designing. TRW Systems has found, in some studies they did for the Air Force, that two-thirds of all errors in software systems come from faulty design; only one-third come from writing down the wrong instruction code. Errors in design are significantly more difficult to track down than coding bugs.

Once the software has been designed, it can be coded. The required functions are manually translated into symbols on paper that represent the instructions to be executed. Since at this point in the project you know both the requirements of the application and the resources available to the computer in the form of the available instructions, it is nearly a rote task to write programs. For each simple thing you must do (say, add two numbers together and then save the sum in some memory location), all you have to do is specify the necessary register transfers in the form of instructions. If your design is robust enough, you may turn this chore over to a lower-level engineer or to a qualified technician. Most often, however, since the design is not that formally complete, the system architect is required to do the coding. The symbolic program is then automatically translated into binary (or octal or hex) form by using an assembler or compiler program (see Chapter 10).

After coding and translating come testing and debugging. Debugging has been called *deblunderizing*. If the design is adequate, debugging will be a straightforward task. Since coding errors make the program behave in ways different from our expectations, they are easy to catch. Design errors, however, do not cause unexpected behavior; since we designed the program that way and it behaves that way, the design errors are significantly more difficult to find.

There is an equivalence between hardware and software activities. Design is design, of course, regardless of the medium of implementation. However, coding is much like making up a wire list for a technician to follow. The actual process of wrapping wire is equivalent to the translation done by an assembler or compiler. And, of course, debugging is like debugging of any kind: Coding errors are as easy to isolate and track down as wiring errors; design errors take much longer, regardless of whether the error is in hardware or software.

Some systems are inherently easy to visualize and comprehend. Full comprehension is absolutely necessary if you are to be able to construct reliable systems.

Program Migration

When programs are first written, novice microprocessor users assume that they will be recorded in ROM and used. However, few programmers, even highly experienced programmers, can write absolutely correct code the first time. Testing, debugging, and correcting of programs are inevitable. If the program is in ROM or PROM, correcting the errors becomes a lengthy and difficult process.

Most initial developments of microprocessor software take place with the program resident in read-write memory (most often semiconductor RAM). After the program achieves a stable state of ''debuggedness,'' it can be transferred into PROM. Even after this process, some latent bugs may remain. It is a good idea, even in high-volume products, to produce initial units with programs stored in PROM. Later, after some field trials have identified all of the remaining bugs, you may wish to commit to mask-programmed custom ROM's.

In conventional random logic (we prefer to call it ''disorderly logic'') systems much of the signal processing is performed in parallel; a 'scope' is an invaluable debugging tool, especially if the status of the system can be frozen at some point in time. The very basic nature of a computer involves the notion of sequence. Therefore, the equivalent to a bunch of status latches in a hardware system might be a group of sequential actions in a computer. Furthermore, the sequential actions may appear in different orders that may imply different intentions and actions.

The human mind is generally conceded to be good at parallel processing, but it finds sequential processing more difficult. In order for us to remember all of the sequential events, we have to have a powerful memory. All too often memory fails us at an inopportune time. All of this implies that during design we need a scheme to help us define all of the sequences that can occur without burdening us with trivia.

We desperately need a means of classifying and structuring the software so that the inherent complexity is well understood. Then the correct hardware/software tradeoff can be made without fear of leaving too much of the software to handle. All of this is necessary while still living within the constraints of the asynchronous real-time demands of the various input and output devices.

Most computer-based projects that fail are poorly understood. If the application is well understood, there is little incentive to bet on unrealistic goals or technologies. Since most applications are new (we seldom design exactly the same thing over again), there is always some part that must be studied in detail. Only by thoroughly understanding the demands of the application can an engineer or system designer hope to be able to bring the product in within budget and to specifications.

There are no magical personality traits that identify good programmers automatically. Nearly anyone can program if he has the motivation to learn how. Programming is so easy to learn that the "programming profession" is just loaded with charlatans who haven't the foggiest notion of how they should really perform.

Most successful microprocessor programmers come from digital engineering ranks. Since they already understand digital logic, learning to control circuitry with an abstract memory content is not very difficult. There are some very competent microprocessor programmers who have migrated from the data processing world, but they are rare. Generally, if their experience has been limited to the common languages like FORTRAN, COBOL, PL/1, and ALGOL, they will be unable to cope with the micro. A *systems programmer* may be of help even if he has no knowledge of electronics. However, he is a rare individual. A programmer who has had some experience in assembly language programming but only on large scale computers will usually be useless to you.

In about half the microprocessor projects we have seen the digital design engineer responsible for the hardware was also the final programmer. In the rest of the cases, these two functions were performed by different people. In a few cases, the hardware was designed without any regard for the software and then the software was "farmed out" to a consultant; in this latter case, it was sheer luck that made the product succeed.

If the digital designer-cum-programmer is new at the programming game, there is a temptation for him to do the easiest thing first. But building the hardware first without any knowledge of the software requirement spells disaster. It is more difficult to maintain the discipline, but it is a surer approach to design and actually code the software first. later, as the designer gains software experience, these two parts of the project can proceed more in parallel.

With separate software and hardware talent, it is essential that the two parts of the team work closely together. If the programmer doesn't have electronics experience, it may be necessary to converse on a somewhat abstract level. However, the common reference point can be considered to be registers. All I/O, for instance, can be defined in terms of registers that can be written and/or read and they are easy for any qualified programmer to understand.

Reputable consulting firms, particularly those that work on fixed price contracts, are reluctant to take on software chores when the hardware is already designed and constructed. They know that the designer is ignorant of the software requirements. These projects usually have pieces of interface hardware that are elegantly simple on the schematic but cause major havoc in software generation and software reliability. These are also the same systems in which the client is unwilling to admit to design blunders and is incredulous when told the estimated programming time required. If you are in this situation, however, you can always find a newcomer who will take on these jobs for the experience. We recommend that you do not take his estimates of elapsed software production time seriously because they are usually vastly understated because of his lack of experience.

All too often, neophyte programmers see the actual machine-language code as the only necessary object of the programming exercise. Experienced programmers know that many preliminary steps must be taken. You can judge the experience level of programmers by finding out how soon they begin writing down instructions to the computer: The novice begins almost immediately and assumes that this is the right thing to do; the more experienced programmer first does a lot of preliminary paper work, producing a series of design documents; actual coding does not begin until much later. In general, the earlier that coding is done the poorer it will be since this most often means that inadequate program design was performed.

The novice programmer typically grasps any "corner" of the intended application (often the one he "understands" best) and begins to chop away at it. If there is to be a keyboard, he will start right out to create a program to read it and convert the characters to the standard code, ASCII. It doesn't occur to him that he doesn't know what to do with those characters after they have been read in. It doesn't occur to him that all the rest of the software will have to be written to make sure that this keyboard scanning program will gain control at least once every 40 ms to avoid loss of keystrokes. It doesn't occur to him that maybe a fully decoded ASCII keyboard might be significantly better for this application.

The experienced programmer knows that quickly rushing off to write code will produce useless software, whether for a large general-purpose computer or for a microprocessor system. He first understands the application (the "problem"), then designs the software system ("what" is done), specifies the steps (modules or "how" it is done), and finally establishes the requirements of each module and how they are used together. Eventually, he will achieve enough of an understanding of the entire system (and its partial evolution at some juncture) to be able to specify the characteristics of the various items, such as the keyboard and the associated software. Coding may take a few hours to complete and debug, but there will be little likelihood that it will have to be torn down and written all over again at the design changes.

In this small pair of scenarios the novice is working upward from the most detailed available level of knowledge toward the eventual system, while the experienced designer is working from system and individual hardware performance specifications downward toward actual software implementation. In the novice's case, the quickly written program is produced with the assumption that it will ultimately prove useful to the whole product under design: This is—at best—a chancy kind of prediction. The experienced designer is betting that at some point the required functions can be implemented in either hardware or software. This is most certainly a surer kind of prediction and is in accord with the mutual two-team review of the system design mentioned previously.

5

Storage Organization

Although it may seem cut and dried, the organization and design of storage facilities for programs and data in microcomputers can be very challenging. Before you undertake any but the simplest "cookbook" design, however, you should probably review the literature on currently available technologies and techniques. Rather than try to show all the ways to design memories we will review the basic structural features of memories for micros and some special considerations you will want to remember for special situations.

As we pointed out in Chapter 1, any storage medium can be characterized as a collection of identical registers, one of which may be selected for reading and/or writing. What we chose to ignore in that basic description was the essential set of memory characteristics about the symmetry of reading and writing. Some memories are "written" only at the factory (mask-programmed ROM's), but others can be written and read at will (RAM's). Other characteristics include the storage medium (dynamic or static), the volatility, and the timing.

Memory Types

The universe of memories can be represented as an *n*-dimensional space. Along one dimension are the potential ranges of speed and along another dimension are the capacities measured in bits per package. The first dimension that any engineer first considers is *read/write symmetry.* This particular facet of memory devices is complicated by the fact that industry practice has managed to apply a malaprop to almost every kind of memory imaginable.

Ignoring the fact that to be useful any memory must be written at least once, memories that are limited to being able to be read are called *read-only memories* (ROM's). A true ROM is made at the semiconductor factory and is delivered preprogrammed according to the customer's specifications. Some ROM's are programmable in the field (PROM's); the customer can buy "clean" ROM's and then "burn in" the specific bit pattern with some special equipment (or have a distributor do it). These memories are all characterized by a number of read cycles that vastly outnumber the number of write operations (one).

When the ratio of the number of writes to the number of reads is unlimited (we prefer to call this *symmetry*), the memory is called a *read-write memory* (RWM). The term RWM has seldom been used in the literature. Instead, the misnomer Random Access Memory (RAM) has been used; actually, of course, a ROM can be a random-access memory, too, but convention is convention.

When the ratio of read to write cycles is large but the memory can be written more than once, the memory is called *Read Mostly* (RMM). There are several examples of these memories, but the most common is a special kind of PROM that can be erased with ultraviolet light; this memory is called *erasable read-only memory* (EROM) or erasable, programmable read-only memory (EPROM). Another technology allows electrical erasure of the entire memory; this memory is called *electrically alterable memory* (EAROM).

ROM's find their most obvious application in program storage for microprocessor applications. Here the permanence of the stored information is an advantage since the programming for a microprocessor-driven product is usually fixed at the time of manufacture and is not frequently changed. RAM's are used for data storage and scratch-pad applications because the information they hold must be continually changed. They can also be used for program storage during the software development phase or in any application in which readily changeable software is a requirement, such as minicomputer systems. RMM's fill the gap between applications that require software storage that cannot be changed (ROM's) and software storage that can be easily changed (RAM's). RMM's find use in those applications in which the software must be changed often enough to make it impractical to throw away the ROM's and buy new ones every time a change is made.

Read-only memories are now available with a great variety of technologies and characteristics. They are available in high-speed technologies such as Schottky-TTL with access times of well under 100 ns and densities of up to 8,192 bits per chip. They are also available in slower, denser technologies such as *N*-channel MOS with access times of from 500 to 1,000 ns and densities of up to 65,536 bits per chip. To obtain maximum density, it is necessary to resort to factory programmed ROM's in which the programming is accomplished by adding or deleting connections in a metalization mask during the manufacturing process. However, user or field-programmable versions (PROM's) are also available at densities of up to about one-half of the mask-programmed versions.

PROM's were originally intended to be used for program development and short-run production. Eventually they were to be replaced by masked ROM's. For this reason, most PROM's available have a pin-compatible masked-ROM twin. However, PROM's are becoming increasingly larger, less expensive, and easier to program (for example, the Intel 2716 is now widely second-sourced), with the result that the cost savings of going to masked ROM's is rapidly vanishing except for very large quantities.

The read-mostly memories are important to designers. Today's technology offers two kinds: EROM's and metal-nitride devices. EROM's are MOS ROM's in which information is stored as charge (or lack of charge) trapped in the gate region of a silicon-gate field effect transistor. The gate region is completely insulated by silicon dioxide so that the trapped charge will not leak off. Charge is written into the gate region by quantum mechanical tunneling that occurs when sufficient voltage stress is applied to the device to be written. Erasure is accomplished by exposing the device to ultraviolet light that imparts sufficient additional energy to the trapped electrons to allow them to tunnel back. Unfortunately, this method of erasure is nonselective and the entire EROM must be erased and rewritten. In addition, the use of ultraviolet light requires that the package have a window that must be made of quartz or other material that can pass ultraviolet light. This, of course, adds something to the chip package costs.

During microprocessor product development there can be a natural progression of the program storage medium from RAM to EROM to PROM to ROM. Ordinarily, once the software is written and debugged (using RAM), it is first stored in an EROM for prototype evaluation. If performance is satisfactory, the program is often transferred to PROM's in order to save costs during initial production. The next step is to change to ROM storage if production quantities become large enough to justify the mask charges. For smaller volume production, EROM's constitute the final storage medium.

The next most common RMM's are the nitride memories. These devices are similar to the EROM's because they also store information by means of charge trapped in the gate region of an MOS transistor. They differ, however, in exactly where and how that charge is stored. In the EROM's the charge is stored in a fully insulated silicon gate region. Sufficient charge is stored to change the FET from "normally off" to "normally on." In the nitride devices, MNOS (Metal Nitride Oxide Semiconductor), FET's are used and the charge is trapped in the high-energy states at the interface between the layers of the dual insulator of the gate region. The net effect of the charge thus stored is to change the threshold of the selected FET. Information is read out by applying a voltage of sufficient magnitude to turn on those FET's with thresholds that have been reduced by stored charge but not high enough to turn on the nonprogrammed devices. The mechanism for programming is again quantum mechanical tunneling induced by voltage stress. However, the reverse tunneling required for erasure is induced by applying voltage stress instead of ultraviolet light to the substrate. This erasure procedure may erase the entire memory or a selected word. The advantage of MNOS memories is that the device is erased electrically and makes reprogramming under program control practical. The major factor that retards the growth of MNOS RMM's is a production problem. The MNOS process is considerably more subject to pinhole oxide failures than the silicon gate process used for EROM's. In addition, since the process is topographically less efficient, MNOS memories require larger chip areas for the same number of bits stored. These two factors add up to considerably less yield and to higher prices for the MNOS devices. Finally, MNOS speeds are not yet keeping up with microprocessor speeds.

The third group of RMM's are the amorphous memories. The basic memory cell of these devices is a silicon film that can exist stably in either an amorphous or a polycrystalline phase. The two phases demonstrate a marked difference in resistivity and may be read out by passing a small current through the device and sensing the voltage drop. Programming of the device is accomplished by applying a relatively long low-current pulse from a high-impedance source (typically 8 mA for 15 ms). The low current restructures the crystal domains producing a low resistivity state. Erasure is accomplished by applying short high-current pulses (typically 250 mA for 5 μs) that disorder the crystalline domains and restore the high-resistance state. Like EAROM's, amorphous memories may be selectively erased; indeed, they must be selectively erased because of the large currents involved. Problems with these devices are both production problems and application problems. Like the MNOS memories, they are large in chip areas and low in yield. In addition, they require rather large and costly decoders because of the magnitude of the erase currents. Lastly, they are available only in a matrix form that requires external decoder, driver and sense circuitry. All this adds up to a total system cost that greatly exceeds either of the other two types of RMM's.

Storage Architecture

A generalized sketch of a memory subsystem in a microcomputer is shown in Figure 5.1. In some systems certain of these basic elements may not be required.

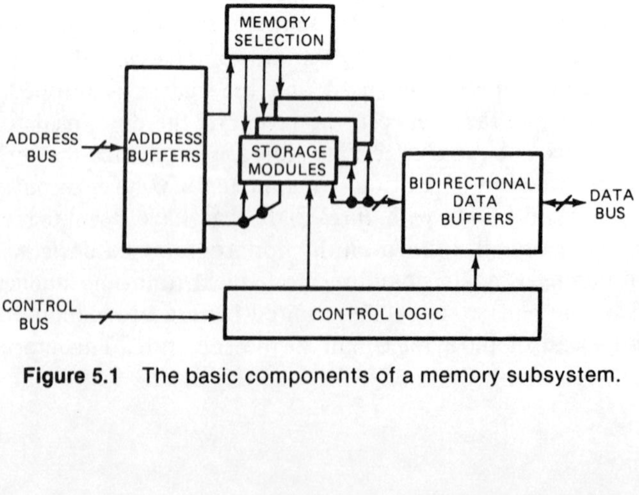

Figure 5.1 The basic components of a memory subsystem.

For example, if your entire computer has only 256 bytes of storage in a single chip, you probably won't require buffers on the address and data bus. If, however, you have a very low-power requirement, your control logic may be extremely complex.

Address bus buffers may or may not be required, depending on the dynamic and static loads the memory chips present to the address bus. If the number of addressed devices is sufficiently small, you may not need buffers. However, it is not only the sum of logic low currents you must consider; each address line input to a chip has a capacitance and all memory chips will be connected in parallel. If timing is important (and in most systems it is), then the memory subsystem's access time may be adversely affected if too many capacitive loads are presented to the CPU's address bus in parallel. In fact, address buffers are required more often for this dynamic loading effect than for the static loading, especially with MOS memories. In some cases, though, it is possible to trade off access time in order to save on the additional chips required for the address buffers. In some microprocessors the pulse rise and fall times are specified at very large capacitive loads; the T.I. TMS 9900, for instance, assumes up to 200 pF. Other processors, such as the RCA COSMAC, have no such specifications and, therefore, you may have to consult the factory for design information. The Intel 8080A has an interesting and useful graph (Figure 5.2) in the electrical specifications. Although timing on the address

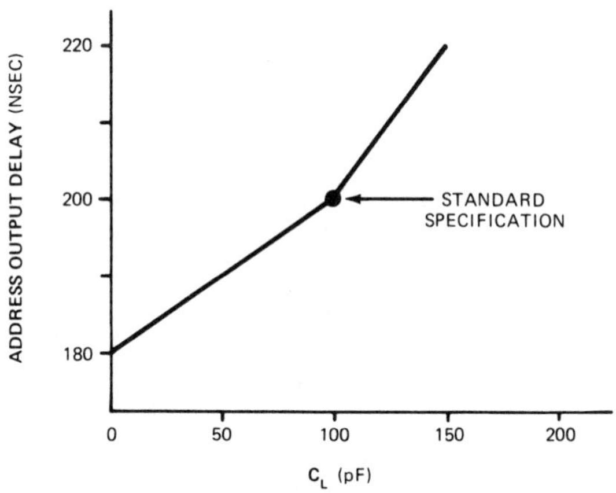

Figure 5.2 Output delay as a function of external capacitive load for the 8080A.

and data buses assumes capacitive loads of 100 pF, you can present larger loads at some additional penalty in output delay. As the graph shows, there is a penalty of about 0.40 ns per picofarad of additional load. Since the 8080A is considered generous on timing margins, it is not unreasonable to expect to be able to design for a 200-pF dynamic load and still have a "worst-case" design.

In many memory systems there will be a trade off in "shape factor" that depends on the relative dynamic or static loadings on the address and data buses.

If your design calls for a 1,024-byte RAM, for example, you may choose to design with eight 1,024-by-1 RAM's, eight 128-by-8's, eight 256-by-4's, or two 1,024-by-4's. The first three all depend on RAM's with 1,024 bits of capacity, but the fourth assumes one of the new 4K static devices. The choice between the 1K and 4K RAM's is clear: one-fourth as many parts may be required. However, a glance at Figure 5.3 will show how two of the smaller memories differ at the system design level. All eight RAM's must rest across the various address bus lines, but different dynamic loads are presented to the data bus in each case. If the data bus is already "loaded" by other parts, you may wish to use the 1k-by-1 memories, each of which will then present only a single load to the bits of bus. However, in this configuration you may have to buffer all ten bits of the address bus because it will see eight loads for the RAM. With 256-by-4 RAM's, each data bus bit sees four loads, and only eight bits of the address bus are loaded by all eight storage chips. The decoder in this example (Figure 5.3) can be considered as a one-load buffer on the address bus.

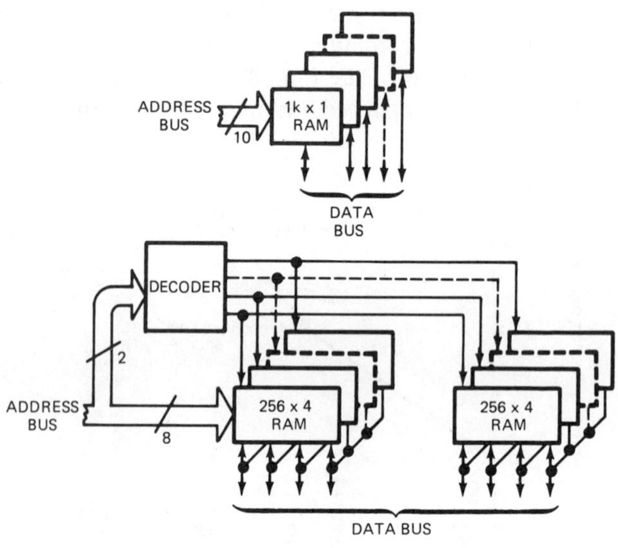

Figure 5.3 Alternatives to organizing storage.

This loading trade off should also be considered in the light of intended expansion capability. If your design will require expansion memory in relatively large chunks, you can elect to use the "taller" memories. If, however, incremental modularity should be in smaller units (say, on the order of 256 bytes at a time), you may want to choose the "wider" memory parts instead.

When you select a storage module, you should coordinate RAM, PROM, and other storage media in order to have the same size. Then, a single simple decoding system can be used (Figure 5.4) to select the storage modules. In many cases, a single decoder can be used to select up to sixteen 1,024-byte "banks;" this de-

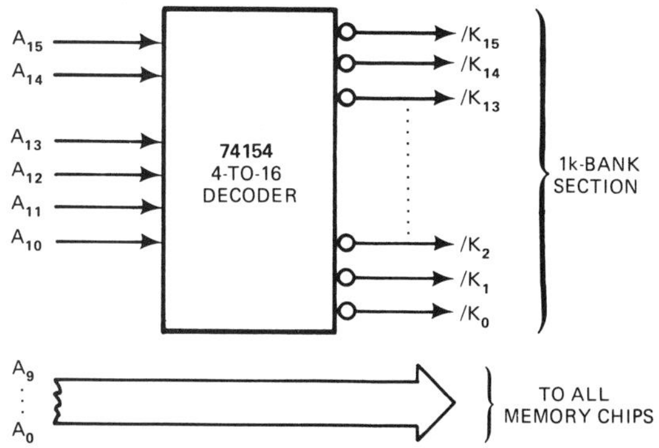

Figure 5.4 A generalized decoder for memory banks.

coder can interface well with the 1k-by-1 static RAM's and the new 1k-by-4 RAM's and 1k-by-8-EROM's.

In selecting RAM's or shift registers for memory usage you must face the question of whether or not you require nonvolatile storage and if so how it should be achieved. Nonvolatility can be approximated by the use of volatile storage medium and some sort of backup battery power supply. Since backup battery supplies are usually costly, efforts should be made to keep the amount of data that must be maintained at a minimum. It should be remembered that it is only necessary to retain power on that portion of the memory that must remain nonvolatile. For long periods of nonvolatile storage or whenever memory size must be large, CMOS static RAM's require the lowest standby power. Many devices now available will retain information at a power cost of 0.1 μW per bit. For shorter periods or for systems in which only a relatively few bits must be stored in this fashion, the choice is frequently a dynamic RAM. Large dynamic RAM's may require standby powers of only from 7 to 10 μW per bit; total standby power consumption, including refresh power and logic, can usually be kept within 25 to 30 μW per bit. For systems like a 4k-by-8 memory in which data need only be retained for an hour or two, this is not an unreasonable amount of power. If, however, the information must be retained for days, CMOS may be the only choice. The MNOS memories are another possible alternative. However, they are sufficiently slow that MNOS EAROM's are often treated as special I/O devices. Instead of connecting the address and control buses, they are tied to output ports of the microprocessor. Reading and writing can continue at a slower pace than normal storage references and under program control.

Speed

In design of a memory for today's microprocessors speed is usually not a prime consideration. Typical eight-bit *n*-channel microprocessors require memory access time of from 500 ns to 1 μs and memory cycle time of from 1 to 2 μs if the processor is to operate at its maximum rate. Occasionally, however, in design of a memory system speed is of prime importance. In such cases, two aspects of memory speed must be considered: access time and cycle time. Access time is the time that elapses from the application of Chip Enable (CE access time) or address (address access time) until the output data is stable and ready for use. In static ROM's and PROM's this is the only speed consideration, but in RAM's and dynamic devices cycle time becomes important. In dynamic RAM's and ROM's considerable amounts of time can be consumed in the clocking required in precharge sense lines and internal buses. This restricts overall machine speed much more than access time alone would indicate. Dynamic RAM's have access times that are competitive with TTL RAM's, but their minimum cycle times are much longer. For example, one 1K dynamic RAM has an address access time (usually the longer of the two) of 80 ns max while one of the 1K TTL RAMs has a maximum access time of 90 ns. If we assume that the output data is to be strobed into a high-speed register and that our addresses are coming from a similar register, we could obtain a new word from the TTL RAM every 100 ns. The minimum cycle time for the NMOS RAM is 180 ns, 80% longer than for the TTL RAM. Since NMOS RAM is dynamic, it must spend at least 80 ns disabled, during which time internal buses are precharged.

If the system design is such that considerable time is spent processing the data after it is read and before another word is fetched from storage, the longer memory cycle times become unimportant and only the access time contributes to the overall cycle time of the system. If, however, the system is such that speed is of utmost importance, pipeline techniques can be used and data can be processed at a rate limited only by the memory cycle time. TTL and ECL RAM's are now available that have access times of typically from 20 to 30 ns, making pipelined processors with data cycle of from 50 to 60 ns practical.

Another consideration for minimizing memory cycle times is for applications that have a preponderance of DMA by I/O devices. If the memory can be cycled at a rate that is a multiple of the processor cycle, twice as fast, for example, then 50% of the memory cycles can be assigned to the processor and 50% can be assigned to the DMA controller with absolutely no degradation of the processor's speed. In addition, if the memory is dynamic, cycles may be stolen either from the processor or the DMA controllers for refresh, allowing whichever has the greater burden to proceed uninterrupted.

Speed can also be used to reduce power consumption. If the required access time of the storage medium of the microprocessor is, say, 2 μs, then a higher-speed nonvolatile memory can be turned only as required. In one recent application, using a CMOS microprocessor, this fact was used to advantage with bipolar PROM's. The RCA COSMAC was selected because of its naturally low CMOS power consumption. When the memories were examined, however, the total power consumption nearly scuttled the project. The production volumes were much too low to warrant the expense and risk inherent in purchasing mask-programmed CMOS ROM's, and programmable CMOS PROM's were not yet available.

Tim Foust and George Bailey of Hekimian Labs designed a neat alternative program store using Signetics' new 2k-by-4 PROM's with the COSMAC. The timing diagram is shown in Figure 5.5. The COSMAC presents the address on the bus and then waits for several clock cycles for memory to have time to settle. At the end of that access time, a clock signal (TPB) is generated, and during the latter half of that signal the data bus contents are clocked into the processor. In this design each clock cycle takes 500 ns. That means that TPB comes up 250 ns before the data is required and stays up during the reading time. TPB's are used to turn on the PROM's. Since they have an access time of only 100 ns, plenty of design margin is left for other timing details. At the worst, the program storage medium is on for only one out of every sixteen clock cycles; the average power consumption is reduced to below 25 mW.

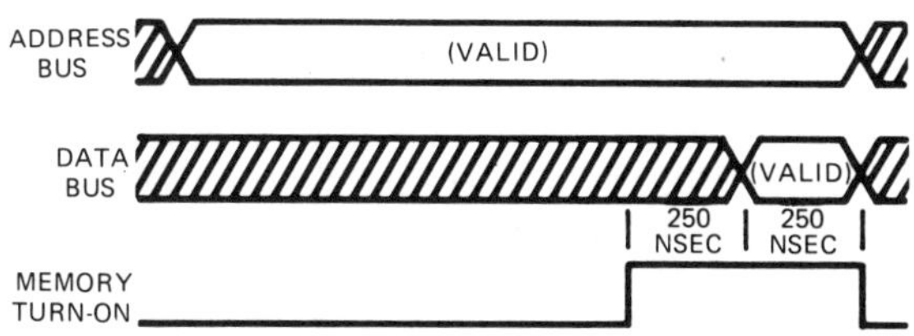

Figure 5.5 COSMAC read-timing used to reduce power consumption of memory.

Microprocessor Memory Systems

A well-designed memory system for a microprocessor often looks disarmingly simple. Designing a simple-looking memory is not as simple as the results may show. There is a bewildering array of storage components for sale and the timing and loading specs for the memory and the microprocessor are often confusing and/or incompatible.

Before you can really start the design, you must ferret out the microprocessor's memory interface characteristics. If several different microprocessors are being considered, the ease with which they interface to memories should be a major selection factor. The microprocessor characteristics of most importance to the memory design are as follows:

- Read access time, or how fast the memory system must present data to the microprocessor after receiving an address
- Write setup time, that is, the duration that the processor holds its output data steady during a write
- Drive capabilities, including the current and capacitive loads permitted on both the address bus and data bus

Once these figures have been established, you can start the design by selecting the program storage components. Mask-programmed ROM's are the least expensive, but they are practical only when you need many copies of the same program. The next step up is EPROM's, which now cost around a penny per bit. These ultraviolet erasable devices are commonly used in light to moderate production volume designs even if erasability is not required because they are less expensive and more compact than fusible link PROM's.

For the RAM's you have a choice between static and dynamic RAM's and, within the static group you have a choice among one, four, and eight-bit wide configurations. At the present time, static RAM's containing 1,024 bits are by far the most popular microprocessor data storage component. They are available organized 128×8, 256×4, and 1024×1; the choice depends on how many words you require. At 1,024 words and up, eight $1K \times 1$ parts are better than eight 256×4 or 128×8 parts because the $1{,}024 \times 1$ configuration reduces the number and capacitance of loads on the data bus.

At this point you can put together a design something like the one shown in Figure 5.6. PROM's and RAM's are included along with some address decoding circuitry. The Intel 2708 PROM is ideal for almost any MOS microprocessor application and is now commonly second-sourced. A single decoder is used to develop chip enable signals corresponding to the first two 1K-sized address blocks. By enabling the decoder with the microprocessor's read timing pulse/(/MEMR)

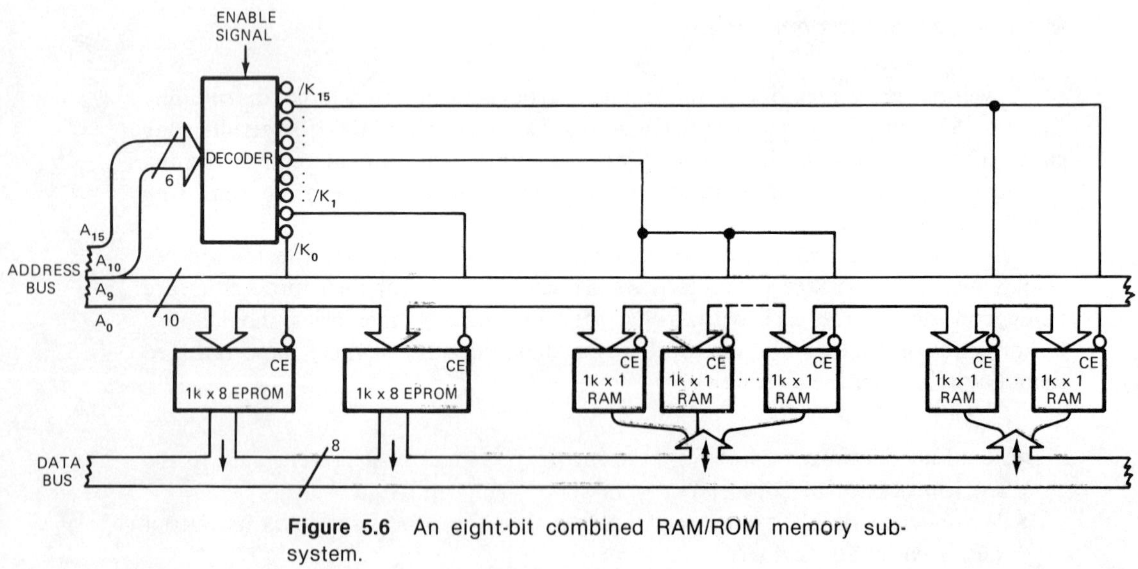

Figure 5.6 An eight-bit combined RAM/ROM memory subsystem.

Saving ROM's

One great and persistent fear with mask-programmed ROM's is that if one minor bug is found, all the ROM's will have to be repurchased and reinstalled in existing equipment. In fact, a little forethought will prevent total loss of ROM's, even if a small error is found. Two strategies can be used.

A nine-bit field-programmable PLA can be used to create a *patch space* for an eight-bit ROM. The inputs are connected across the address bus. When a byte is to be replaced in the ROM, the inputs are programmed to respond to that address and the outputs are programmed to generate the new eight-bit value; the ninth bit is set to zero when the PLA has no valid output; When the PLA's ninth bit is high, that signals the gating logic to ignore the ROM's output and use the PLA's instead.

A more software oriented approach can also be used. The subroutines that are called by other subroutines are never called directly but are called through a transfer vector instead. A *transfer vector* is a table to subroutine addresses held in a PROM. Since all references to a faulty subroutine will be "caught" by that subroutine's entry in the transfer vector, all that needs to be changed is that one address. To patch a bad program (see Figure A), the appropriate word in the PROM is changed so that future references all go to a new place in memory. In most designs the patch space will be found in unused areas of the PROM itself.

If the PLA approach is used for patching, the PLA need not be programmed or installed unless a lingering bug is actually found. If the PROM approach is used, at least the transfer vector must exist in PROM to start with. However, more than one PLA and/or PROM may be designed into the manufactured product as an unfilled socket for future expansion.

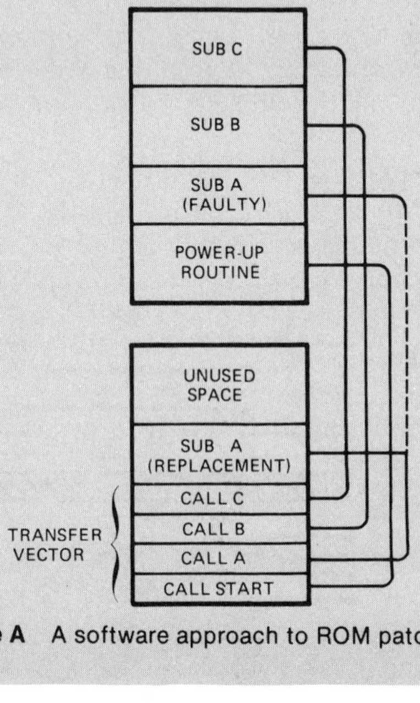

Figure A A software approach to ROM patching.

you get the only timing signal required to control a PROM. The /K0 signal, for instance, means "read from the zeroth 1K block." Although this signal is low, the first 2708's three-state output buffers are enabled and address lines A_0 through A_9 select the word that is presented to the bus. If A_{10} and A_{11} were **01** instead of **00**, the /K1 decoder output would go low and select the second PROM instead. When several more PROM's are needed, the design can be extended by using a four-to-sixteen decoder.

In this example 2102A RAM's are combined in pairs to make 1K-by-8 blocks. Chip enable signals corresponding to 1,024-word pages are developed by the same decoder as used with EPROM's. During memory write pulses /MEMW the selected chip pair accepts data from the bus and stores it.

In any but the smallest systems, address buffers will be needed between the microprocessor and the memory system because microprocessors invariably have rather poor drive capability. It is common to find that the microprocessor can provide neither the voltage, current, nor capacitive drive needed by the memory sytem! Hex TTL buffers may be inserted if all of the memory components will accept TTL levels. Most EPROM's, however, need a higher "logic one" voltage than TTL provides. The answer here is an eight-bit buffer designed for MOS interfacing such as Intel's 8212 or the equivalent T.I. 74S412.

Direct Memory Access

Efficient designs often require that devices other than the microprocessor have the privilege of access to memory. Certain time-critical devices, such as refreshed video displays, may be designed to read directly from memory without recourse to the microprocessor because the required data transfer speed is higher than the processor can support. In these cases, some special control signals may be required to prevent the processor from referring to memory during the outside access. At the same time, all of the microcomputer's buses must be able to be placed in a nonoffending state.

To gain access to memory, some "handshaking" must be designed in as an interface between the DMA requesting device and the DMA granting device (the processor). This essential timing is shown in Figure 5.7. The DMA REQ signal is generally designed in negative logic so that it can be pulled down from a variety of

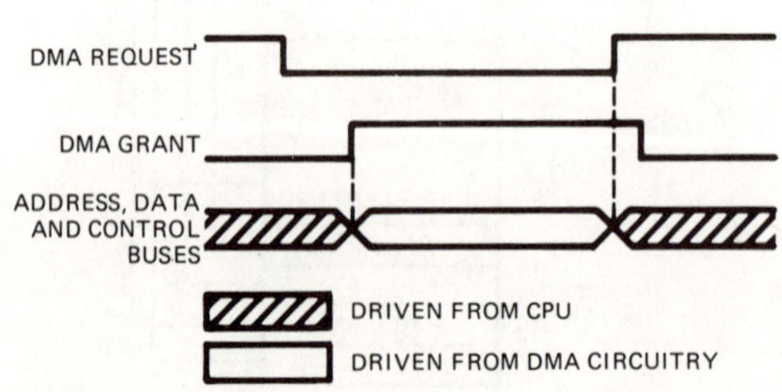

Figure 5.7 Timing for direct memory access.

sources; the DMA GRANT signal is usually positive logic. The time delay from DMA REQ to DMA GRANT depends on the microprocessor and the particular instruction sequence that it is executing at the moment. Some microprocessors can be held off the memory buses almost immediately while others may require several microseconds. The worst-case response time for DMA requests should be studied carefully before you select a processor.

When the processor responds with DMA GRANT, the CPU's address, data, and control buses may all be in the high-impedance state (or they may not, depending on your particular processor). If any of these signals are buffered, you must use the DMA GRANT signal to control these buses. The ultimate objective is to make sure that the address, data, and control buses are not being driven from the CPU. At that time (the leading edge of DMA GRANT), the external equipment can drive the buses to cause the appropriate memory action. Generally, the release of the /DMA REQ signal will signal the end of the external request; sometime later the DMA GRANT signal will be deactivated from the processor. Certain microprocessors are sticky about how long you are allowed to hold down /DMA REQ; holding it down too long may cause loss of register contents in the processor.

Processor-controlled timing and DMA do not work well together. The actual elapsed time for the execution of a particular instruction sequence may vary greatly from one invocation to the next because of the "random" DMA activity. However, if you can cope with the jitter that DMA may introduce, you can still use the processor for timing-dependent applications.

Memory Selection

The size of memory in a microcomputer is dictated by the application. Some trade offs are possible if the processor is fast enough, but generally the program size and required data storage will be firm. The problem for the engineer is to discover what those size factors are. If you have never programmed before, you will find it difficult to guess.

There are only two basic rules in specifying the memory size:

1. Break the size of the problem down into pieces you *can* estimate,
2. Always leave room for more memory to be added to the design.

It is a good idea to estimate program sizes on the basis of probability. A form is a good idea to help you regularize your thinking process. We estimate program and data sizes independently, since programs can reside in ROM but data can't. Each function to be handled in software (or module, if you can adequately partition the software from experience) is identified and written down. Then the program and data storage requirements (generally in words) are estimated. A new estimate is calculated for each probability figure. In the 50% column, for instance, we declare that the requirement has about an equal chance of being larger or smaller than the specified value. In the last column we write down the estimate in which we have 95% confidence; there is a 95% probability that the requirement will be smaller than the specified value and only a 5% chance that it will be larger. Summing each column will yield the best estimates of storage requirements. The "spread" between the 50% and 95% confidence columns will identify how firm or shaky the estimates are. If the 95% column is about twice the 50% column, then we are about right.

Data space is nearly always easier to estimate than program size. If you are to refresh a 2,000 character CRT from memory, then you know how many characters worth of storage you'll need for that function. However, program sizes depend on your programming skill and the cleverness in the hardware. The only way to estimate program sizes without extensive experience is to actually write some code. The more completely you write the program for the specific function, the better your estimate will be.

Size is an important factor in selecting memories because it will dictate the breakpoint in the tradeoff between memory chip size and timing and control complexity. The larger the memory chips, the less important the cost of timing and control circuitry becomes while the more important the cost of the memory chips themselves become. For typical small memory arrays used in many microprocessor applications, there is little advantage in using smaller memory chips because they require more control circuitry.

Memory format, however, is a different thing entirely. In an application that clearly requires a 4K×8 RAM, the problem usually boils down to which 4K×1 shall we use. When the memory is 2K×8, however, the choice is less obvious. We are faced with a choice between using sixteen 1K×1 chips (rather common and inexpensive), eight 2K×1 chips (half of which are not needed). The potential advantages of using the 4K chips are system expansion and the possibility that there will be a price reduction in 4K memories. These advantages may or may not justify the added current expense.

Applications in which an eight-bit processor manipulates lots of eight-bit binary data but also requires storage of many seven-bit ASCII characters or four-bit BCD digits are not unusual. It is possible to configure the memory with some locations holding eight-bit words and still others holding four or seven bits. If the requirement is for 512 eight-bit words and 1,024 four-bit words, we have several choices: Obviously, we can use 2K×1 or 1K×1 chips to configure our memory as 2K×8 and waste % of the bits; we could repack the four-bit words into pairs in software and build a 1K×8 memory; we could configure the memory just as the processor requires by using eight 256×4 RAM's. Other choices are also possible. Most of the choices are economic. Because prices change rapidly in today's markets, it is extremely difficult to choose which of the options are the most economical.

6

Data Structures and Programming

The design of computer programs is complicated because there is no commonly agreed upon design notation or language. Circuit diagrams are almost universal in their format and acceptance; there is no real software equivalent. Flow charts are often cited as the programmer's equivalent to the schematic, but only by the very naive. Flow charts are not even adequate to the task, even though we continue to teach the concepts of flow charting to new programmers. Flow charts are to software what the sketches of the 1910's were to electronics: Those old drawings of breadboards with parts nailed down and all the parts completely drawn in perspective bear no resemblance to the schematics that the electronics industry has now adopted. Just as the old perspective drawings loaded the mind with unessential detail (like the relative placement of d.c. parts on the board) and obscured much important data (like the power rating of the components), so flow charts are ineffectual. The burdensome notion of drawing different functions in strictly regulated box sizes and shapes completely ignores the fact that *data* structures are more important to good design than are *program* structures. Since flow charts don't allow us to describe important and powerful arrangements of data in memory, they actually inhibit good designs from maturing.

An alternative is emerging in the form of the principles of something called *structured programming.* We are not going to debate here what the term means, but we can expect the power of the concept to continue unfolding over the next several years. Suffice it to say that practitioners of the technique rate it as excellent. We will not rigorously define structured programming or even the various techniques used with it (such as program proof or verification). We will introduce the concepts by example and then suggest some further reading to improve your skills.

At the outset, it must be made perfectly clear that there are two underlying principles of program design:

1. The concern at this point is with clear and unambiguous documentation of the design without regard to implementation details.
2. The trade offs between hardware and software (and within software, between data and procedure) are of paramount interest.

Binding Time

There is one basic premise about data that should be reviewed: If we assume that data values are variables (if they are constants we can consider them just as special parts of the program), then we must ask when the variable is bound to a particular value. This is called the *binding time* of a variable.

Generally, software variables have *names,* just like variables in algebra. When we discuss a particular variable we generally refer to it by its name in both software and algebra. A variable name PI might have a universally recognized non-repeating decimal value in the world of mathematics, but it can assume a whole range of different precisions and accuracies in a computer. Similarly, the concept of a character (say, the letter "R") is well understood, but the specific representation in a computer may be several different binary bit patterns depending upon which code we elect to use for our alphabet.

Generally, the *structure* of a variable must be bound at the time the computer program is designed. Since it is imperative that all of the procedures agree on the structure of shared data values, we must have some agreed upon way of describing the data structures. The *value* of a variable may be bound at many different times. We might choose to bind the value of PI to 0110010010000011111110 in some particular program at design time (for it is unlikely to change). But, the variable that holds a digit from a numeric keyboard that is read in during execution of the program cannot have its value bound prior to execution since the value depends on which key is struck. Some variables, such as addresses that are destinations of jump instructions, are bound at the time of assembly or compilation; a "jump to XYZ" instruction becomes a "jump to 1234" when the assembler establishes the location of XYZ to be 1234.

In general, the earlier you can bind values to variables, the smaller and faster your program will be. Obviously, you will have to defer binding some of the important variables, but you can bind others earlier. Early binding of variables means a loss of generality; therefore, you will have to make an intelligent and informed design decision. You will be able to make that decision when you know what the intention of the program is. If you intend to change the program in the future, you will probably want to reserve binding to a later point in time. If you need execution efficiency, you may have to bind earlier.

Data-Procedure Trade Offs

Now we can define the essence of the data-procedure trade off: Data structures provide fast acquisition of small amounts of information (thus falling on the side of efficiency), while procedures provide slower computation of large amounts of information (and so provide generality). Using the square root function example again, we can see that there are many possible solutions to providing the requisite values. If memory costs were truly zero and if execution time were of paramount interest, we would be wise to opt for binding the values of the square root at design time. This solution would take the form of a table of square root values. The value of the argument itself can be used to index this table in order to select the appropriate answer.

If, however, the number of square root values is too large to fit into memory as a static array, then we need to implement a procedure to do that work. The procedure accepts some value and then computes the value's square root. Because many more machine cycles are required for computation (using any of the known algorithms), the procedure will be slower than a table search. However, it also requires substantially less memory space to hold the procedure than to hold the table of all possible high-precision square root values.

Consider, for a moment, the computation of a square root on eight-bit integers. There are only 256 possible numbers and so 256 possible square roots. The fastest solution is to precompute the 256 square roots and store them in successive bytes in memory. The value for which the square root is required is treated as an integer index in the range 0 ... 255; indexing into the table (i.e., computing the address of the desired square root by adding the value of the argument to the starting address of the table) will yield the required result quickly and without much procedure. Alternatively, imagine that we need to compute the same function on sixteen-bit integers; now the table will have to be 65,536 sixteen-bit words long. This requirement should probably be met with a procedure that uses one of the known strategies to compute square root from the supplied argument value. Of course, we could also opt to solve for the square root in hardware and use input/output instructions to send out the argument value and then read in the result (that is a minimum software solution with small procedure and almost no data structure).

Any problem can be solved with a large enough data structure. Similarly, we can compute everything as required and avoid the use of data structures altogether. However, practical problems are solved by an intelligent mixture of both. During design you should not concern yourself with *how* you're going to implement the needed functions, but you should be concerned with *what* those needed functions are going to do. The notation sqrt(x), denoting the function of taking the square root of **x**, is perfectly ambiguous for us. It is clear that the square root is needed, but the notation implies either an array full of values named sqrt with a subscript named x, or it implies a procedure named sqrt (much like the functional notation of mathematics) with the argument x. Therefore, at this top level of design we safely ignore the internal complexity of the square root function and concentrate on how that value is used.

Up to this point we have used the words *data structure, table,* and *array* in an intuitive manner, but in order to demonstrate nontrivial applications of data structure choice and design, a more careful exposition is required.

Data can be organized into records, lists, and arrays. A *record* is a collection of several data items of identical or different data forms. When many records are alike in structure and format, they can be combined into *lists* and *arrays.* Each data object that is neither a member of a list nor a member of an array is considered to be a *record.*

A *list* is the most fundamental kind of data structure in the digital world. Other data structures are special kinds of lists. A list is made up of several items, all of which are usually of the same form. Each item consists of a data record and a reference variable (Figure 6.1). The data record retains information of value to

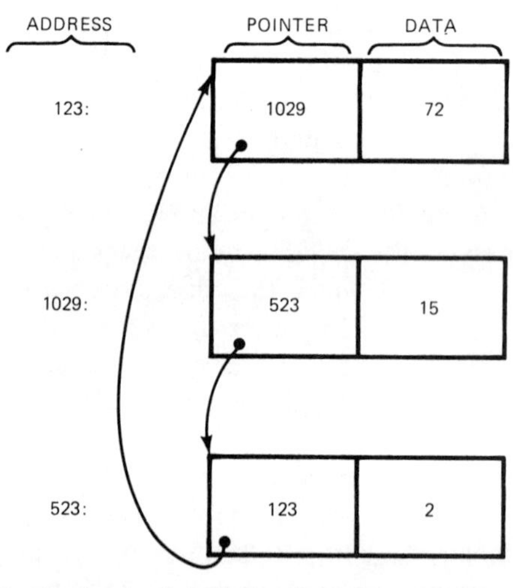

Figure 6.1 A simple list that might be composed of six different storage words.

the program, and the reference variable provides a means for accessing other data items in the list. In some cases, only the reference part of the list item exists; its mere existence is information enough. If the addresses of related items are not carried in the data item, the structure is not a list and some program must make the link between one data and another.

In a practical, random-access storage medium (main or disc storage) a list is usually created out of contiguous locations. The reference parts and data records are usually adjacent, but not necessarily (Figure 6.2). The pointer must be large enough to be able to refer to other items in the list; the rest of the list item must be large enough to hold the entire data record. Note that the reference items in the list need not refer to adjacent data items; this is an important property of a list. By simply changing the pointer, the programmer can cause the order of data to be changed without actually moving it in storage.

	POINTER	DATA
1001:	1009	3
1003:	1005	5
1005:	1007	8
1007:	1011	13
1009:	1003	21
1011:	(?)	34

Figure 6.2 A list in storage representing the sequence (3, 21, 5, 8, 13, 34).

A list has a potential maximum size that can be statically defined in the program. This is the amount of space to be reserved in the storage medium for storage of the list elements. However, when the procedures are executed, the instantaneous number of actual list elements may be less than or equal to this maximum. A design notation should provide an indication of the maximum and minimum number of items that may be in the list at any point in the program. In the example the list may have as few as zero members (none) or as many as six members.

Now, if the list defined contains pointers that always refer to adjacent data items, and those references need never change in the program, some efficiencies may be introduced. The explicit reference parts of the data structure can be removed and replaced by a small procedure (Figure 6.3). This procedure is used to advance from one data record to the next. Instead of using the (no longer existing)

	IMPLIED POINTER	DATA
1001:	1002	3
1002:	1003	5
1003:	1004	8
1004:	1005	13
1005:	1006	21
1006:	(?)	34

Figure 6.3 An array, a special case of a list.

reference part, the current address and the data record size are used to compute the next record's address.

The number of available data record spaces in an array is generally fixed. Since the individual data records are generally randomly accessible, some way of uniquely identifying the records is required. In most cases, the record spaces in the array are arbitrarily numbered (say, from 1 to 6) and a subscript to the array-name is used to refer directly to data records. Programmers write subscripts as numbers in parentheses. The third item in a table of ASCII characters might be written as "TEXT (3)." Arrays generally use less storage space than lists for the same amount of information, but the relationships among the various data records are less flexible.

A telephone system provides an excellent opportunity to define and use rich data structures. An example is in the handling of the way calls are recorded while on hold. In one particular system there is only one hold key on the telephone instrument and there are no buttons for selecting among incoming calls. By depressing the hold button you can regain the dial tone and place another call. When you hang up from that second call, the held call will begin ringing you back immediately. In the midst of the second call you may wish to put the party on hold and place a third call. Originally, the system specifications called for an unlimited number of calls to be allowed to be placed on hold by any telephone at any time. This meant, in the simplest sense, that if there were 100 telephones in the system, then each telephone would have space in central memory for recording the extension numbers of up to 99 other telephones; that would total 9,900 bytes of RAM for this one feature.

The original solution proposed suggested using an array of 10,000 bytes of RAM. Each telephone instrument would have had 99 bytes associated with it for recording all of the calls on hold; an additional byte would count the number of calls on hold by each telephone. That solution was rejected because it was too costly.

The original project engineer decided, in the absence of any experience or design ability, to ignore the specifications and allow only 2 calls on hold at any one time for any one instrument. That meant that only 200 bytes of RAM had to be reserved for all 100 telephones. However, good design practice dictates there be no unilateral change of specifications. When this particular "solution" was disclosed, there were howls of protest from prospective customers.

What is needed is a way to store large number of calls on hold, but without permanently allocating a large amount of storage space to each telephone instrument. Programmers know that the list offers just that dynamic arrangement. But how many calls might be on hold? That is worth some study and investigation.

We need to implement a worst-case design. It would be disastrous to the product if some party who was trying to put a call on hold corrupted the entire system. Since one party cannot be expected to know how many other calls are already on hold, there must be enough space to record each and every held call. In a 100-telephone system there can never be more than 99 calls on hold (one telephone calls all others and successively places each on hold). Therefore, we must provide a list of at least 99 entries.

Because the extension numbers are in the range of 0..99, we will tend to use one byte of memory for each recorded call on hold; an additional byte is necessary to point to adjacent elements of lists. This means that we can initialize space in RAM to a bunch of two-byte list elements. The two bytes are called the *datum* and *pointer* of the element.

We begin our data structure design by assigning 198 bytes (hopefully contiguous, although they may be separated somewhat arbitrarily) as our list area. The entire set of pointers is initialized so that each list element points to its neighbors; the last item points to zero so that we can detect when we have removed the last item from this list of "free" data objects. There is maintained somewhere in memory a data value that is a pointer to the top of the list of unused data elements; that variable is named FREE (Figure 6.4).

At another place in memory we allocate one byte per telephone instrument in an array named HOLDQ. These bytes are initialized to zero. Whenever a call is placed on hold, HOLDQ will be set to point to some list element in the list space; the extension number of the call on hold will be stored in that list element's datum byte. Now, a list of telephone extensions on hold can be maintained for each

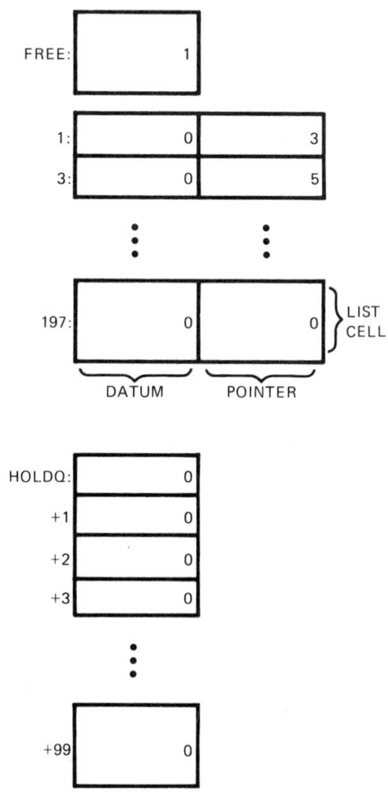

Figure 6.4 Storage arrangement of lists to solve the telephone program.

telephone; the entire scheme requires about 300 bytes of memory, but the number of calls on hold is not artificially limited.

Start with the assumption that extension number 3 is talking with extension number 28 and the first party puts the second party on hold. The sequence of these steps is shown in Figure 6.5:

1. The current value in the <u>HOLDQ + 3</u> location is saved in a temporary place (say, <u>X</u>).
2. The value in <u>FREE</u> is placed into <u>HOLDQ + 3</u> so that the top of the hold queue for extension number 3 is now pointing to some free-space list element.
3. The list element is removed from the free-space list by copying its pointer value into <u>FREE</u>. Now, only <u>HOLDQ + 3</u> points to that no-longer-free list element.
4. The extension number to be held, 28, is stored in the datum byte of the new top-of-queue list element.
5. The list element's pointer is set from <u>X</u>. This appends the old hold queue (if any) to the top list element; this creates a Last-In/First-Out queue of calls.

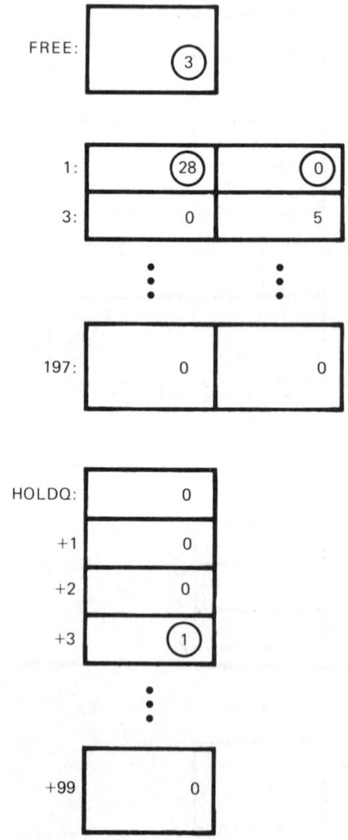

Figure 6.5 The contents of storage after extension #3 puts extension #28 on hold.

Notice that we can continue to do this sequence for each call placed on hold. The calls can be for different telephones and there can be any arbitrary number of them for any one telephone.

When a call is taken off hold, the analogous steps are performed in reverse. The topmost call in some list pointed to by the appropriate hold queue will be removed from that list of held calls and returned to the free-space list.

In this one example we have used scalars (FREE), arrays (HOLDQ), and lists. These are important concepts.

Software Reliability

A word about reliability: Example programs like these are nearly always simpler than you would actually implement. To avoid obscuring the underlying concept with what might be red herrings, we have ignored some special end points. For example, what would happen if the free-space list is exhausted and someone wants to place a call on hold? It is absolutely essential that every part of the program that can acquire an element from the free-space list check the variable FREE and take some action if the value of FREE is zero. In a finite-state machine you can return to the overall main loop and let the other FSM's execute; when this FSM regains control you will probably find that some space has been relinquished and is now available. This is representative of the special care you should take with software examples you find elsewhere. In general, as in this example, avoid inductive logic (that is, assuming something to be true, for example, the availability of unallocated space). If you don't practice what the professional programmers call *defensive programming,* you leave yourself open to field failures that occur all too seldom to be measurable but often enough to be troublesome.

Finite-State Machines

A powerful tool for describing microprocessor software is the finite-state machine (FSM) model. It is especially appropriate for systems that are "driven" by large numbers of successive external events. If the microprocessor is interfaced to a large keyboard that has many function keys, you can be sure that the FSM model will be useful. If the micro is connected to many external sensors, the conditions or changes of which are all important, the FSM will be a powerful tool. Frankly, the only problems we found that could not be effectively simplified by the FSM approach were trivial anyway. The FSM is a tool to help you convert ambiguous system specifications into unambiguous respecifications that can be easily converted into computer programs. A very large application is usually modeled as a set of intercommunicating FSM's instead of one huge FSM for both conceptual and computational ease in refining the overall design.

Most finite-state machine examples are relatively trivial, but the concepts are directly applicable to very large applications. One of the most important classes of application is the sensing of external events in real-time. At any given point in a program some external stimuli may be safely ignored. Simultaneous but unrelated stimuli may require separate finite-state machines; these are easily implemented in software. Because of the need to make many kinds of error tests for extraneous input signals, flow charts of these complicated processes become unwieldy. State diagrams, however, can be a strong simplifying influence in these cases.

As an example, imagine that a designer must control a light bulb whose switch must be debounced. A four-state FSM (Figure 6.6) can describe a circuit to de-

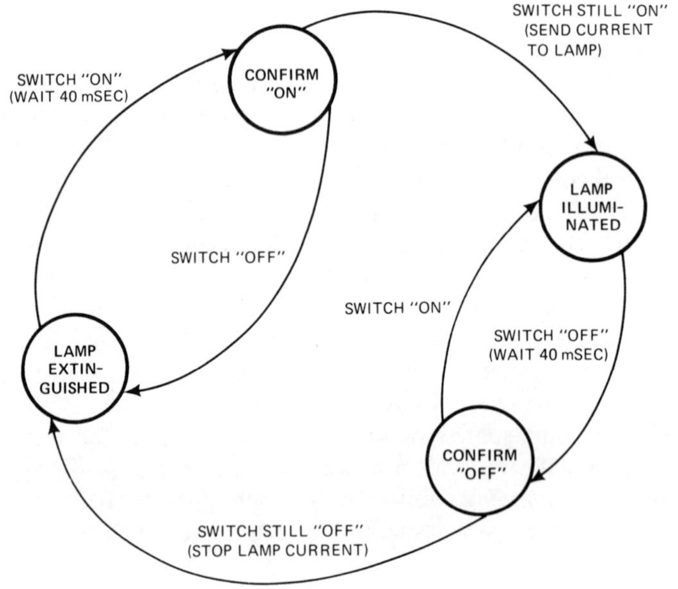

Figure 6.6 A debounced switch FSM.

bounce a switch. Two of the states are the desirable, stable states (switch on with indicator lamp on and switch off with indicator lamp off) and the other two states are transitory, unstable states that always lead to a correct stable state. We will assume that all significantly troublesome switch bouncing is finished within 40 ms after the switch position is changed. One implication of this assumption is that since we don't care how many times the switch contacts bounce during this initial 40 ms, we don't design our FSM to tell us how many bounces. A more serious implication is that real trouble may result if our guess of 40 ms is low by say from 10 to 20 ms. Such a misguess is an example of trouble at the design (actually the "switch application") level and it points out that teamwork is essential between digital designers and software designers.

Implementing a finite-state machine requires some engineering decisions. Basically, these decisions are based on whether events are detected and how

State Machines: The Concept of State

Each object in a digital system can exist in one or more *states.* A state is nothing more than one of the modes or conditions that the object can be in at any point in time. A light bulb can be turned *on* or *off;* these are two states a light bulb can assume. The light bulb can also exist—temporarily—in a condition of being illuminated or being extinguished; these *transitions* from state-to-state are conveniently ignored in state machine theory application without penalty. The switching circuit design penalty for a badly designed transition can be a "hazard" or a "race" condition. These do not occur in software because software is sequential on all of today's microprocessors. In digital systems of interest to us here the objects can take on a *finite* number of discrete and identifiable states. Any digital system that can be characterized by describing all the possible states in which it can exist is called a *finite-state machine.*

Finite-state machines can be imagined as small hypothetical computers that have a few well-defined and discrete possible actions and conditions. Consider, for a moment, a trivially simple digital machine and some small number of conditions and actions: A light switch that controls a light bulb is about the simplest kind of digital machine we can imagine. The system (i.e., machine) can exist in two *states;* the light bulb can be illuminated or extinguished. For the purposes of this description we intentionally ignore the details of the transition from *off* to *on* and vice versa; during those transitional times there may be some flickering of the lamp, but it is of no concern to our understanding of the two-state machine. (See Figure A).

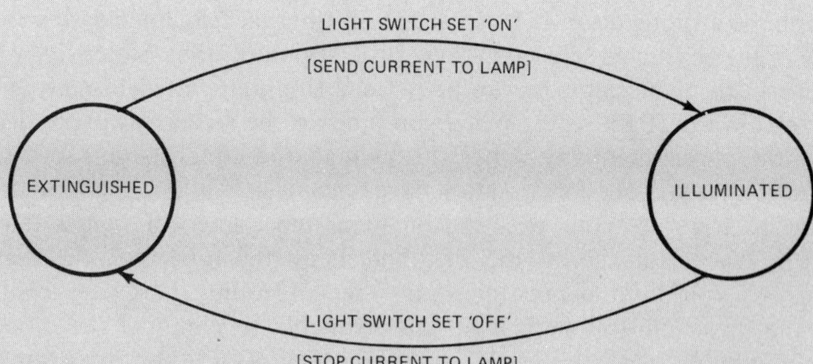

Figure A

The lamp control has a finite number of states (two) and transitions from one state to the other. The states are drawn as circular *nodes;* the directed lines that connect these nodes (called *edges* by the purists) describe the external events or actions that can allow the state of the FSM to be changed. Along with the actions are some effects that need to be noted: Setting the light switch *on* must also cause current to be sent to the bulb. As a convention, we will enclose the consequent actions to be taken in parentheses. Each line is terminated with an arrowhead that specifies the direction of the transition between the two specified states. In the *extinguished* state, for example, we can ignore every other stimulus except the "Light switch set 'ON'" event because this is the only action arrow leaving this state. Furthermore, if no stimulus is sensed that will cause the state to be changed, then the FSM is assumed to remain in the same state.

actions are taken and states are recorded in hardware or software. The design may depend heavily on whether the real quantity of switches and light bulbs number nearer one than 100. To control one light in a room, you would probably install a wall switch (hardware). To control the street lights of a city, you would probably use electronics. To control a whole musical light show, you would probably opt for computer (software) control.

The objective of a state diagram is to allow the designer to be concerned with what needs to be done instead of with how to do it. Instead of rushing into deciding how to implement a poorly understood system, the engineer uses state diagrams to help him understand the application. This is a nontrivial accomplishment.

State tables for trivial examples are easy to draw and understand, but state tables for real-world problems become unwieldy very quickly. A good example is the telephone at your desk. If it is part of an internal telephone system, other extensions can be dialed directly. Actually, six important states in which the telephone instrument can exist can be defined (Figure 6.7a). Normally, your telephone rests in the IDLE state. When you pick up the receiver, the physical equipment of the phone company senses this change and connects you to a source of dial tone so that you get confirmation of service; it also attaches a *tone decoder* to your line to translate your push-button tones into electrical signals that can be processed. Once you depress the first button on the tone pad, the dial tone is stopped. As you keep depressing keys, the controlling hardware continues to collect the digits until enough digits are available to compute the other party's extension number. The JOINING state is transitory; if the extension you are calling is idle, the central equipment gives you an audible ringing signal to listen to and starts ringing the other party's bell. You are left in the AUDIBLE-RING state until the other party answers; at that time you are both put into the TALKING state in which you remain until one of you hangs up. This forces the party who hung up into IDLE. On some systems both parties are returned to IDLE even

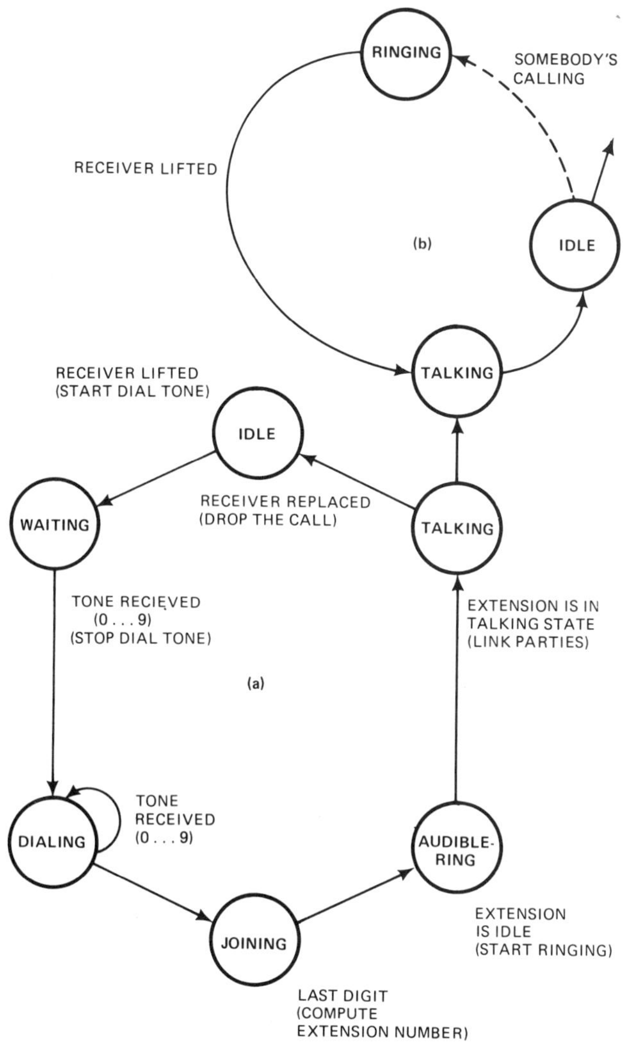

Figure 6.7 (a) FSM for a simple single telephone. (b) An automatic, externally-induced state change.

though only one hung up. On others systems one party moves to the WAITING state when the other hangs up.

This finite-state machine describes the main and important states of any simple telephone instrument. However, a one-telephone system isn't very interesting. It is imperative that there be several telephone instruments, each represented by its own FSM. This means that in a 100-telephone system, we can conceive of having 100 asynchronous and cooperating finite-state machines, each of which may be a state totally distinct from the others. However, when a finite-state machine is described for one telephone instrument, it applies to all of them. We have reduced the level of complexity in the design to the level of a single instrument.

When it is in the JOINING state, the telephone of interest interrogates the status of the other party. Once that party has been determined to be IDLE, it is imperative to place that FSM into some other state. This implies a need in each FSM for a state that corresponds to the physical condition of being rung by a caller. We call this the RINGING state (Figure 6.7b). The state transition that takes place between IDLE and RINGING is one that the FSM does not make itself; this transition occurs "magically" because of the actions of some other FSM (that of the originating party). In Figure 6.7b we show this relationship with a dashed line. When the party being rung lifts the receiver, the telephone is placed in a state so that it listens to the caller. When the FSM for the originating party is next activated, the called party is in the TALKING state and so the two parties listen to each other.

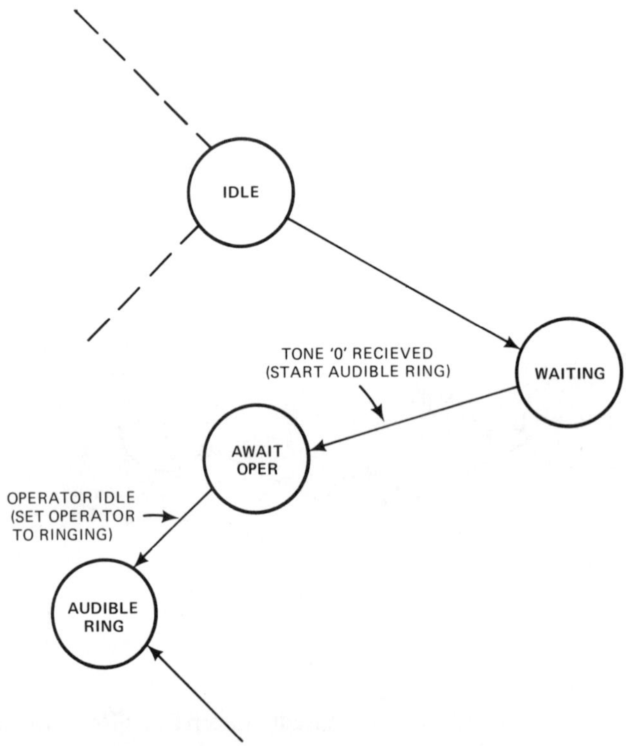

Figure 6.8 A new state to handle a special case.

There are always special cases to be handled in every design. These special cases cause headaches in implementation if they are poorly understood. When special cases are fully understood, they cease to become special cases. Their features tend to be absorbed by the overall design of the system. In a telephone system, dialing the operator is a classic example of a special case. If you have ever noticed, you have probably never gotten a busy signal when you called the operator. Even if the operator was busy you were supplied an audible ringing sound. Our state diagram in Figure 6.8 shows that by introducing another state called AWAIT-OPER the calling party gets into this state by dialing zero; this state may be transitory if the operator is found to be IDLE. However, we may become "trapped" here until the operator becomes free. In practice, there is an additional complication not shown here that arranges the calls in first-come, first-serve order; however, the principle remains the same.

There are numerous shortcuts that a telephone user can take. If an error is made, for example, or if the other party never answers the phone, we'd like to be able to abort the call by hanging up. There are many states from which the call can be aborted. Furthermore, the transitory JOINING state has more than one possible outcome; two new states are added for calls made to busy extensions and to extensions that do not exist (what will happen if a party dials his own number?).

Our simple telephone system has rapidly grown to contain ten discrete states and nineteen different possible state transitions. And we haven't gotten to the hard part yet. What about outside trunk calls? And special services, like conferences and calls on hold and forwarding and ... and ... and ... ? A practical design will exceed fifth states. If becomes clear that we cannot easily talk about state diagrams for real systems with typical complexities. There ought to be a better way to represent a large FSM. There is: a state table.

State Tables

A state table is a handwritten or typewritten equivalent of the state diagram. State diagrams are good for sketching the general objective and for communicating among small informal groups. The state table, properly written, can be the formal documentation of the predesign effort, and it is almost always the preferred representation for large FSM's. (See figure 6.9.)

Reading Programs

A note about the reading programs: You would not expect to glance at a complex schematic diagram and incorporate unfamiliar parts and comprehend it all at once. Therefore, don't expect to absorb program examples without some effort and study. Each program you read adds to your kit of tricks and techniques; it is one of the most efficient ways of communicating experience.

Each program and state table presented here is worthy of some of your time. Don't leave an illustration unless you understand it thoroughly.

CURRENT STATE	CONDITION	ACTION	NEXT STATE

Figure 6.9 A table for describing an FSM.

A state table is made up of four columns that are labeled as follows:

1. Current state
2. Condition (or event)
3. Action
4. Next state

The *current state* is an arbitrarily assigned name that represents one of the named circles in a state diagram. To keep typing rules reasonable, we usually limit these state names to fifteen characters or less. The *conditions* or *events* are the things that can cause a state transition. When the specified condition prevails or the event occurs, the specified *actions* are performed and the FSM's are placed into the state named in *next state.*

The state table provides more room for detail about the meanings of the conditions/events and the actions to be taken than does the state diagram. In the state diagrams we leave out many details because of space and physical layout limitations. In a state table we specify all of the conditions and actions in as much detail as we know at this stage. For example, in the telephone system FSM described earlier, the IDLE state is left whenever the telephone's receiver is lifted. However, in a practical system there is only a small number of tone decoders installed. If these are all in use, the telephone can't be issued a dial tone because the user might begin dialing too soon. In the state table we can state this combination of events (OFF-HOOK and TD-FREE) explicitly, or we can introduce a new and temporary state, check CHECK-TD, just for the purpose (Figure 6.10).

When a state has two or more possible conditions, we arrange them in order of intended testing. In the case of the CHECK-TD state, it is proper to check the telephone to see if the call has been aborted before trying to assign a tone decoder. That way, if the call has been aborted, we don't deny someone else access to the toner decoder.

It should also be apparent that there can be null actions. In the case of the IDLE to CHECK-TD transition, there is nothing to be done except change the state of the FSM. This turns out to be one of the most important properties of finite-state machines. Embodied in the state is the distillation of all the important

CURRENT STATE	EVENT OR CONDITION	ACTION	NEXT STATE
IDLE	OFF-HOOK & TD-FREE	ASSIGN DECODER; START DIAL TONE	WAITING

OR

IDLE	OFF-HOOK		CHECK-TD
CHECK-TD	ON-HOOK		IDLE
	TD-FREE	ASSIGN DECODER; START DIAL TONE	WAITING

Figure 6.10 Alternative ways can be used to describe the same set of states and events.

defines what things have happened in the past that are of interest to us. In the CHECK-TD state, for example, we know that the telephone is not idle and off the hook. Similarly, we know that the receiver is supposed to be on the cradle in the IDLE state. If it isn't we immediately leave the *IDLE* state the next time the conditions are checked.

Designing the FSM

Designing the finite-state machine for an application is an important programming step. It requires the programmer to thoroughly understand the application and to seriously design the program prior to doing any actual coding. Because the FSM description is application-oriented instead of programming-oriented, system analysts and sophisticated user representatives can read and comment upon it before coding is undertaken. This can assure adequacy of the program before it is written.

The finite-state machine descriptions do not spring full-grown from the mind. Each FSM is the result of a lot of careful thinking, rethinking, and paper shuffling. To construct an FSM, we begin with a gross sketch that outlines a typical input. This is usually drawn on a chalkboard or sketch pad. There is no value in trying to complete the diagram at this time because, just as with flow charts, minor changes may require redrafting.

For each state in the diagram, we think up a reasonable and meaningful name. Since a state is a condition of being, these names should be nouns or adjectives—not verbs. Now, we rule off several pieces of paper into three more columns, like the form shown in Figure 6.9 & 10. It is probably best to make up a form and duplicate it; most practical FSM's require from 50 to 100 states and in redrafting we will use up at least twice as many pages. At the top of each page we transcribe one of the state names from the draft sketch. For each state, we transcribe the conditions and next state from the sketch to the forms.

Now the paper shuffling begins in earnest. We pick an arbitrary state and begin working on it. We should not pick a very common state like the first or last state. In real-time programming we shouldn't choose the idle or waiting state because these states have so many possibilities that we won't be able to make a decision. Instead, we pick a simple state.

For each state, we ask the question, "What important things can happen in this state?" We write down each and every possible event or input condition. All possible events that could occur and all of the important data variables that ought to be checked by the program in this state should be described. Once all the state transitions are defined, we describe the actions that should take place when the transition takes place. We must be sure to specify a successor state in the third column of the form. Each time we declare a new state, we make up a new page for it and add it to the gross sketch.

We find that randomly proceeding through the pages of the state table is the easiest thing to do. Where we discover two very similar states, for instance, we may wish to revise all the states that refer to these two states so that they can be reduced to a single state. We should look for completeness on each page. Each state should consist of all relevant events and conditions explicitly stated. Each condition must have a successor state defined. All of the states named in column 3 must have pages with that name in the sheaf of state descriptions.

Once we have added four or five new states to the gross sketch, we redraw this expanded gross sketch as sketch 2. Then we check the state name sheets against the latest sketch to ensure agreement. As the number of states in the sketch increases, we find it fruitful and time-saving to concentrate on a set of related states, and we attempt to completely define these more accurately. Once this is done, we move to another set and so forth.

Conditions are normally given as short names that stand for complex hardware and/or software sequences. We describe the meanings of those sequences on a dictionary page (See Figure 6.11). As new conditions are needed, we add them to the dictionary. The condition dictionary is used to decide which input schemes ought to be used. Each of the conditions refers to inputs or to variables in memory. By thorough study we can decide which ought to be in hardware and which ought to be in software. A particular condition may be tested directly (i.e., is the bit *true*

OFF-HOOK	TELEPHONE RECEIVER IS OFF-HOOK (LIFTED)
TD-FREE	THERE IS AT LEAST ONE TONE DECODER FREE
DIGIT (1-9)	TONE DECODER HAS DETECTED ONE OF THE DIGITS 1. . . 9
DIGIT-0	TONE DECODER HAS RECEIVED ZERO DIGIT
LAST DIGIT	THE DECODER HAS SENSED AND RECORDED ALL OF THE DIGITS FOR A CALL

Figure 6.11 A simple condition dictionary for an FSM.

or false?) or through a complex sequence of instructions or even through another small FSM that needs to be separately described.

In any event, the condition dictionary describes all of the inputs needed from the outside world and all of the data variables that must be kept throughout the system. As the need for data variables is determined, actions that must be taken to set or compute those variables should be verified. If the specified variables are not set by the appropriate actions in the state table, these actions must be added for completeness and accuracy.

The *action* entries of the state table describe which data variables are set and which output ports will be required. Again, there is a hardware/software trade off to be established. For example, the following action in an application's state table is totally ambiguous: "Type the word out to the terminal." We must still decide which kind of terminal, which speed, which code and format, and whether the bit pattern is created by hardware (say in a UART chip) or is in software. However, the general need for output like this is often specified in the original system spec. The data variables that are set by actions in the state table, however, are on a more detailed, limited range level. This level should be verified by assuring that the variables that appear in the table are used in other conditions or actions in the table.

Finally, all of the states should be verified. Does every state named in the *next state* column of the state table appear in the *current state* column? Is there a path to each and every state? Does each state have a potential transition to another state? If there is a state that goes only to itself as a next state under any condition, care must be taken that other conditions will normally occur that will switch this state to another state. It is also a good idea to make a state-transition chart. This chart is generally made up on one page and all the states are listed down the left side of the page and across the top. The left side labels the current states; the top labels are for next states. For each state transition in the table, we mark an x in the chart. Some logical patterns will emerge that can lead us to oversights and errors in the state table itself.

When we analyze the state transition we may find that two columns may have identical entries. That is because an FSM is allowed to have two nearly identical states with similar but not absolutely identical actions. Since each state carries the implied history of what has happened in the past input sequence, two nearly identical states may exist to distinguish between two different past input conditions that are no longer recorded anywhere else in memory. This condition is a tip-off that we can use a subroutine that is called from both places in the program. This subroutine will save space because we won't have to write the same piece of code twice.

Just as computers can have subroutines, so can finite-state machines (since computers are nothing more than overgrown FSM's anyway). If two states in a large FSM have similar structures but with subtle differences, then the two states can share a common subroutine described as another FSM. There are other procedures for minimizing the number of states in an FSM, but they are fairly obvious. The common subroutine is an example of one form of minimization.

Once the FSM has been designed, it should be transcribed onto punched cards or some other computer-editable medium so that copies and updates can easily be made. Printed copies should be distributed to analysts and users for review. It is not an impractical idea to plant an obvious error or two, just to see if the document gets read.

The act of creating a finite-state machine is nothing more than solidifying original specifications. If the formal documentation of an FSM can be distributed to knowledgeable readers, the final quality of the product is likely to be much higher. It is easier to catch design errors before coding instead of after coding.

Deciding What to Model

In any system of reasonable complexity likely to be seen by the microcomputer designer, description of the whole system would lead to unreasonably large FSM tables. In the first example, for instance, we modeled the actions of one particular telephone instrument. Now, obviously, a one-telephone system isn't going to offer much variety in communication possibilities. What's really needed, in the final equipment, is a system that allows an FSM for each separate telephone instrument. However, when modeling the process we simply treat one telephone instrument because we know that all the others are identical.

The first rule in creating the FSM model is to select the repeated design elements and model them only once. A system with multiple keyboards and matching displays, for example, should be described with but one FSM that documents a one-keyboard/one-display system. If these replicated subsystems can cooperate with one another (as the telephones do when one party calls another), then some extra states (and "phantom" transitions to them) may have to be introduced.

It is also possible to break down a large FSM into a "master" machine and several "slave" machines. Remember, these finite-state machines are conceptual devices only; therefore, this master-slave relationship need bear no resemblance to any future hardware design but can resemble the software structure. A master FSM with several slave FSM's will still require only one microprocessor.

When some complex sequence of events leads to some set of well-defined set of outcomes, you can usually partition that into a separate FSM model. Each of these smaller models can be independently documented and implemented, but they will eventually just be different pieces of software in the same microcomputer. In the design of a point-of-sale terminal, for example, you might define a separate FSM for the set of functions related to data communications. Since the overall FSM for the whole terminal simply refers to that FSM by name, it is apparent where that subfunction is invoked.

Uses of the FSM

Once you have created a model of your eventual system it's time for some review and critical design decisions. First, since the FSM is described in easily readable terms, the nontechnical users or their representatives should be given the oppor-

Program Design Goals

There are many kinds of programs that get written during the course of a microcomputer project. There are "quickies" that are written to stimulate the new hardware or to find faults. There are "prototype" programs that are written to demonstrate feasibility and to provide some limited capability to show off the product features. There are "drivers" that are usually designed in concert with the design of the I/O hardware; these programs become parts of other and larger programs. Finally, there are "production" programs that end up being included in the delivered product. Each of these kinds of programs has different attributes. Quicky programs to diagnose hardware (or suspected hardware) faults don't have to consider all potential conditions, for example. If a quicky program is unreliable because it doesn't test for invalid conditions, there's no harm done. However, the I/O driver programs need to be totally reliable so that future programs may rely on them; you can afford to spend a lot of time verifying that all the potential troublesome conditions and events are taken care of in this kind of software.

The first step in designing any computer program, whether for micro, mini, or huge machine, is to establish your goals. You can have a concise program, or one that is fast, or one that can be written and debugged in a short time. It is impossible to achieve all of these goals simultaneously. Actually, the situation is confused in most real projects because the goals change through the life of the design cycle; if you change those goals by intent (instead of just letting them happen haphazardly), you are in control of the situation.

There are several attributes of a good computer program, many of which are listed here. You may have some other factors that you feel are important; they should be added to this list. To establish the goals of your software development effort, pick some important time points. In most microcomputer projects key events are at three instants in time: when the hardware has been completed but not yet debugged; when the hardware is in prototype form, ready to be demonstrated; and when the product is about to be finalized for production or shipment. The list of goals you establish for the first event will probably have "quick programming" at the top of the list, while space and time efficiencies will be near the bottom. "Reliability" will be a key issue when you are about to demonstrate the product, whereas that factor is normally unimportant earlier in the project. Finally, you may find "minimum size" at the top of your own goals list at the end of the development effort.

Nobody can specify the list of goals for you. However, studies (such as Weinberg's, reported in *Datamation,* November, 1972) have shown that you need this list of goals to succeed. Without these goals established, each person will apply a personal set of goals that may vary with the slightest whim. Once the list of goals has been established, be sure that everybody on the project knows what they are. When you change your set of goals, be sure to promulgate that information, too.

tunity to read and modify the model. It is not difficult for a reader who has experience in a particular field to pick out flaws in your FSM, particularly in matters of style. That is, your proposed model may call for some particular external sequence of actions that violates a long-standing practice among users; user review will point out needed changes and can spare you much future grief.

You should aim to achieve a written approval of the design embodied in the FSM description. It protects you, as the designer, from future claims of misunderstanding. Because of the responsibility it places on the person or group who reads the description, the approval process ensures that the FSM model will actually be studied.

Once the specifications for the product have been formalized in an FSM model, design can begin in earnest. To implement each condition and each action you have to start making some hard decisions about the hardware/software trade off points. These decisions come after the specs have been approved, not before. The whole object of the FSM method of describing systems is to avoid overlooking required features in the hasty pursuit of implementation.

CURRENT STATE	EVENT OR CONDITION	ACTION	NEXT STATE
IDLE	OFF-HOOK	ASSIGN TONE DECODER; START DIAL TONE	NEED-TONE
NEED-TONE	ON-HOOK	RELEASE TONE DECODER; STOP DIAL TONE	IDLE
	DIGIT (1-9)	RECORD FIRST DIGIT; STOP DIAL TONE	DIALING
	DIGIT-0	STOP DIAL TONE; RELEASE TONE DECODER; START AUDIBLE RINGING; SET OPERATOR AS PARTY	AWAIT-OPER
DIALING	ON-HOOK	RELEASE TONE DECODER	IDLE
	DIGIT (0-9)	RELEASE TONE DECODER; COMPUTE EXTENSION NUMBER; SET NEW NUMBER AS PARTY	JOINING
JOINING	PARTY-INVALID	START REORDER TONE	HEAR-REORDER
	PARTY-BUSY	START BUSY TONE	HEAR-BUSY
	PARTY-IDLE	START AUDIBLE RING; START PARTY'S STATE TO RINGING; START PARTY'S INSTRUMENT RINGING	HEAR-RING
AWAIT-OPER	PARTY-IDLE	SET OPERATOR'S STATE TO RINGING	HEAR-RING
	ON-HOOK	STOP AUDIBLE RING	IDLE
HEAR-RING	ON-HOOK	STOP AUDIBLE RING; SET PARTY'S STATE IDLE	IDLE
	PARTY-TALKING	STOP AUDIBLE RING	TALKING

Figure 6.12 A finite-state table excerpt for the telephone system.

Translating FSM to Program

Each finite-state machine can very easily be turned into program code for a particular microprocessor. The condition dictionary defines the hardware/software interface and, hence, the required hardware to implement the necessary input ports. The action dictionary will also have to be defined in terms of the output ports affected by each specific action. The software is the code that is written to exercise the inputs and outputs in accordance with the rules of the FMS tables of Figure 6.12.

In a single FSM, as you might use with a simple process control system, each state becomes the name of a unique subroutine. Each condition within that routine

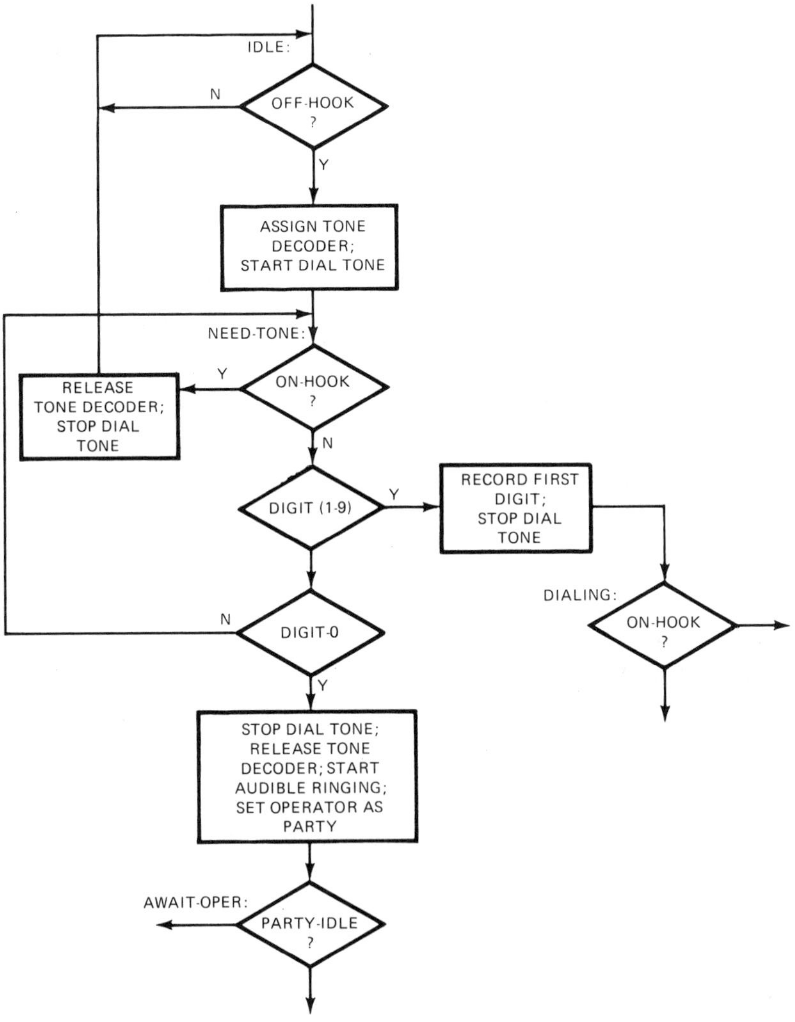

Figure 6.13 Partial flowchart derived from FSM of figure 6.12.

is some sequence (simple or complex) of input reading, data referencing, and conditional jumps. If the conditional jumps result in no change in state, the sequence ends with a jump back to the top of the subroutine for repetitive execution. When a particular condition for specified combination of conditions is satisfied, the code that will implement the actions is executed and the new specified state is jumped to. It is even possible to translate an FSM into a flow chart if you feel more comfortable with that representation (Figure 6.13).

The usual approach to program design using a finite-state machine model is to create the FSM and associated dictionaries at one time, along with the definition of all data structures that the FSM will expect to have recourse to. After the FSM and data structures have been closely examined, the data structures can be defined in terms of primitive programs that operate upon them, and the FSM can be translated into code for the microprocessor of interest. It is possible to design the vast majority of programs in the FSM form without considering the specific microprocessor being used. The FSM represents the *requirements.* When data structures are defined, however, you are making a conscious selection between data and procedure. This choice should be made with a specific microprocessor in mind so that efficient use of unique features can be designed in.

Design Sequence

It is now clear that the first thing you should investigate is the organization of the data that your program will be processing. Given the data structures and the specifications, the procedures are functionally defined for you—you only have to discover their actual form. Since the specifications describe what must be done and since the data structures define representations of data to be manipulated to meet those specs, you must implement procedures that operate on that data in order to achieve those specs. You still have some latitude in selecting algorithms, but the design of the structure is done.

An *algorithm* is "a prescribed set of well-defined rules or processes for the solution of a problem in a finite number of steps", according to the American National Standards Institute (ANSI). If, for example, you have to search a table for specific information (an associative table, the software implementation of a content-addressable memory), you will discover that there are literally hundreds of algorithms that you can use. These range from the simplest linear search of the array (inspecting each item in turn) through dichotomizing searches (examining the midpoint to divide the effective table in half) and randomizing schemes (using the data itself as an index to a randomly organized array). Selecting the algorithm is often tightly coupled to the notion of selecting the data structures. Certainly, some algorithms require specific data structures for operation. However, the two can often be separated. If you have to search an array of data, use the simplest possible algorithm early in the design process. Then, after you have the software up and working, you can replace the algorithm with one that is closer to your set of final software goals. This new algorithm usually does the job faster or with elegance, but it is often more complicated than the first choice.

Don't be afraid to introduce some "scaffolding" at this point. Some extra software that "instruments" your program so that you can monitor its behavior can save you many hours of debugging. An easy way to do this is to insert halt instructions after each sequence of conditional tests. The halt should never be executed (because you have programmed control away from it), but if it is, you know what is wrong.

Another powerful tool is the execution history. This history is kept for a short period of time, and it is easy to keep with an FSM. If there is an error, you can easily reconstruct the sequence of events that led to the error.

Each time the FSM changes state, you can record the prior state (and perhaps some other data of importance) in a "circular" table in RAM (see Figure 6.14).

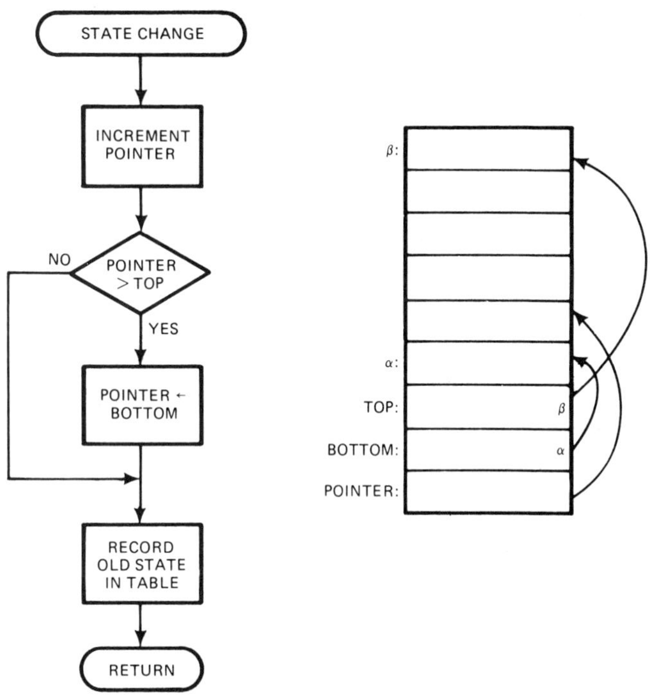

Figure 6.14 A circular table for keeping history.

The size of the table may be large or small, depending on the available memory and the maturity of the program. During early debugging you may wish to use some additional RAM in the prototype just to be able to keep a detailed history. Later, as the program becomes less error-prone, you can reduce the size of the table to only a few entries. During the field trials for a product, for example, only the few unused words at the end of RAM may be allocated to history keeping.

What is recorded in each position of the circular table depends on your program. If you change states by jumping to another subroutine, this stage-change recording subroutine may simply record the top of the return address stack that contains the most recently specified return address. In this case, use a subroutine call to the next state instead of a jump. At the beginning of the new state call the history-keeping subroutine that will remove the return address and put it into the circular table. If your states are handled as indices to a transfer vector, you may wish to record the state number in the table. In addition, you may wish to record a key data variable, especially if the performance within a state depends on that variable. It will make reconstruction of the events leading up to the failure much easier if you have data to augment the state identification.

Analyzing the execution trail is easy. Start at the place in the table addressed by the pointer and work backward. For each history table entry, write down the name or function of the state represented; write them down from the bottom of the page upward. When you are done, you will have recovered the execution trail. A brief study of the trail will usually uncover some invalid or inappropriate state transition for the input signals you know were provided. Look at the code for the state that the program was in prior to that transition to see where the fault lies.

The Walk-through

A design is not complete until it has been reviewed. You should plan to spend a day or more with an experienced colleague and "walk through" your program. Since you are no longer concerned with the design of the hardware (it is hopefully frozen by your software), you need to review the software with someone who has extensive programming experience, preferably on microcomputers (or, lacking that, on minicomputers).

Whether you start with the lowest level routines and work upward or start with the highest level routines and work downward, you should go through the entire software system from one end to the other. You are not looking for coding tricks to add to the software; you are looking for design flaws. Pay particular attention to the handling of error cases. Look at each loop and be sure that it works correctly on the first and last iterations. Be sure that each conditional test can have two outcomes (because at least one of the variables changes).

You may also get some ideas on how to improve the software at this point, especially if the reviewer has programmed a system like yours before. Resist making impulsive changes. Record them so that you will be sure to remember how to improve your program if and when you need to. But, changes that are consequences of this review should be made only to correct known deficiencies, not to add new features.

This walk-through is considered heretical by many novice programmers. Experienced programmers welcome the opportunity (after all, the practice did start with that master programmer, John von Neumann). It is one of the best ways to share programming experience, and the reviewer tends to learn a lot too. The purpose of this exercise is not education—it is to uncover design flaws.

7

Input/Output Interfaces

Next to software, the design of practical interfaces between the microcomputer and external equipment is usually the designer's biggest challenge. The processors are not difficult to understand, and memory is certainly easy to configure. The problem with input/output interfaces is compounded, of course, by the set of decisions that have to do with whether a particular function should be accomplished with a minimum of hardware or a minimum of software.

Interface design can be as complex as you want to make it. However, by partitioning the problem into small pieces, you will find that interface design is just as simple as any other kind of system design task. However, the opportunities to be clever abound. If the very nature of the microprocessor robs the creative designer of the ability to synthesize whole designs, input/output interfacing restores it—in spades. A simple interface can often be the cleverest. To drive a meter, for instance, most novice microprocessor designers would install a digital-to-analog converter with sufficient accuracy. A clever designer would drive the meter directly (Figure 7.1) and use software to control the computer's output with the appropriate duty cycle.

This apparent waste of a computer's capabilities is characteristic of many successful microcomputer system designs. If the computer has nothing better to do—use it. In any system that contains a computer, any circuitry must justify its existence by being less expensive than the equivalent software or by performing functions that the computer is too busy to handle. In the case of the meter, the software to generate a controlled duty cycle output might be trivial, but software to directly control the meter pointer would have to account for mass, momentum, inductance, and time. This, of course, would be a needlessly complex solution.

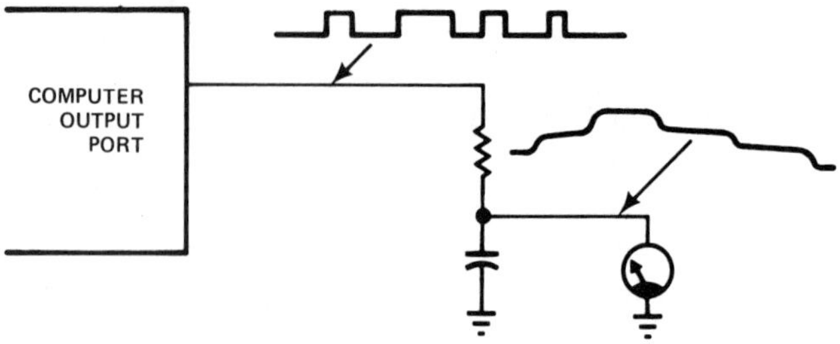

Figure 7.1 An analog output from a digital computer.

In many real-time control applications, microcomputers are hard pressed to keep up with the incoming data. Here, unique hardware is often added to help the computer by slowing the effective data rate. In one application, incoming pulses from many optical tachometers had to be counted by scanning these inputs fast enough to detect every pulse; that would have consumed too much execution time. The demands on the processor's time were relaxed by feeding each pulse stream into a four-bit counter that the computer could read. The input data rate was thus slowed by a factor of sixteen. The software determined the number of new pulses received by subtracting the previous counter reading from each new reading; this eliminated the need for circuitry to clear each counter after a reading.

The microcomputer system design is continually faced with hardware-software trade offs of this sort. There is a broad spectrum from one end (largely hardware with minimal software) to the other (mostly software). It is the engineer's job to select the most economical of an almost limitless variety of possibilities in that spectrum. The kind of thinking required to deal with these choices takes some getting used to, especially if the engineer is not sure how a task would be performed in software. We all tend to reach for the comfortable tools first. Finding the best combination of hardware and software requires the ability to estimate the cost and speed of each approach as well as an appreciation of how each decision will impact on other portions of the design. It is clear that the bank of counters accepting tachometer pulses will considerably simplify the software in that product. However, a decision to feed a meter with controlled duty cycle pulses might force all of the software in that system to conform to unacceptably rigid execution time patterns.

These are the kinds of design problems that must be tackled near the beginning of any microprocessor development project. Frequently, one has not even established which processor will be used in the design. That, in fact, is one of the many decisions that must come out of the initial design studies. But determining the techniques to be used in getting information in and out of the computer system is a much more important area and will probably have more impact on the economics of the system. Input/output (I/O) design is full of opportunities for the clever and creative designer. There are surely many great ideas still to come in combining hardware and software to create economical interfaces.

I/O Ports

External equipment that is connected to a computer always makes use of one or more paths terminated at what are called *ports.* The external equipment may be as simple as a rank of toggle switches or as complex as another computer. Regardless of the external equipment's own complexity, we must standardize the way communications are handled so that the new equipment can be easily added to the design.

A *port* is a register that can be selected to exchange data with the computer. The port is selected by executing an input or output instruction. If we execute the instruction OUT 18, for instance, we are selecting output port number 18 to receive a copy of the binary word already prepared in some register, usually the microprocessor's accumulator. In an eight-bit wide microprocessor the output port typically consists of an eight-bit latch and the circuitry necessary to generate the required strobe. If eight lamps are connected to the Q-outputs of the eight-bit latch, the programmer can directly control the lamps by establishing the required binary pattern in the accumulator and then loading the output latch with the OUT instruction. The output latch holds the pattern until the next OUT 18 instruction occurs.

An input port in such a system may consist of nothing more than an eight-bit buffer with three-state capability. That is, in addition to generating high or low logic levels, the outputs can be thrown into a high-impedance condition. This makes it possible to connect many similar buffers onto a shared bus into the computer. No more than one port is enabled at a time. When that port is active, generating high or low logic levels, all other input ports must be in the off state in order to avoid an electronic tug of war.

From the programming viewpoint, an instruction like IN 34 causes the word at the named (numbered) input port to be loaded into a standard location. Again, this is usually the microprocessor's accumulator. In the simple case, the eight input wires might be connected to eight toggle switches. The input instruction causes bits in the accumulator to be set or cleared, depending on the position of associated input switches. The program can analyze the switch pattern and take appropriate actions. Later we will see that the input and output lines associated with a program controlled port do not necessarily carry binary numbers or on/off bits. These ports are just general-purpose highways for a wide variety of tricks.

Port Control

Some microcomputers provide input and output ports on the CPU or storage chips. Intel's four-bit products and Fairchild's F-8 do it that way. With other microprocessors, the ports must be designed by the engineer. In these cases, the microprocessor provides a combination of signals that are to be used to select ports and control the direction of data transfers.

Different addresses are sometimes used for each direction; this avoids having to send direction signals through the scarce package pins. More commonly, direction-specifying signals are used; they can be named *inpulse* and *outpulse.* It is often necessary for the designer to generate these signals from still other signals provided by the microprocessor. During output operations, *outpulse* occurs when the data word to be transferred is ready on the microprocessor's data bus. The *outpulse* signal must be routed to one of the system output ports to enable it to latch the output data from the bus. The *inpulse* signal defines the time during which an input port may drive the data bus. The microcomputer will store the data that is on the bus when the trailing edge of *inpulse* occurs.

In addition to the direction pulses, a microcomputer must provide an address bus that specifies a port address. If the software commands an output transfer to port 18, the address bus lines will hold the binary value 18. The address bus contents are decoded and simultaneously gated with *outpulse* (or *inpulse,* depending on direction) to generate the required input/output action.

Although simple NAND/NOR logic can be used with each input/output port to enable data transfers, it is easier to decode many addresses with a single decoder. A single 74154 decoder will provide us with sixteen different I/O select signals; these can be combined with *inpulse* and *outpulse* to select one port in each direction (Figure 7.2).

Note that although the input and output ports are addressed identically, they are separate and distinct. It is not necessary to relate like-numbered input/output

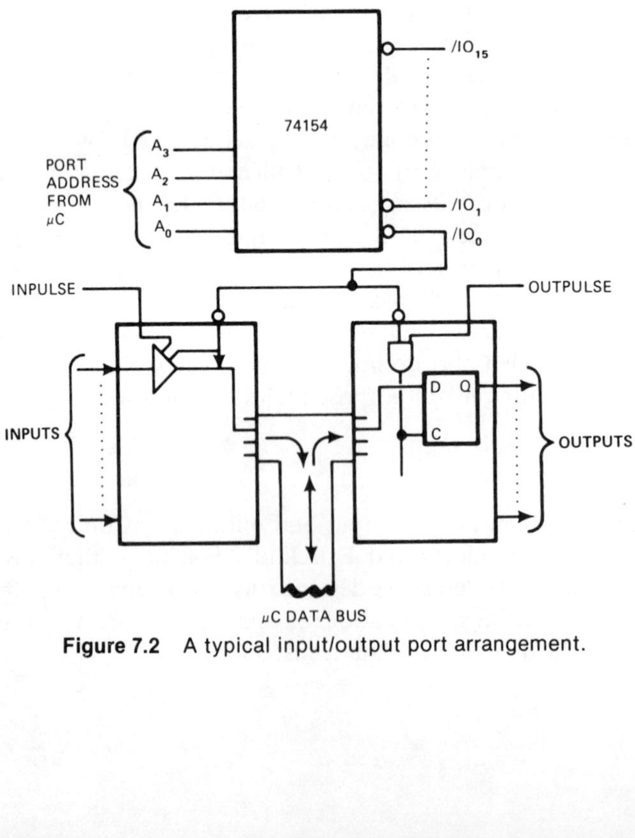

Figure 7.2 A typical input/output port arrangement.

ports to communicate with a single input/output device, although sometimes it is convenient to do so.

Incidentally, some output transactions do not actually involve use of the data bus at all. The signals, each controlled by an input or output instruction from the computer, can be used as narrow pulses that can be controlled from the software. These strobes are often useful output signals, especially when controlling the timing of external devices.

Using Storage Addresses

Because every computer must have instructions that move data in and out of storage, the use of special instructions to perform input and output is not strictly necessary. If ports are constructed to behave like storage locations, the storage transfer instructions will also perform I/O transfers. Systems built this way allow the programmer to apply the full capabilities of the computer's instruction set to I/O ports as well as to stored data. If storage locations can be directly incremented, shifted, tested, and so on, I/O words can be handled with the same agility.

On the hardware side, the use of storage addresses as I/O ports offers mixed blessings. On the system level, the use of common control and address buses for all elements makes for better flexibility and expandibility, but, the storage address bus is usually wider than the I/O address bus, which may lead to more complex address decoding logic. However, if a range of addresses is reserved for all I/O (say, all addresses with the most significant address bit true), decoding can be dramatically simplified. Treating I/O devices as storage locations probably offers clear advantages in designs that are expected to be adapted to a wide variety of tasks.

LSI Ports

Manufacturers are beginning to offer complex accessory chips for use with microprocessors. Some of these are general-purpose programmable ports that can be configured as inputs, outputs, or bidirectional interfaces. Others are special-purpose circuits designed to handle popular interfaces such as telephone lines, terminals, and keyboards.

In the first category, Motorola's 6820 Peripheral Interface Adapter (PIA) the first to appear. (See Figure 7.3). The PIA is a forty-pin IC designed for combit programmable ports plus an interrupt and a multipurpose control line for each of these ports. The PIA is connected to the microprocessor's address and control buses and it always responds to read or write operations to its addresses. Each port includes three registers that can be written to or read by any memory-reference instruction. Ports look like storage locations to the microprocessor. Only one of these three locations is actually accessible to I/O devices, but it can be used for input, output, or even some of each. The other two registers allow the programmer to define pins as inputs or outputs by loading certain bit patterns.

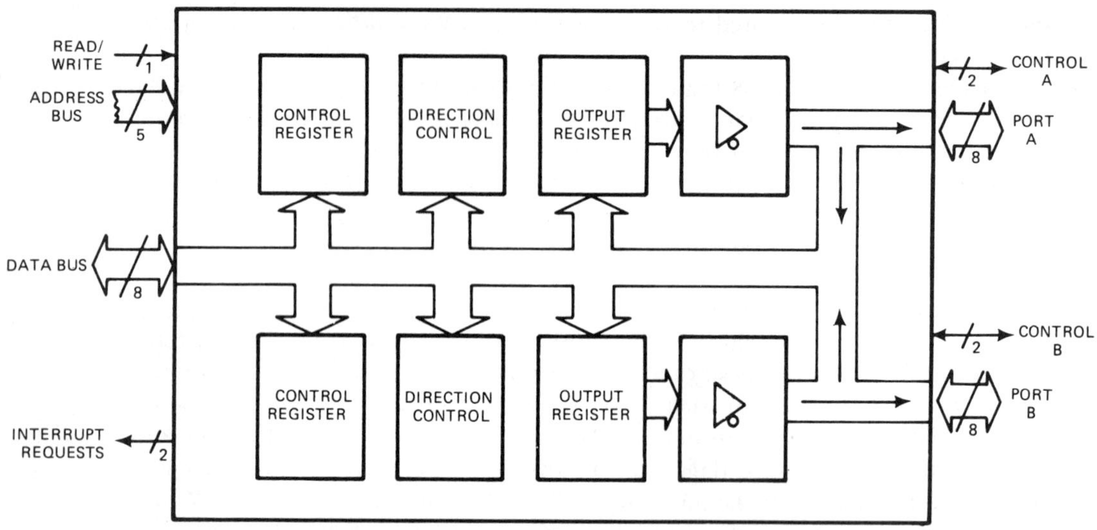

Figure 7.3 Block diagram of the registers in an LSI I/O port, the Motorola Peripheral Interface Adapter (PIA).

Each port's control register, for instance, has one bit position that, when set to one, allows interrupt requests to be passed along to the microprocessor. A second control register bit "tells" the PIA whether to generate the interrupt on the rising or falling edge of the signal connected to the port's interrupt input. If the interrupt happens, a third bit position in the control register will be set: The software reads all control registers to find out whose bit is set and thus who interrupted. Finally, the act of reading a control register automatically clears this interrupt bit. This means that once the software has noticed it, the interrupt flag voluntarily gets out of the way so that other interrupts can perhaps get through. Other control bit positions and patterns allow the programmer to use the multipurpose line as a second interrupt request line (complete with masking, transition direction, and flag, as before) or alternatively as an output. In the output mode this line can further be specified to be directly under program control or to automatically generate an interrupt acknowledge pulse at just the right time.

The direction register included in each half of a PIA is loaded with ones or zeros that enable or disable their respective output drivers. Only if there is a one in the appropriate position in the direction register will a bit written into the output register actually be fed to the port pin.

In most applications the PIA is "configured" to the required modes by initialization programs that run each time power is applied to the system. Thereafter, the PIA is treated as a conventional input or output port. Because of its ability to handle most programmed port requirements without external circuitry, the PIA can often reduce the complexity and chip count of supposedly "routine" interfaces. Additionally, the PIA's interrupt control circuitry makes it possible to construct systems that require multiple interrupts with no additional circuitry. Such systems, however, are limited to software polling speed to locate the interrupting peripheral.

Rockwell's PPS-4 and -8 family features the 10453 Peripheral Data Controller (PDC), which is very similar in abilities to Motorola's PIA. The Rockwell device connects directly to either of their microprocessors and includes four pins that are strapped high and low to tell the chip which I/O addresses to respond to. In addition to handling programmed input and output, the PDC can work in conjunction with another PPS family chip to provide direct access to memory for high-speed peripherals.

In order to offer similar I/O capabilities, Intel introduced the 8255A, also a forty-pin programmable chip. This device uses the input/output signals and instructions in 8080-based designs to provide either two eight-bit ports with several additional control signals for each or three eight-bit ports without control signals. In addition to basic input and output transfers, the 8255A introduces a couple of new twists: First, interrrupt flags from up to four 8255A's can all be read simultaneously because part of the initialization programming "tells" each chip to use different bit positions to report its flags. Second, instructions can be sent to a port to individually set or reset only one of its eight output bits. This is particularly handy in industrial control applications in which one-bit outputs are frequently needed to control lamps and relays. Both of these features will tend to make some programs smaller and faster.

Specialized Ports

A new class of microprocessor support circuit is beginning to appear. These LSI devices are special-purpose ports that are designed to interface a particular microprocessor to a particular (or particularly common) peripheral. UART's (Universal Asynchronous Receiver/Transmitter) and USRT's (for synchronous data) that work directly from their microprocessor's buses are available from Motorola and Rockwell. Intel has a similar unit for the 8080 that will handle both kinds of data transmission modes in one chip. These chips make it a trivial chore to connect the microprocessor to phone lines, terminals, or any of the hundreds of products that use the E.I.A. RS-232 interface standards. Since this interface has been sensed by the semiconductor vendors as the most commonly required interface, it is the most widely available type of specialized port.

To see what the future may hold in the way of these interface circuits, one need look no further than Rockwell's current family. In addition to its variety of general-purpose programmed ports, Rockwell has two kinds of specialized interfaces that work directly with its PPS-series processors.

The first is a combined keyboard-display interface that scans and debounces keys and simultaneously runs a multiplexed numerical display. These functions are required in at least half of the microprocessor-based products being built today. They can be (and frequently are) performed in software, but they consume relatively large amounts of execution time. At least two or three interface chips are usually needed, even when the software is doing most of the work. Thus an LSI port that handles the whole task can simplify both hardware and software. In simple products that have execution time to spare, software scanning will certainly be less expensive. But computers can do much more clever things with their time. If you have many clever tasks to do, a little scanner in a chip will let you do more of them.

Rockwell's other special-purpose port is designed to control a low-cost printer made by Seiko and used in a number of printing calculators. More of these kinds of packaged solutions can be expected in the future from many manufacturers, but they will naturally be limited to interfaces that offer reasonable hopes of being extremely popular with the high-volume crowd. Cassettes, floppy discs, and even CRT interfaces are now all available from a variety of makers.

Synchronization

Microprocesor peripherals often have rigid synchronization or timing requirements. It is not enough just to throw data at a port. With the microprocessor and the external devices all operating asynchronously, the process of transferring data must be controlled so that no data can get lost "between the clocks." The simplest method of dealing with this is electronic *handshaking.*

In a handshaking interface the circuitry that is to receive a data word must first indicate its willingness to do so with a ready *signal.* If the receiver is ready, the transmitter sends the message data along with a pulse suitable for latching it in the receiver. The same signal is used to clear the receiver's ready flip-flop. It is up to the receiver to notice that the new data has arrived and do something about it. When it is all done, the receiver will once again set READY.

When the receiver and transmitter systems are operating from different clocks, care must be taken in the design of the receiving circuitry to make sure that the status signals never lie. In our circuit, (in Figure 7.4) for example, the data receiving latch must present the new data at its outputs simultaneously with, or before, the trailing edge of READY. If the data latch did not operate this way, the receiving system might be speedy enough to occasionally react so fast to the ITS HERE signal that it reads old data just before the new data appears at the latch outputs. This situation must be designed out. If the problem occurs, it will generally be just frequent enough to be troublesome, but not frequent enough to catch.

Microprocessor system designers may meet the handshake interface very early in their new careers because most system prototypes will need some kind of terminal. The teletypewriter works one bit at a time and cannot be hurried. When the microcomputer is ready to print something, it must work at the terminal's speed. If the interface includes UART (Universal Asynchronous Receiver/Transmitter communications interface) chips to handle parallel-to-serial conversion, the UART will indicate that it is ready for a new character by setting a *buffer empty*

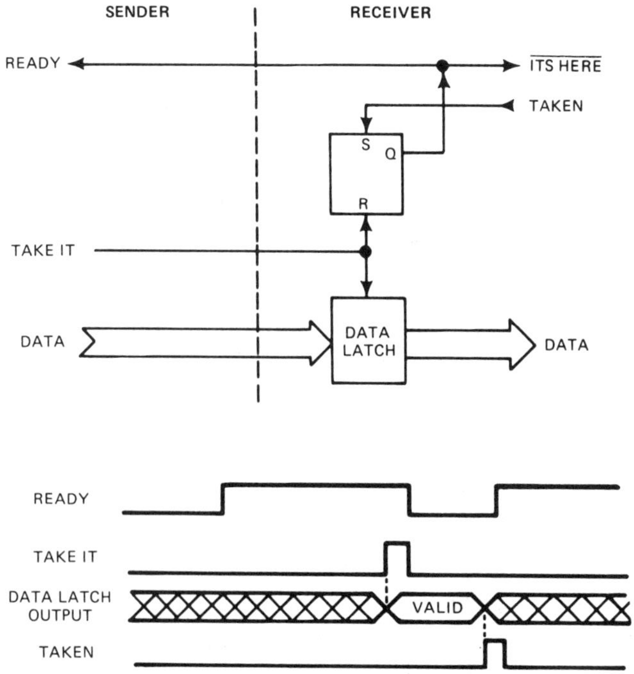

Figure 7.4 A simple handshaking interface for synchronization.

signal. (See Figure 7.5.) The software must not output a character unless this bit is set. Note that the output port latch in this interface can, if logic levels permit, be the UART itself. Any complex chip that accepts data and a load strobe can be connected to the microcomputer's data bus and can utilize the decoded load pulses. Shift registers are often connected this way when it is necessary to bring out a large number of bits, say, for a panel full of indicators.

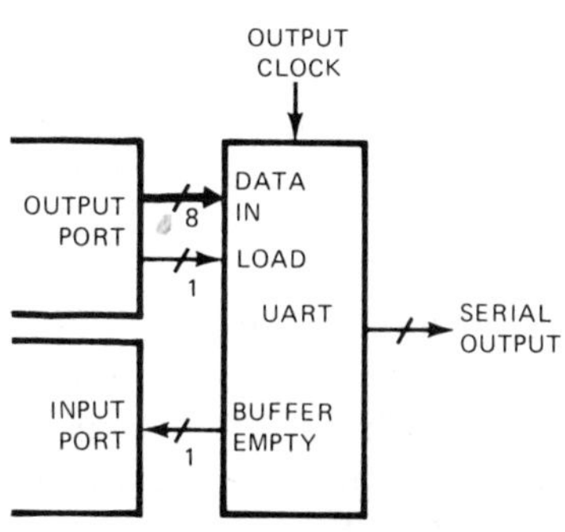

Figure 7.5 An output device with inherent data buffering.

Within the UART transmitting circuitry resides another popular synchronization circuit called a *double buffer.* See Figure 7.6. Its function is to give the data source—the microcomputer, here—as much time as possible to produce the next output character until the previous character was completely shifted out of the UART's output register. But at that time the printer is ready for a new character right away. If it takes a few milliseconds for the software to notice the *buffer empty* flag, the printer must wait for the microprocessor and the printing operation may slow down. Adding the buffer register solves the problem. Now, as soon as the output register is empty, it is filled from the buffer register by the UART control circuitry. The printer never misses a beat and the computer has one entire character transmission interval in which to refill the buffer.

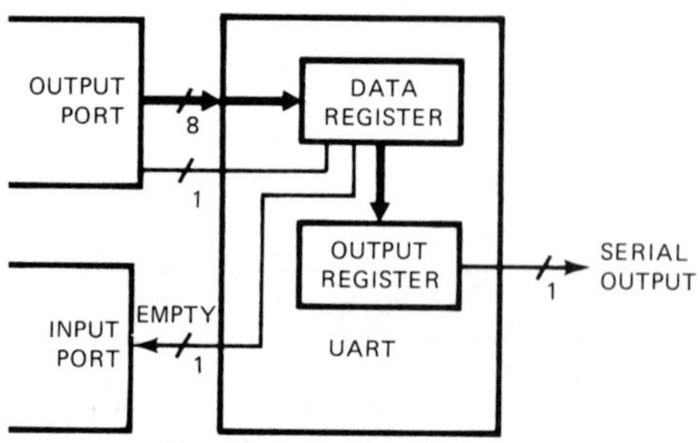

Figure 7.6 An expanded UART with double buffering.

Burst Data

Handshakes and double buffers allow interfaces to cope with fairly steady data rates. But what if data appears in bursts? The microprocessor may be able to keep up only with the average data rate; meanwhile, incoming data may have to be "stacked up" somewhere.

There are two different kinds of irascible data generators: those with predictable patterns and those without predictable patterns. The first kind might be one of the simpler punched card readers; a burst of data of predictable size (the card) is followed by a predictable pause while the next card is readied. There are several solutions to this kind of data transfer problem. The data can be stacked up externally in a pair of shift registers. While one register is being filled at the high burst speed, the second is being read at the lower average speed. This is called *double buffering.* Much the same thing can be done in the microcomputer's memory with DMA. While the software is digesting memory area A, area B can be filled directly from the card reader. At the end of each card, the processor and the DMA controller both shift their attention to the opposite area. This technique is called *ping-pong buffering.* A third technique uses interrupts (to be analyzed shortly). Finally, an MSI component known lovingly as a "FIFO," rhyming with Fido, should be considered. (See Figure 7.7.)

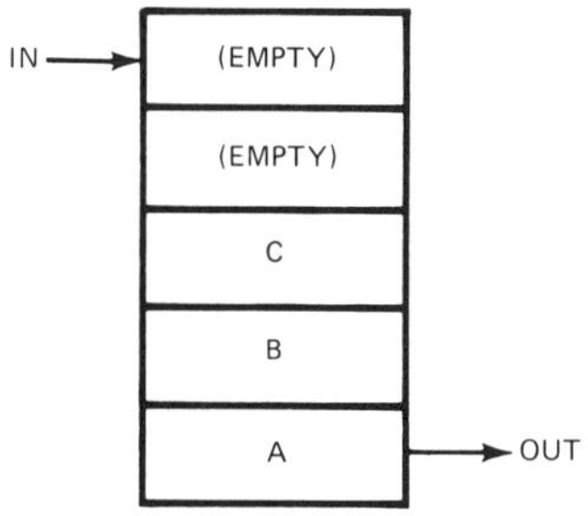

Figure 7.7 Representation of a FIFO.

First-In/First-Out (FIFO) registers have several words of capacity. As words are entered at the top, each place is compared with the next lower place; if the lower place is empty, the data is moved there. In this way, data is placed into the first (lowest) empty cell. When a word is removed from the bottom cell, an empty cell is created and all data falls down one place. Separate clocks are provided for shifting in and shifting out, and no synchronization is needed between the separate clocks. A data source like the card reader pours in data as fast as it can; the microprocessor can independently pull data out the other end at its slower rate. As long as the FIFO has enough capacity to hold the worst-case disparity between input and output, all is well. If the FIFO becomes completely empty or full, appropriately named pins on it let you know so that the processor can react appropriately. Other signals are usually provided that allow any number of FIFO's to be placed in series, making the buffering capacity longer. Of course, a FIFO can also be implemented in RAM with software control.

The other intermittent data generator, the unpredictable one, crops up at the input of controllers that deal with a large number of asynchronous but identical inputs: elevator call buttons, vehicle detectors, incoming telephone calls. When one has peripherals like these, he must cope with the fact that all or none of them occur at once. Some kind of external storage is generally needed in this system to to keep track of pending service requests.

The simplest way of handling these multiple inputs is to use time-division multiplexing (Figure 7.8). Each external signal source is represented as a point in a

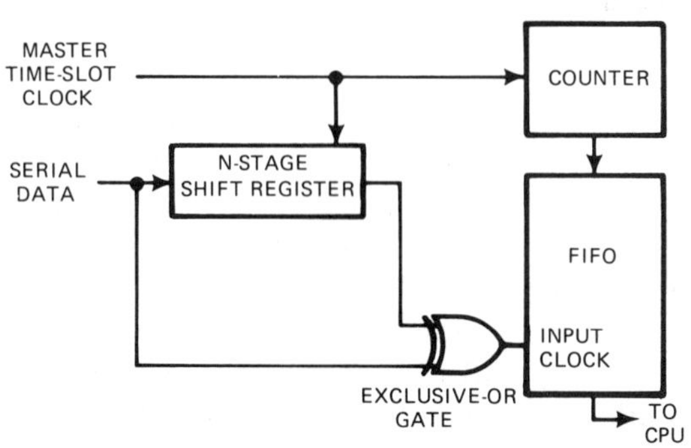

Figure 7.8 A circuit to multiplex many inputs into a processor.

time-division multiplexed frame. A common clock is assumed. The serial data is fed into a shift register and held until one full time-frame has passed. When a *change* is detected, the current time-slot counter is recorded in a FIFO; this number indicates that only events of actual importance are fed into the processor itself. Since the processor need not spend an appreciable amount of its time scanning inputs to see if something important has happened, better service can be afforded to the "active" peripheral devices.

Information Transfer

The realm of design tricks that the control of time unfolds has already been briefly exposed in some of our earlier examples, such as the D/A converter made up of an RC network (Fig. 7.1). Interfacing requires such new thinking that we have learned to completely ignore conventional transducers and interfaces. For years transducers have been sought that would directly produce signals suitable for digital systems. Although some progress has been made with some transducers, the microcomputer goes more than half way in providing a digital system that can interpret or generate almost anything a transducer requires. The microcomputer's computational power will make many formerly difficult or expensive interfaces much more practical.

In order to address interfacing problems in an imaginative fashion, we have developed a catalog of all of the possible ways to encode (or modulate) data with information. Effective use of this catalog requires that the information or actions to be interfaced to the microcomputer be thought of not as signals but as physically observable things. If you start out wondering how to interface a tachometer to a microcomputer, you're on the wrong road. Go farther out. What you should be seeking is a way to interface the shaft's rotational speed to the microcomputer. Then, once you see that the computer's tools are logic levels and time, search for a detection technique that somehow converts the RPM into a combination of these commodities.

Conditions that can be detected on one wire (by suitable hardware or software) are limited to four: logic levels high and low and transitions up or down. We will simply call these possibilities *detectable conditions* and concentrate on what can be done with them.

On-or-Off Status The presence or absence of a detectable condition is clearly the most basic information input imaginable. Similarly, on output, setting a single bit true or false is an easy way to control external devices. The load on the software, however, is rather high, particularly if transitions are to be detected on input. To detect a low-to-high transition, for example, means that the software must verify the low condition before looking for the high condition; each state may have to be read in and confirmed as a protection against noise. On output, some software decoding may be required to be able to set the output bits appropriately. For example, one output bit might directly control a LED; if that LED is one of seven in a seven-segment digit, then the software must decode the desired digit into seven such bits so that this particular one can be set on or off.

Time-Dependent Status Noting the time at which a particular detectable condition arises provides both the fact of occurrence and the time of occurrence. The time may be directly useful, but it is more often an analog for some other information such as the *place* of occurrence. In any time-division multiplexing system each transmitting device is usually associated with some particular point in space (and the equipment located there). These systems may require the software to maintain an external real-time clock to determine the when of the event; ideally, the real-time clock is a counter that can be read to determine the relative time of the event.

Elapsed Time The time that elapses between two detectable conditions is information in itself. In its simplest form this technique can be used to generate and detect pulse-width modulation. Corollary techniques that can be derived include frequency, phase, pulse-position and duty-cycle modulation. It is a most fertile ground for clever ideas. A simple cassette recorder interface (to be explained later) uses these concepts.

With the use of more than one wire, three more information encoding schemes arise. They all depend on the logical or time-dependent relationships among the wires.

Patterns on Wires The patterns on a set of two or more wires at a point in time can convey parallel information. One of the most obvious examples is the presentation of a binary number. Data can be presented to the computer (or from it) in the form of BCD digits or virtually any other code. When the patterns are limited to a one-of-*N* code, there is inherent decoding. With a broader code, decoding must be provided by software. A rotary switch can be presented to the computer as a one-of-*N* code. A keyboard array is usually combined with some decoding logic so that multiple responses may arrive simultaneously. The keyboard, of course, has to be decoded in software to interpret the specific keys depressed. The rotary switch is inherently self-decoded in this scheme.

Time Interrelationships The sequence of detectabled conditions on the wires also contains information. The data that separate wires might not all be in synchronization. From this can be derived information about which signal arrived first. Certainly, in the process control field, signals abound with these kinds of properties.

Sequential Data When multiwire data does arrive in sync, the order of these patterns carries information. The appearance of a pattern that represents a number followed by a pattern that does not represent a number is important to many applications; calculators work this way. In general, any data communicated between a computer and a human will be in a sequential multiwire form.

Using these basic concepts from information theory is often a new experience. Heretofore, when an engineer needed a particular information transformation capability, he consulted catalogs to see if such a part existed. In the absence of such a part, the problem became one of accomplishing the function in just a few packages. However, when a computer is used, another dimension is introduced. This is the nucleus of the hardware/software trade off.

The competent designer usually begins by looking for the simplest possible interface from a raw data source. Once the data is transformed into a computer-compatible form, the software can perform all decision making and data reduction. Next, the software task is estimated. This usually results in the discovery that we need about 10 s of execution time per second ... so, back to the drawing board.

Now, reviewing the list of possible input schemes, we select another appropriate opportunity, one that is more complex, perhaps, but one that offers more information in parallel. Since this affects the software positively, we can reestimate the impact. This process is repeated until a satisfactory trade-off point is reached that has enough margin for error that we won't get trapped if our software turns out to be more complex than we imagined.

Similar procedures are applied by the engineer in designing output signal sources. We tend to start with the simplest form in order to minimize engineering time and manufacturing cost; we discard simple alternatives only when we demonstrate to our satisfaction that the software would be unreasonable or impossible.

A Design Example

The easiest way to understand the hardware/software trade off issues in interface design is by example. In the example that follows the simplest kind of interface is developed between a microprocessor (say, the 8080) and a Burroughs' SELF-SCAN (registered trademark) display panel. This simple example is drawn from a larger series of application notes published by Burroughs; these notes can form a good study in the potential trade offs that exist in interfacing a single product to micros.

As a basic display medium, the SELF-SCAN display provides one or more lines of display capability. Each line is made up of seven horizontal rows of dots. The number of dot columns determines the number of characters in a line. Although the characters are presented in a 5×7 dot matrix pattern, the basic format has a two-column space between characters so that there are 222 columns on a thirty-two-character display, 138 columns on a twenty-character display, or 111 columns on a sixteen-character display (not 224, 140, or 112, since the last character does not require the added two-column space).

Four models of the SELF-SCAN display (Figure 7.9) incorporate thirty-two-character memories to alleviate the need for refreshing. The characters to be displayed are presented to the display one at a time. As they are received they are

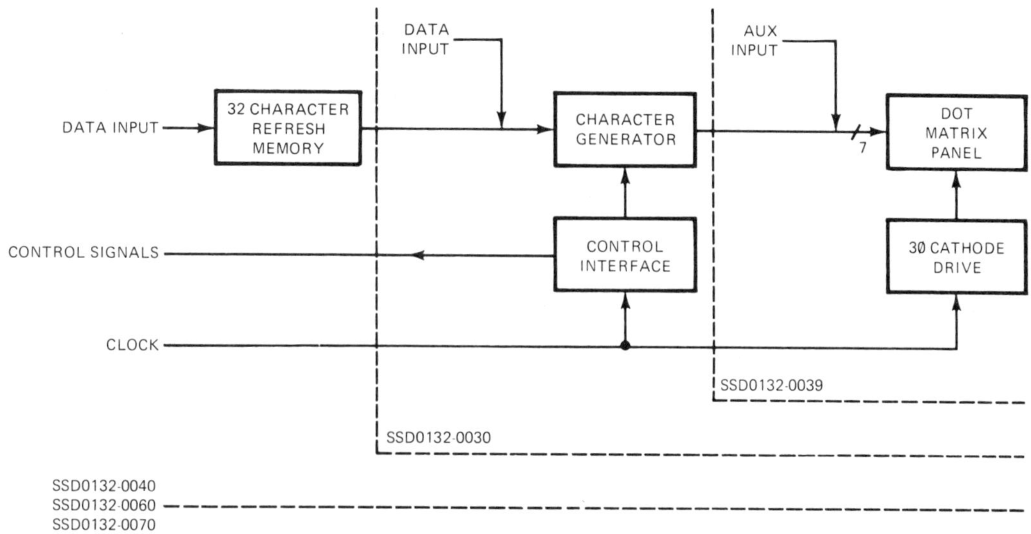

Figure 7.9 SELF-SCAN models and features.

stored in a local memory and then retrieved and decoded as necessary to present the proper dot patterns on the display. These four models of the SELF-SCAN display have unique features:

SSD0132-0040: 64-character set, left-to-right entry
SSD0132-0060: 64-character set, right-to-left entry
SSD0132-0070: 128-character set, right-to-left entry
SSD0132-0081: 128-characters in PROM/ROM, right-to-left entry

Each of these models will display characters across the panel area. However, the character set is made up of six-bit data for the -0040 and -0060 and seven-bit data for the -0070 and -0080. As each new character is sent out to the display, all prior characters are shifted over one place and the new character shows up on the rightmost (leftmost, for the -0040) position.

To interface to any of the memory version SELF-SCAN display panels, the input of the SELF-SCAN panel are connected to the outputs from the computer. Then, as the computer presents output signals, the SELF-SCAN panel will sequentially display them.

Data is passed between the microprocessor and the SELF-SCAN display panels with memory under the aegis of a handshaking interface protocol. When data is presented to the SELF-SCAN panel, the microprocessor sets the DATA PRESENT signal low and then back to high. Further data transfer is inhibited until the SELF-SCAN panel signals that it is ready by setting DATA TAKEN low; this will occur no sooner than 33 us after DATA PRESENT has been set low. A timing diagram is given in Figure 7.10, the general connection diagram in Figure 7.10a, and the necessary software for an 8080 in Figure 7.10c.

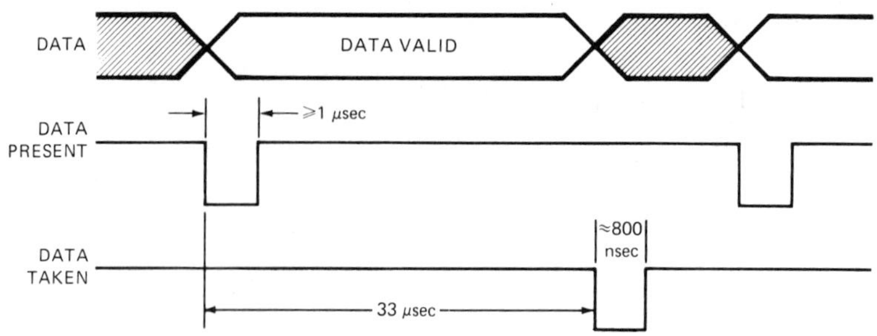

(a)

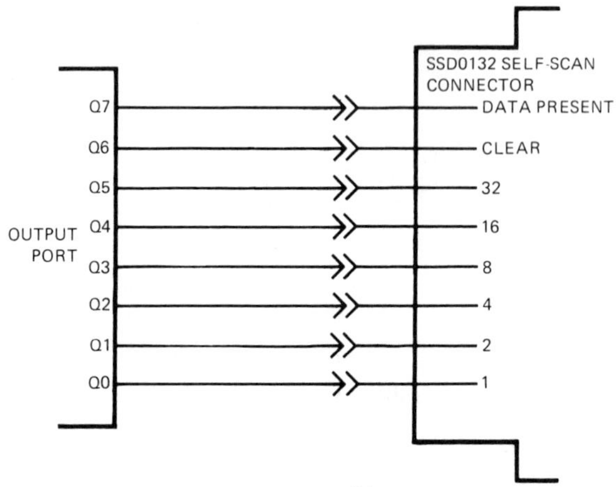

(b)

```
;SSOUT ISSUES CHARACTERS TO A SELF-SCAN WITH MEMORY
;
;     UPON ENTRY, A-REGISTER CONTAINS ASCII CHARACTER
;     TO ISSUE. A-REGISTER IS NOT PRESERVED. THIS
;     ROUTINE EXECUTES FOR A MINIMUM OF 48 MICROSECONDS
;     WHEN OPERATED WITH A 500 NSEC CLOCK PERIOD. THAT
;     ASSURES AT LEAST 55 MICROSECONDS BETWEEN PERIODS
;     THAT DATA-PRESENT IS TAKEN LOW.
;
;     THE TWO MOST-SIGNIFICANT BITS OF OUTPUT SHOULD BE
;     SET HIGH DURING POWER-UP INITIALIZATION.
;
SSOUT:      ANI   Ø7FH           ; REMOVE MOST-SIGNIFICANT BIT
                                 ; (I.E., SET DATA-PRESENT LOW)
            ORI   Ø4ØH           ; MAKE SURE CLEAR IS HIGH
            OUT   SSCAN
            ORI   ØBØH           ; SET MOST-SIGNIFICANT BIT ON
                                 ; (I.E., SET DATA-PRESENT HIGH)
            OUT   SSCAN
            MVI   A, 3           ; COUNT OFF SOME TIME
            DCR   A
            RZ                   ; RETURN WITH A-REGISTER ZERO
            JMP   $-2            ; GO BACK AND DECREMENT AGAIN
```

(c)

Figure 7.10 (a) Timing for SELF-SCAN panel with memory. (b) General microprocessor interface for a SELF-SCAN with memory (c) Simple SELF-SCAN output routine (SSOUT).

A single eight-bit output part is used to pass the six data bits, the CLEAR, and the DATA PRESENT control signals. Notice that the DATA TAKEN signal is not used in this simple interface. Since the DATA TAKEN signal is known to occur no sooner than 33 us after the data is presented to the display, by executing some NO-OP instructions you can assure that sufficient time is allowed.

The entire display contents can be effectively changed instantaneously by writing out the thirty-two characters in a loop.

In the 8080A all the characters can be written out in less than 3 ms too fast to be seen by the human eye. The data to be displayed is placed character by character in a thirty-two-byte area of memory. Whenever the display data is to be changed, the output subroutine is invoked to issue all thirty-two character out. The "show a line" subroutine is given in Figure 7.11.

```
;SSMSG PRESENTS A MESSAGE ON A SELF-SCAN WITH MEMORY
;
;       SSMSG ASSUMES A 32-BYTE AREA THAT IS ADDRESSED BY
;       THE (H,L) REGISTER PAIR. (H,L) POINTS TO THE FIRST
;       BYTE. DATA IS ASSUMED TO BE STORED IN ASCII.
;
;       (H,L) NOT PRESERVED.
;
SSMSG:  PUSH  B
        MVI   B,32
        MOV   A,M          ; GET THE BYTE TO BE DISPLAYED
        CALL  SSOUT        ; SHOW IT
        INX   H
        DCR   B
        JNZ   SSMSG+3      ; CONTINUE 32 TIMES
        POP   B            ; RESTORE SAVED REGISTER
        RET
;
;SSCLR CLEARS THE SELF-SCAN DISPLAY
;
SSCLR:  MVI   A,Ø8ØH       ; SET CLEAR LOW TO CLEAR DISPLAY
        OUT   SSCAN        ; ISSUE CLEAR SIGNAL
        MVI   B,20
        DCR   B            ; WAIT (TIMING ESTABLISHED BY DISPLAY)
        JP    $-1
        ORI   ØBØH         ; TAKE AWAY CLEAR-LOW
        OUT   SSCAN
        RET
```

Figure 7.11 Subroutines to issue 32 bytes to SELF-SCAN (SSMSG) and to clear display (SSCLR).

This simple interface will work with any of the displays with memory, whether left-to-right or right-to-left entry. Generally, data is displayed exactly as presented, one character at a time. This single character entry-and-display mode is particularly useful when the display is used in conjunction with keyboard inputs from an operator. However, in many applications, different kinds of data are presented in fixed positions on the display surface. For example, the first few characters might be devoted to a product type code. In these applications, single character data entry is not advantageous.

Finally, the backspace function, so useful when interfacing the SELF-SCAN panel with conventional random logic, can be set to blank and the buffer address pointer (the register that points to the next space in the thirty-two-byte buffer area) can be decremented.

Remember, however, that all these functions can be handled in hardware, with consequent savings in both program and data storage space, if the additional output port bits are available.

Some of the functions that are not already provided in circuitry of the SELF-SCAN panel can be provided in software. A prime example is *blinking*. It is possible to make the entire SELF-SCAN panel blink on and off at some rate by using the control lines provided (BLANK DISABLE). In some applications, however, the designer would like the flexibility of selecting only certain characters to blink or having different blinking rates at different times.

One way to institute and control blinking is to use a periodic timer interrupt to the 8080A. This interrupt can execute a small program to change the status of the display to effect blinking. In the 8080A it is particularly easy to generate RST 7 (restart 7, hex FF) instruction in response to an interrupt. If the 8228 System Controller and Bus Driver is used with the 8080A, pull up pin 23 of the device ($\overline{\text{INTA}}$) to +12 V to cause an RST 7 to be generated in response to an interrupt on the INT input of the CPU. For typical systems, the timer should interrupt once every 100 ms or so; a timer controlled for 60 Hz power can be made to generate an interrupt at about the right period by counting the normal 16.6 ms period six times before interrupting.

A blinking control byte is used in software to establish the particular duty cycle to be used. During each interrupt the blinking control byte is rotated one bit place and then the least-significant bit is used to control blinking. If the bit is zero, this part of the eight-phase cycle will cause data to be displayed. If the bit is one, blanks will be emitted in places where characters are to blink. To allow for selective blinking of specific characters, the most-significant bit of the data characters is used for control purposes. Characters that have a zero in that bit position will never blink; characters that have a one in the most-significant bit position will blink on and off at the rate specified in the blinking control byte.

Blinking duty cycles are specified in the special blinking control byte. If the control byte is zero, then all blinking is suppressed. If all characters are marked for blinking and the control byte is all ones, the entire display will remain cleared. A simple on/off, 50% duty cycle is controlled by setting half the bits of the control byte on and half off:

1111 0000.

To blink on and off rapidly so that the characters are alternatively blank and nonblank at the interrupt timer's rate, the following pattern may be used:

1010 1010.

Complex patterns can also be used. In the example in Figure 7.8 the characters blink twice for each display cycle. The characters appear briefly and blink, and then they appear for a longer time and then blink:

1100 0100.

The software that will recognize and use the blinking control byte is shown in Figure 7.12. Here, we assume that the control byte is stored at the address just below the first byte of the thirty-two-character buffer where data is held for the display.

```
;SSRST ISSUED BLINKING OUTPUT TO SELF-SCAN DISPLAYS
;     BYTE JUST BEFORE THE FIRST BYTE OF DATA BUFFER
;     CONTROL THE BLINKING RATE.
;
          ORG   56          ; RESPOND TO INTERRUPT AND RST 7
          PUSH  PSW         ; SAVE CPU REGISTERS
          PUSH  B
          PUSH  H
          LXI   H, SSBUF-1  ; GET BYTE BEFORE DATA
          MOV   A,M
          RLC               ; ROTATE LEFT ONE PLACE
          MOV   M,A         ;    AND RESTORE FOR NEXT TIME
          ANI   1
          MOV   C,A         ; SAVE THE BLINK CONTROL BIT
          MVI   B, 32       ; COUNT OUT 32 CHARACTERS
SSNXT:    INX   H           ; ADDRESS THE NEXT CHARACTER
          MOV   A, C
          RAR               ; PUT BLINK-CONTROL BIT INTO CARRY
          MOVE  A,M         ; FETCH DATA BYTE
          JNC   SSNBL       ; IF BLINK BIT IS ZERO, DISPLAY CHARACTER
          CPI   Ø8ØH        ; SEE IF THIS CHARACTER IS MARKED
                            ;    WITH A BIT SPECIFYING BLINKING
          JC    SSNBL       ; YES. GO DISPLAY IT
          MVI   A, ' '      ; TIME TO SUPPRESS THE CHARACTER
SSNBL:    ANI   7FH
          OUT   SSCAN       ; ISSUE OUT THE SELECTED CHARACTER
          ORI   Ø8ØH        ; RESET DATA-PRESENT BIT
          OUT   SSCAN
          DCR   B           ; CONTINUE FOR ALL 32 CHARACTERS
          JNZ   SSNXT
          POP   H
          POP   B
          POP   PSW         ; RESTORE REGISTERS
          EI                ; RE-ENABLE INTERRUPTS
          RET               ; RESUME INTERRUPTED PROGRAM
```

Figure 7.12 A selective-blinking routine for SELF-SCAN, using interrupts.

An Analog Interface

Another example of an input/output circuit worth study is the digital-to-analog interface between a micro-computer and a common audio cassette recorder. This interface can be used for the program storage and retrieval mentioned in Chapter 3.

There have been several simple circuits published for interfacing cassette recorders to micros, and there are many companies that sell such interface controllers. Some interfaces require several chips and a high-quality recorder but others are more primitive. However, all of them are easy to understand and build. One circuit, with software for the 8080A, is shown in Figures 7.13 and 7.14. With the appropriate software in memory, you can execute one routine to read or write tape. (This circuit originally appeared in *Popular Electronics,* September, 1975.)

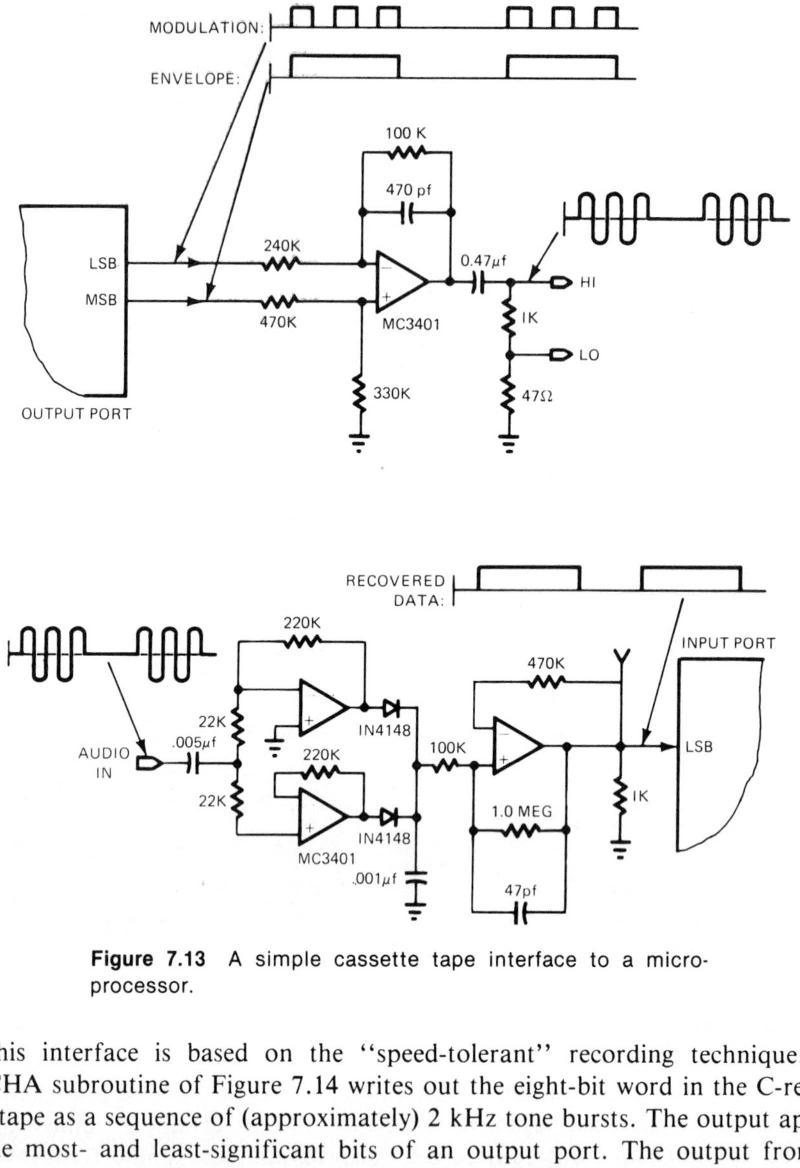

Figure 7.13 A simple cassette tape interface to a microprocessor.

This interface is based on the "speed-tolerant" recording technique. The WRCHA subroutine of Figure 7.14 writes out the eight-bit word in the C-register onto tape as a sequence of (approximately) 2 kHz tone bursts. The output appears on the most- and least-significant bits of an output port. The output from the MSB is named ENVELOPE; it is true during the period of the tone burst. The output from the LSB is called MODULATION and is a software-controlled square wave. The op amp converts the TTL-level signals into a 2-kHz sine wave burst that can be recorded on any tape recorder. The HI output is about 2 V peak-to-peak; the LO output is about 50 mV.

Input from a cassette playback is reconverted into a digital signal by the three remaining op amp sections. The first two sections form a full-wave rectifier; the

```
MAXRL     EQU    200          ; MAXIMUM RECORD LENGTH
XXSYN     EQU    16H          ; SYNC CODE
XXSTX     EQU    2            ; START-OF-TEXT CODE
XXETX     EQU    3            ; END-OF-TEXT CODE
XXBCC     EQU    0            ; BLOCK CHECK CHARACTER
TAPEO     EQU    3C05H        ; TAPE OUTPUT ADDRESS
TAPEI     EQU    3C00H        ; TAPE INPUT ADDRESS
; THESE TAPE I/O ADDRESSES ASSUME MEMORY-MAPPED I/O
;
;
;  THE WRITE ROUTINE WILL TRANSFER MEMORY TO
; CASSETTE TAPE. THE STACK CONTAINS ENDING ADDRESS,
; TAPE ID BYTE, STARTING ADDRESS. FORMAT OF DATA
; WRITEEN ON TAPE IS:
;
; S          S S C I  A A          D     E B B
; Y....      Y T O D D D    . . .  A . . . T C C
; N   (32)   N X U    R R          T      X C C
; C          C   N    U L          A
;                T
WT:       POP    H            ; (SAVE RETURN ADDRESS)
          POP    D            ; (D,E) :=ENDING ADDRESS
          POP    B            ; (C) := TAPE ID
          XTHL                ; (H,L) := START ADDRESS
          MVI    B,O          ; (B) := BLOCK SIZE (BYTES)
          PUSH   B
          PUSH   H
          INX    D            ; (D,E) := ENDING ADDR + 1
;  COMPUTE THE NUMBER OF BYTES IN THIS RECORD
WT1:      CALL   MTST         ; IF (D,E)=(H,L) THIS IS
          JZ     WT2          ;       LAST BLOCK
          INX    H
          INR    B            ; INCREMENT BLOCK COUNT
          MOV    A,B          ; SEE OF MAX BLOCK SIZE REACHED
          CPI    MAXRL
          JNZ    WT1          ;       IF NOT, KEEP COUNTING
WT2:      XTHL                ; STACK NEXT START, RETRIEVE
          DCX    D            ;  THIS ONE
          PUSH   D            ; SAVE ENDING ADDRESS
;         AT THIS POINT, B=COUNT, C=TAPE ID,
;         (H, L)=STARTING ADDRESS, AND STACK IS SET FOR
;         A RETURN TO -WT- AFTER WRITING THIS BLOCK
          PUSH   B            ; SAVE COUNT AND TAPE ID
          MVI    D,32         ; SET TO WRITE 32 SYNC CODES
WRSYN:    MVI    A,XXSYN      ; ISSUE THE SYNC CODES
          CALL   WRCHA
          DCR    D
          JNZ    WRSYN        ; CONTINUE UNTIL ALL OUT
          MVI    A,XXSTX      ; OUTPUT THE START-OF-TEXT
          CALL   WRCHA
          POP    D            ; RETRIEVE COUNT (D), TAPE ID(E)
          MOV    A,D
          ADI    3            ; ISSUE COUNT + 3
          CALL   WRCHA
          MOV    A,E
          CALL   WRCHA        ; ISSUE THE TAPE ID BYTE
          MOV    A,H
          CALL   WRCHA        ; ISSUE THE HIGH HALF OF LOAD ADDRESS
          MOV    A,L
          CALL   WRCHA        ; ISSUE THE LOW HALF
          MOV    A,D          ; IF DATA COUNT IS ZERO,
          ORA    A
          JZ     WRWLF        ;  GO WRITE END OF BLOCK
WRBLK:    MOV    A,M          ; GET NEXT DATA BYTE
          CALL   WRCHA        ; WRITE IT TO TAPE
          INX    H            ; ADDRESS THE NEXT BYTE
          DCR    D            ; DECREMENT THE BLOCK COUNT
          JNZ    WRBLK        ; WRITE REST OF BLOCK OUT
          INR    D            ; SET D NON-ZERO SO EOF WON'T
                              ;  BE WRITTEN OUT THIS TIME.
WRWLF:    MVI    A,XXETX      ; OUTPUT THE END-OF-TEXT
          CALL   WRCHA
          MVI    Z,XXBCC      ; OUTPUT SPACE FOR A BCC,
          CALL   WRCHA        ;  IN CASE ONE IS ADDED LATER
          MVI    A,XXBCC      ; OUTPUT NEXT BYTE OF BCC
          CALL   WRCHA
          MOV    A,D          ; GET COUNT BYTE
          ORA    A            ; IF ZERO, THIS WAS THE ZERO-LENGTH
          JNZ    WT           ;  RECORD, SO
          RET                 ;  WE ARE FINISHED.
;  COMPARE (D,E) TO (H,L)
MTST:     MOV    A,H          ; IF (D,E)=(H,L) SET -Z-
          CMP    D
          RNZ
          MOV    A,L
          CMP    E
          RET
;  THE FOLLOWING SEQUENCE WILL WRITE AN UNLIMITED NUMBER
; OF SYNC CODES ON TAPE, UNTIL THE CPU IS STOPPED.
WTPS:     MVI    A,XXSYN
          CALL   WRCHA        ; ISSUE A SYNC CODE
          JMP    WTPS         ;  AND DO IT AGAIN.
```

```
;  WRITE THE BYTE IN THE (A) REGISTER OUT TO TAPE,
; LEAST SIGNIFICANT BIT FIRST. AFTER THE EIGHTH BIT,
; WRITE A STOP BIT.
;
; VARIABLES (WRWAI) AND (WRLEN) CONTROL DATA RATE
; (WRWAI) DEFINES THE PERIOD OF EACH MODULATION HALF-
; CYCLE: (WRLEN) DEFINES THE LENGTH OF EACH DATA BIT.
; DATA RATE, IN BITS PER SECOND, IS COMPUTED AS:
;                          1000000
;        BPS = ------------------------------------------
;              (15 WRWAI + 64)  ( 6 WRLEN - 1)  C
; WHERE (C) IS THE 8080 CYCLE TIME IN MICROSECONDS.
; FOR THE PARAMETERS SHOWN HERE, BPS = 364.
;
WRWAI    EQU   29              ; 2400 HZ IF C=0.5 MICROSECONDS
WRLEN    EQU   2               ; REDUNDANCY: TWO CYCLES PER BIT
WRSHT    EQU   255-WRLEN-WRLEN+2 ; (MUST BE ODD)
WRLNG    EQU   255-WRLEN-WRLEN-WRLEN-WRLEN+1 ; (EVEN)
;        GET THE NEXT DATA BIT TO TRANSMIT
WRCHA:   STC                   ; JAM IN THE STOPPER BIT!
WRCHX:   RAR                   ; GET THE NEXT LSB
         MOV   C,A             ; SAVE OTHER BITS FOR LATER
         MVI   B,WRLNG         ;     (FOR DATA "1")
         JC    WRBST           ; IF "1", GO WRITE OUT THE BURST
         MVI   B,WRSHT         ;     (FOR DATA "0")
;        WRITE A TONE BURST OUT TO TAPE
WRBST:   CALL  WRTIM           ; WRITE OUT FIRST HALF-CYCLE
         JZ    WRFIN           ;     (GO DO THE LONG PART NOW)
         CALL  WRTIM           ; WRITE OUT SECOND HALF-CYCLE
         JNZ   WRBST           ;     (KEEP GOING)
         STA   TAPEO           : TERMINATE THE MODULATION
         MVI   B,WRSHT         ;     (GO DO SHORT PART NOW)
         JMP   WRDLY
WRFIN:   STA   TAPEO           ; TERMINATE THE MODULATION
         MVI   B,WRLNG         ;     (GO DO LONG PART)
;        WASTE TIME TO WRITE OUT NO MODULATION
WRDLY:   CALL  WRTIM+4         ; JUST DELAY, DON'T WRITE
         JMP   $+3             ; (WASTE A BIT MORE TIME)
         MOV   A,A             ; (WASTE SOME MORE TIME)
         JNZ   WRDLY
;        PREPARE THE NEXT BIT FOR OUTPUT
         MOV   A,C             ; RETRIEVE THE CHARACTER
         ORA   A
         RZ                    ; IF ZERO, CHARACTER IS DONE
         JMP   WRCHX
;        TIMING DELAY LOOP FOR CONTROLLING MODULATION
WRTIM:   MOV   A,B             ; GET THE COUNTER WORD, THE
                               ; LSB OF WHICH IS CHANGING
         STA   TAPEO           ; WRITE OUT THAT CHANGING BIT
                               ; AS THE MODULATION
         MVI   A,WRWAI         ; SET UP A WAIT PERIOD
         DCR   A
         JNZ   $-1
         INR   B               ; UPDATE THE COUNTER
         RET
;  THE READ ROUTINE WILL TRANSFER TAPE INTO MEMORY.
; DATA WILL BE ENTERED INTO MEMORY STARTING AT THE
; ADDRESS GIVEN ON THE TAPE AND PROCEEDING SEQUENTIALLY.
;  IF VALID EOF RECORD FOUND, THIS ROUTINE EXITS
; WITH (Z) SET. OTHERWISE, (Z) IS CLEARED TO IN-
; DICATE AN ERROR OCCURED.
RDBLK:   MVI   C,128           ; SET BYTE STOPPER BIT
         MVI   E,XXSYN         ; PRESET (E) TO SYNC CODE
         CALL  RDCHC           ;     AT OUTSET, READ ANY 8 BITS
         MOV   Z,C
         CMP   E               ; CHECK FOR SYNC CODE
         JZ    RDSYN+2         ;     FOUND ONE
;        DIDN'T FIND SYNC.     TRY WITH ONE MORE BIT
RDNXT:   ORI   1               ; SET TO READ ONLY 1 BIT
         MOV   C,A
         JMP   RDBLK+4         ; GO TRY NEXT BYTE
;  SYNC HAS BEEN ACHIEVED. NOW READ AND IGNORE ALL
; SYNC CODES AND QUIT ON AN STX. STX WILL BE ALLOWED
; ONLY AFTER AT LEAST ONE MORE SYNC CODE IS FOUND
RDSYN:   MVI   E,XXSTX
         CALL  RDCHA           ; READ NEXT BYTE
         MOV   A,C             ; TEST FOR SYNC
         CPI   XXSYN
         JZ    RDSYN           ; SCOOP UP SYNC CODES
         CMP   E               ; CHECK FOR STX NOW
         JNZ   RDNXT           ; LOST SYNC-GO RETRY
         CALL  RDCHA           ; GET BLOCK SIZE INTO (E)
         MOV   E,C
         CALL  RDCHA           ; READ ID BYTE
         CALL  RDCHA           ; READ LOAD ADDRESS INTO (D,C)
         MOV   D,C
         CALL  RDCHA
         MOV   L,C             ; SAVE ADDRESS IN (H,L)
         MOV   H,D
         MOV   A,E             ; GET COUNT BYTE
         SUI   3
         MOV   E,A
         RZ                    ; IF LENGTH WAS 3, THIS WAS EOF
RDATA:   CALL  RDCHA           ; READ IN NEXT DATA BYTE
         MOV   M,C             ;     AND SAVE IT IN MEMORY
         INX   H               ;     AND ADVANCE MEMORY ADDRESS
         DCR   E               ; STOP WHEN COUNT IS EXHAUSTED
         JNZ   RDATA
         CALL  RDCHA           ; READ IN THE END-OF-TEXT
         MOV   A,C
         CIP   XXETX           ; ERROR EXIT IF NOT ETX
         JZ    RDBLK
         RET
```

```
;  READ A BYTE FROM TAPE INTO (C) REGISTER. (C) IS
; LOADED LEAST-SIGNIFICANT BIT FIRST INTO THE MOST-
; SIGNIFICANT POSITION.
;
;  SAMPLE PERIOD FOR INCOMING DATA IS SET BY (RDTIM)
; IF (RDTIM) IS 7, AND THE 8080 CYCLE TIME IS 0.5
; MICROSECONDS, THEN SAMPLES WILL BE 100 MICROSECONDS
; APART.
RDTIM    EQU   7          ;SAMPLE EVERY 100 USEC
;        SET UP NORMAL WORD-SIZE STOPPER
RDCHA:   MVI   C,128
         LDA   TAPEI      ;AWAIT DATA "0" CONDITION
         RRC              ;    BEFORE LOOKING FOR A
         JC    RDCHA+2    ;    LEADING EDGE
         CALL  RDBIT-2    ;WAIT FOR ONE SAMPLE PERIOD
         JC    RDCHA+2    ;    THEN CONFIRM A "0"
;        FIND AND CONFIRM LEADING EDGE OF DATA BURST
RDCHC:   CALL  RDCHN      ;LOOK FOR, CONFIRM LEAD EDGE
         MVI   A,1        ;CONFIRMED. START COUNTING
         MOV   B,A
;        RAMP UP (B) REGISTER UNTIL TRAILING EDGE
RDCH3:   ADD   B          ;INCREMENT THE RAMP COUNT
         MOV   B,A        ;SAVE THE RAMP COUNT
         JC    RDCHE      ;    (BAD DATA: PULSE TOO LONG)
         MVI   A,RDTIM+1
RDCHR:   CALL  RDBIT      ;GO READ THE NEXT SAMPLE
         MVI   A,1
         JC    RDCH3      ;IF SAMPLE = "1", COUNT
;        CONFIRM TRAILING EDGE
         NOP              ;(FOR TIMING)
         CALL  RDBIT-2    ;CONFIRM
         MVI   A,2
         JC    RDCH3      ;EARLIER "0" WAS JUST NOISE
         MVI   A,-2       ;START THE RAMP DOWN
;        COUNT DOWN AFTER TRAILING EDGE
RDCH5:   ADD   B          ;DECREMENT RAMP COUNT
         MOV   B,A
         JNC   RDCHO      ;DATA BURST SHORT; DATA = "0"
         MVI   A,RDTIM+1
         CALL  RDBIT      ;READ IN NEXT SAMPLE
         MVI   A,-1
         JNC   RDCH5      ;STILL "0", CONTINUE COUNT
;        CONFIRM CLOCK (NEXT LEADING EDGE)
         NOP
         CALL  RDBIT-2    ;GET SAMPLE TO CONFIRM
         MVI   A,-2
         JNC   RDCH5      ;EARLIER "1" WAS JUST NOISE
;        FOUND NEW LEADING EDGE; DATA = "1"
         MOV   A,C
         RAR              ;INSERT "1" INTO THE BYTE
         MOV   C,A
         RC               ;IF THAT WAS STOPPER, (CY) ON
         MVI   B,2
         MVI   A,RDTIM
         JMP   RDCHR      ;GO CATCH THE THIRD SAMPLE
;        COUNTED DOWN TO ZERO; DATA = "0"
RDCHO:   MOV   A,C        ;INSERT "0" INTO THE BYTE
         RAR
         MOV   C,A
         JNC   RDCHC      ;GO WAIT FOR LEADING EDGE
;        AT END OF BYTE. BE SURE TO AWAIT THE
;        LEADING EDGE OF THE NINTH BIT, A "0"
RDCHN:   LDA   TAPEI      ;LOOK FOR LEADING EDGE
         RRC
         JNC   RDCHN
         CALL  RDBIT-2    ;GO CONFIRM LEADING EDGE
         JNC   RDCHN
         RET
;        SET UP TIMING DELAY FOR READ SAMPLE PERIOD
         MVI   A,RDTIM+2
RDBIT:   DCR   A          ;DELAY
         JNZ   RDBIT
         LDA   TAPEI      ;READ AN INPUT BIT
         RRC              ;    AND PLACE INTO (CY)
         RET
;        TAPE READ ERROR ROUTINE. CLEAR CARRY TO
;        REPORT AN ERROR
RDCHE:   INR   A          ;(A) WAS ZERO: CLEAR (Z)
         RET              ;ERROR RETURN
```

Figure 7.14 8080 software to control the cassette data transfers.

third is used as a Schmitt trigger. The output, presented to the computer on the input port, is the recovered ENVELOPE signal.

The input routine, RDCHA, reads in each bit as a duty cycle; while the ENVELOPE is high, the subroutine counts up and while the ENVELOPE is low, the routine counts down. If the duty cycle is less than 50% (the routine counts down more than up), the data is a "0." Otherwise, the data is a "1." All timing is done in software.

The routines RDCHA and WRCHA are known as *physical input/output routines* because their operation depends expressly on the particular external hardware to which the ports are connected. These routines operate on a single eight-bit byte at a time. The other two subroutines, WT (Write Tape) and RDBLK (Read a Block) are called *logical input/output.* They read and write several bytes at a time in a mutually agreed upon format. Notice that we could easily change the "physical I/O" details without affecting the "logical I/O" operation so long as "physical I/O" faithfully accepts and reproduces eight-bit bytes. This is an example of good programming practice.

The format that WT and RDBLK agree upon is illustrated in Figure 7.15. Each block begins with 32 ASCII SYN characters that are designed to allow the soft-

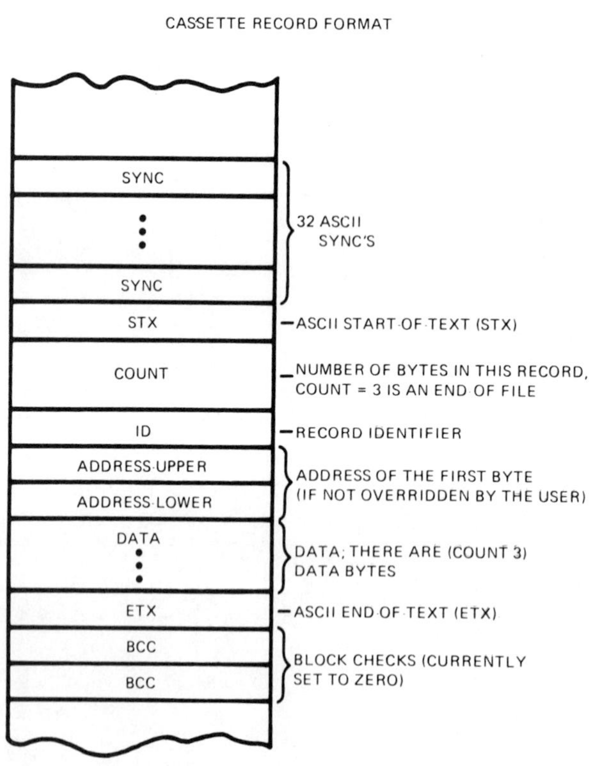

Figure 7.15 Logical input/output data format on cassette.

ware to get into sync with the moving data. The first character after those characters is an ASCII STX character, and then there is a byte that represents the number of bytes in the record (including the ETX and two block-check character spaces at the end). Each record may be identified by number so that several different programs, each uniquely identified, may be stored on the same tape; space for that number is included on the tape.

Since most programs are in object format, it is important to know where they are to be loaded into memory; the next two bytes specify that. Up to 200 bytes of data to be loaded into those storage locations follow the address. The record ends with the ASCII ETX character. The last two bytes are always zero, but you may write out a complex block-check character to provide for error protection if you wish.

With the constants given, this cassette interface will read and write at about 365 bits per second.

You will want to use your external program storage medium several ways. First, each time you create a program you should save it for future use, especially if the program is large. If you have just entered a 1,000 byte program into RAM, you should write it out to the external medium so that you have a backup for your volatile memory in case there is a power failure. Also, you may want to be able to exchange program tapes with colleagues.

The Future of I/O

It is in the structure of the input/output scheme that the creative engineer will find the greatest outlet. It is also the part of the design that most apparently shows the effects of poor design. Fortunately, however, poor input/output design is seldom disastrous.

When designing a project for volume production, it is a wise practice to design at least two paper alternatives for input/output. One design should emphasize the software control of minimal hardware; the other should utilize more hardware to relieve the software. The software-oriented design should be tried first. Then, if the software "runs out of gas," you can retrofit the more expensive solution. By designing both at the outset, you can implement the majority of the software in a fashion that is independent of the specific input/output details.

These decisions will become both simpler and more difficult in coming months. It will become significantly more difficult to choose among microprocessors and their families of input/output parts as each vendor tries to reach into unique markets with new offerings. Once your choice is made, however, many of the interfaces you build will become a simple matter of wiring a couple of chips together.

8

Real-Time Software

Probably the largest single problem facing the newcomer to microprocessor software is understanding how to "orchestrate" a wide variety of asynchronous input/output devices. Most of the programming literature is based on the assumption that the input/output interfacing (hardware and software) is done for the programmer. Of course, in a microcomputer, that is seldom true.

If you have one or two peripheral devices connected to your computer, the problems are relatively simple. However, if you have a wide variety of devices to contend with, your grasp of the problem begins to slip. At the same time, if the general nature of the external equipment is such that it isn't important when you service it, you can create a simple program. However, peripheral equipment is seldom so easy to use. If you must accept data from a keyboard or an A/D converter, your software must be designed to examine the input port frequently enough to avoid losing data; you no longer can program assuming that "things will happen fast enough."

If you are faced with a problem like the one shown in Figure 8.1, you can get a real sinking feeling in the pit of your stomach. It is clear that each input/output port must be "serviced" with some software frequently enough to keep the users happy. For example, to avoid loss of keystrokes, it will generally be necessary to read the input port connected to the keyboard about once each 40 ms. Somehow, the CPU must be prevented from getting into a program and staying there for more than 40 ms.

One of the first acts of analysis, which is highly dependent on the application needs, is to determine which things must be done on time, how long each one is going to take (in hardware and/or software), and the relative priorities of each

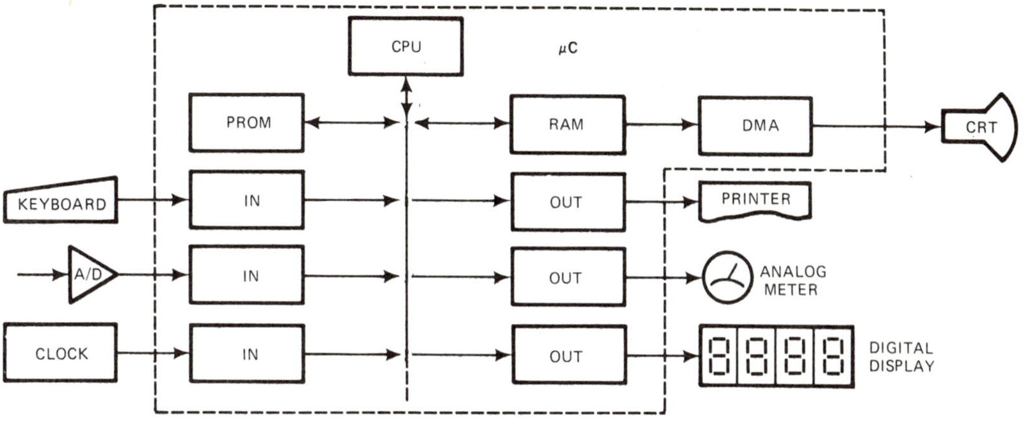

Figure 8.1 A complex microcomputer with various I/O demands.

task. In this particular example, input signal servicing has been specified (Table 8.1) to have priority over output servicing. Following industry practice, we establish the need to scan the keyboard once every 40 ms. Using our estimates and experience, we can estimate that (with the particular hardware we have designed for this computer) each keyboard reading process will take 2 ms. This means that the keyboard will be examined 25 times per second, with a total of 50 ms out of each second (5% of the available resource of time) consumed in this one function.

Table 8.1 A typical real-time task list for the system in Figure 8.1.

FUNCTION	PERIOD (mSEC)	EXECUTION TIME (mSEC)	PRIORITY
SCAN KEYBOARD	40	2	2
READ A/D CONVERTER	100	0.5	3
READ CLOCK	15	0.1	1
UPDATE CRT DISPLAY	1000	55	6
PRINT CHARACTER	100	0.1	7
DISPLAY ON METER	50	0.1	4
UPDATE LED DISPLAY	40	0.2	5

It is clear that the software must be written to activate the subroutine that handles the keyboard at least once each 40 ms. That is, instead of being able to handle the keyboard whenever we get around to it (i.e., arbitrary time), we must conform to "real time." Nearly all microprocessors are used in applications that require cognizance of real time. This should be contrasted with most large-scale computer systems in which most (or even all) of the software executes without regard to the time elapsed on a master global clock.

There are some simplifications that can be introduced. The scanning of the keyboard and the updating of LED displays both have periods of 40 ms; perhaps these two can be activated as one function. The major problem, however, is still the obvious disparity between one function that must be activated once every 15 ms and others that have periods of up to 1 s.

An apparently useful approach might be the one shown in Figure 8.2. A "super program," known as a *Supervisor,* is assigned the responsibility of "deciding" which function to activate next. Each function is implemented as one or more subroutines; the Supervisor processes a table that specifies which subroutine to

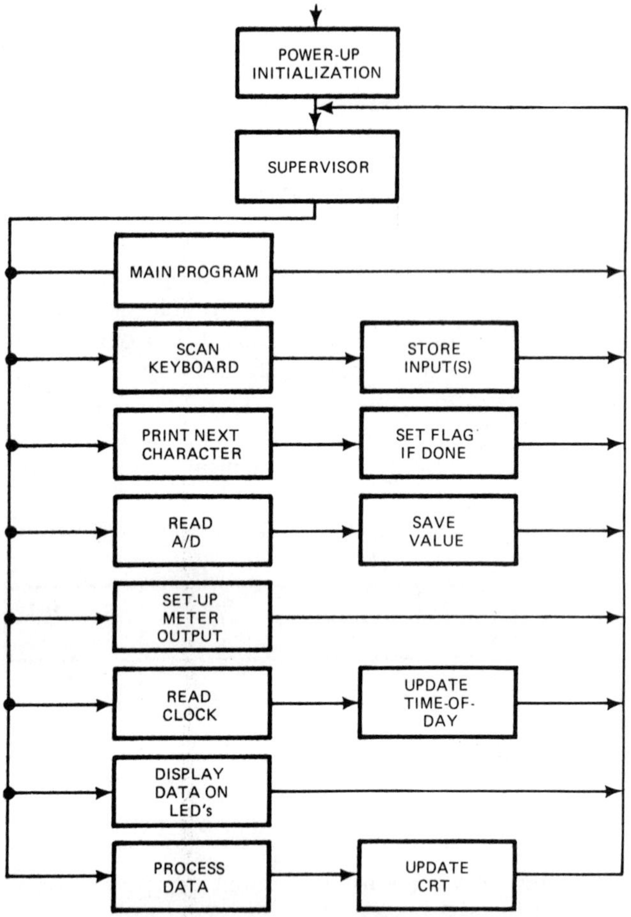

Figure 8.2 One simple real-time system based on a supervisor.

activate next. However, each subroutine must be written to execute no longer than the shortest period in the entire system; in our example, no subroutine may be allowed to execute for more than about 15 ms. This is a severe limitation on some functions. In fact, it may be impossible.

Another problem also surfaces. The subroutines are all neat and simple input/output interfaces, but they must be able to communicate with one another. Each subroutine may be a "producer" of data of one kind and a "consumer" of data of another kind. Between "producer" and "consumer" it is absolutely necessary to have agreement on format, allowable values, and location of the data. All of these "linkage conventions" must be defined for each subroutine so that each neighbor can be written to conform to common agreements.

Interrupts and Polling

There are basically two ways of allowing multiple asynchronous input/output events to occur with apparent simultaneity in a microprocessor. If the computer is equipped with an interrupt scheme, any ongoing program can be designed to be temporarily suspended while some more urgent action is taking place. If interrupts are not present, or perhaps if present but undesirable to use, then some external status checking or polling of status can be used to achieve the same effect.

In polling it is imperative that no single part of the program execute for such a length of time that it prevents another subroutine from being activated frequently enough to do its assigned task. The supervisory approach of Figure 8.2 can be modified to isolate the time-dependent from the time-independent subroutines. The Supervisor can then cycle amongst the independent subroutines as necessary to accomplish the task of the microprocessor. Each of these tasks is designed to execute in some maximum time period that is less than the time required for the highest frequency input/output subroutine. At the end of each subroutine's execution, control is returned to the Supervisor. At that point, the Supervisor "decides" whether to activate one of the time-dependent subroutines or to allow another of the independent subroutines to execute.

You can see that this primitive control can, in some cases, present a large programming problem. Each subroutine must be written within the scope of some large set of overall specifications, yet simultaneously live within the allowed time constraints imposed by this software structure. In fact, in simple applications in which the microprocessor is not so nearly taxed, this scheme can work very well. If, however, your computations show that it is possible that you will have to strain to fit it all in, interrupts may be the only viable alternative.

The concept of interrupts is a good one, but it must be applied cautiously. Programs that depend on interrupts and the associated software required to work with them are generally at least one order of magnitude more difficult to test and debug than simpler programs. To be forewarned is to be forearmed.

An interrupt is a way of producing a hardware subroutine call. When some external condition (called the *interrupt*) occurs, some pin is raised on the CPU chips. This causes some subroutine located at a specific, fixed address to be executed. Since the program that was in execution at that time cannot continue while the CPU is used to execute the special subroutine, we say that the program has been *interrupted.* The subroutine that is executed is called the *interrupt service routine.*

A computer that has an interrupt capability can be very responsive to its environment. Interrupts are frequently used to allow several different asynchronous events to be coordinated by the same computer. When some external event must be communicated to the processor (e.g., the passing of one clock interval, or the completion of some task, or the demand for service), the event is sensed and held in an interrupt latch (Figure 8.3). The latch is provided in case the CPU is busy and cannot respond immediately. The CPU could, for example, be busy servicing an immediately preceding interrupt. When the CPU acknowledges the interrupt, the interrupt latch can be cleared.

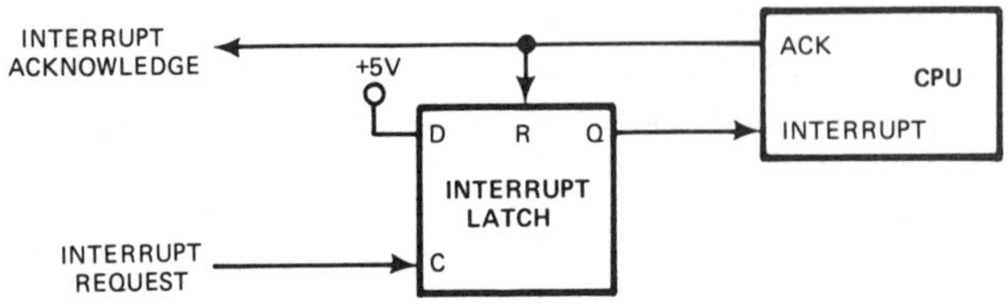

Figure 8.3 A simple one-level interrupt interface.

From here on, details of behavior vary, depending on the product, but the resulting action is always a transfer of control to special programs written just to handle the interrupt. When the interrupt program is through, the last instruction in it must cause the interrupted program to resume exactly where it left off.

The microprocessor must provide a way to first save and then later restore all registers and status bits as they were when the interrupt occurred so that the interrupted program's data will not be corrupted. In Motorola's 6800 all of this is performed automatically for the user. Other processors make the interrupt program responsible for maintaining continuity for the interrupted program. Most such processors use the stack (Figure 8.4). The first thing done by an interrupt

```
INTERRUPT PROGRAM
PUSH  PSW        ; SAVE (A) & FLAGS
PUSH  B          ; SAVE (B, C,)
PUSH  D          ; SAVE (D, E)
PUSH  H          ; SAVE (H, L)
•
•
•
•
(INTERRUPT PROCESSING)
•
•
•
•
POP   H          ; RESTORE ALL
POP   D          ; (NOTE ORDER)
POP   B
POP   PSW
EI               ; RE-ENABLE INTERRUPTS
RET              ; EXIT
```

Figure 8.4 A small interrupt service routine.

Intraprogram Documentation

Every good book on programming exhorts the novice programmer to add comments to programs which can aid in understanding in the future. There are two sets of rules that you should always follow:

1. All comments embedded in the code along with the source statements should explain *why* something is being done, not *what.* Next to a compare instruction, for example, the comment should say, "SEE IF LOOP IS FINISHED YET," not something like "COMPARE WITH ACCUMULATOR."
2. Each subroutine should be preceded by a textual "header" that explains the entry conditions, exit conditions, and the transformation that is done to the data. A list of the required resources is also important.

An example of a well-documented program and a poorly documented program compared side-by-side will serve to explain the difference.

```
; COPY.
;   THIS ROUTINE COPIES ONE STRING OF
;   BYTES FROM ONE PLACE IN MEMORY TO
;   ANOTHER.   AT ENTRY, THE STACK HOLDS
;        SP:     (RETURN ADDRESS)
;        SP+2:TARGET ADDRESS                     (T)
;        SP+4:ENDING ADDRESS OF SOURCE FIELD (E)
;        SP+6:STARTING ADDRESS                   (S)
;   THIS PROGRAM MOVES THE BYTES IN LOCATIONS
;   (E) THROUGH (S), INCLUSIVE, INTO LOCATIONS
;   STARTING AT (T).
;   THIS ROUTINE DESTROYS CONTENTS OF ALL
;   CPU REGISTERS.
CPY:     POP    H          ; SAVE RETURN ADDRESS
         POP    B          ; GET (T) INTO (B, C)
         POP    D          ; GET (E) INTO (D, E)
         XTHL              ; GET (S) INTO (H, L)
CPY1:    MOV    A, M       ; GET NEXT BYTE TO BE MOVED
         STAX   B          ;   AND PUT IT AWAY
         INX    B          ; ADVANCE TO NEXT TARGET
         CALL   MTST       ; SEE IF WE''RE DONE YET
         RZ                ;   WE ARE.  GO BACK.
         INX    H          ; ADVANCE TO NEXT SOURCE
         JMP    CYP1       ; CONTINUE FOR ALL BYTES
; COMPARE (D, E) TO (H, L) ; SET ALU FLAGS
MTST:    MOV    A, H
         CMP    D
         RNZ               ; NON-EQUAL, SO RETURN
         MOV    A, L
         CMP    E
         RET               ; Z-FLAG IS SET NOW
```

```
; COPY FROM MEMORY TO MEMORY. ADDRESS
; ON THE STACK.
COPY:
         POP    H     ; GET ARGUMENTS
         POP    B
         POP    D
         XTHL
CPY1:    MOV    A, M  ; MOVE MEMORY TO ACC
         STAX   B     ; STORE AWAY ACC
         INX    B     ; INCREMENT B REGISTER
         CALL   MTST  ; COMPARE
         RZ           ; ALL DONE
         INX    H
         JMP    CPY1  ; GO BACK TO TOP OF LOOP
MTST:    MOV    A, H  ; GET H
         CMP    D     ; COMPARE WITH D
         RNZ          ; RETURN IF ZERO
         MOV    A, L  ; GET L
         CMP    E     ; COMPARE WITH E
         RET          ; RETURN
```

Figure A Examples of intra-program documentation.

program, then, is a PUSH of all registers and status information to the stack. The program can then freely use the processor's registers and ALU to handle the interrupt because the original contents will be restored later with POP instructions. After the interruptable state of the computer is restored, interrupts can be re-enabled (the RI instruction in this example). Ideally, EI should not take effect until after the return instruction is executed. In today's processors, however, an interrupt may strike enough stack space if this does happen.

When interrupts are used to transfer data in or out, the following tasks must be handled by the interrupt program:

1. Save the contents of all registers to be used during the interrupt.
2. If more than one potential interrupt exists, identify the one that needs service and invoke the appropriate software.
3. Acknowledge the interrupt so that the interrupting device can release the interrupt pin on the CPU.
4. Perform the required input or output transfer or whatever it is that is supposed to be done.
5. Check to see if this is the last in a series of interrupts. If it is, inform the main program that, for example, a whole record has been read in.
6. Restore registers and status bits to the way they were at the time the interrupt struck.
7. Enable interrupts. Reenable interrupts that were locked out to prevent interference and then return to the interrupted program.

With most microprocessors, almost all the hardware and software contributing to this chain of events must be provided by the designer.

You will occasionally need more than one interrupt in the system. You might, for example, have a periodic clock driven from 60 Hz that produces an interrupt every 16.67 ms and a communications channel that may interrupt sporadically to cause some data transfer. Most microprocessors have some way of handling multiple interrupt sources, but all of them are common in one respect: They must have some way of identifying which interrupt has occurred. There are two ways: *vectoring* and *sensing.* In vectored interrupts, several different subroutine addresses are allocated in the design of the CPU, and some way of setting the specific address upon interrupt is provided. In this design, like the 8080 and the 9900, for example, some extra pins or control signals are used to allow the specification of one of a discrete set of addresses. There is a complication too: since two interrupts may arrive from different sources at the same time, some way of priority ordering is essential to "serialize" them. The common priority encoder chips (Figure 8.5) are used for this purpose. For all of the inputs, if there are two or more active at one time, only the highest (or lowest, depending on the design) numbered will be allowed to reach the output.

In other designs, when an interrupt strikes, it is necessary to interrogate the potential interrupters in order to determine the source. The necessary electronic

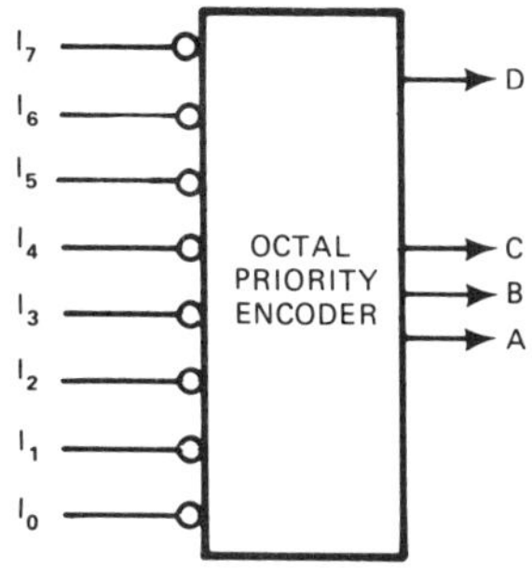

TRUTH TABLE

INPUTS								OUTPUTS			
I_0	I_1	I_2	I_3	I_4	I_5	I_6	I_7	A	B	C	D
H	H	H	H	H	H	H	H	X	X	X	L
L	H	H	H	H	H	H	H	L	L	L	H
X	L	H	H	H	H	H	H	L	L	H	H
X	X	L	H	H	H	H	H	L	H	L	H
X	X	X	L	H	H	H	H	L	H	H	H
X	X	X	X	L	H	H	H	H	L	L	H
X	X	X	X	X	L	H	H	H	L	H	H
X	X	X	X	X	X	L	H	H	H	L	H
X	X	X	X	X	X	X	L	H	H	H	H

Figure 8.5 Priority encoder for interrupt resolution.

circuitry is shown in Figure 8.6. The functional equivalent of this interrupt system will be found in the Motorola 6800 and similar devices. Each interrupt source has an isolated interrupt request latch. The interrupts are distinguished from one another by the SENSE line. All of these SENSE lines are connected to individual bits of an input port so that the CPU can read them in to resolve the priority. The CPU acknowledges individual interrupts by using an output port, each bit of which is connected to a different interrupt request latch. The latches are cleared under software control. An additional elaboration is provided by the ENABLE input to each interrupt circuit. By connecting these ENABLE logic signals to an output port (which, itself, has a latch), individual interrupts can be caused to be ignored by the hardware, but under software control. Although this system creates additional software overhead, it provides more flexibility in some cases.

Communication between an interrupt program and the main programs that rely on it can be accomplished with a *semaphore.* When the interrupt program has

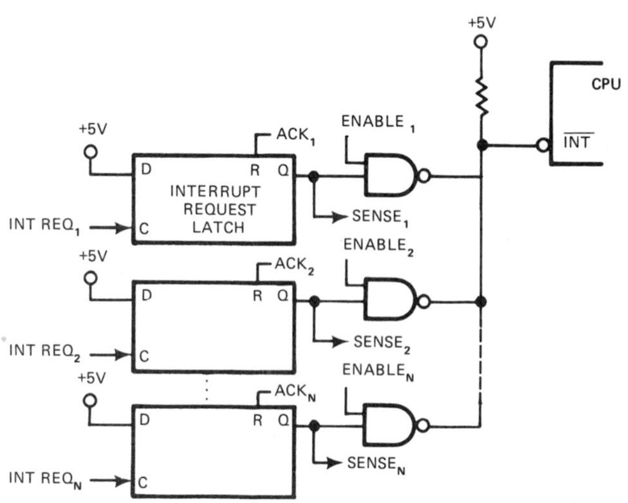

Figure 8.6 Sensing of multiple interrupts.

completed a long drawn-out task after numerous interrupts, it signals this fact by putting a code in some agreed upon location in memory. The main program occasionally checks the location to see, for instance, if it is allowed to set in motion another long drawn-out task. Frequently, a *semaphore* is really some counter used routinely by the interrupt program to keep track of its task. If it counts the number of columns read from a card, the main programs can check the same counter to see if the process has terminated. There must be some way, however, to prevent the two routines from getting out of sync; the incrementing and decrementing and examination of these semaphores must not be interruptable. The operation of fetching a word from memory, incrementing, and restoring must be uninterruptable. Some processors can do this in one instruction, which, of course, is ideal.

Timing

Real-time systems necessarily imply that time must be accounted for between important events. Therefore, in real-time microprocessor products some timing control will be essential.

Some output events require the generation of a simple short pulse. This is done most easily by setting an output bit with one instruction and then resetting it with another. Some micros even have the ability to do this in one instruction. Other output tasks, however, need pulses of some specified time duration.

So long as the required pulse width is very short, one or two instructions can create the necessary pulse. If the required pulse width is as long as a few instruction cycles, then instruction sequences that do nothing but delay can be used to time the operation. Some computers don't have no-operation (NOP) instructions, but others do. Certainly, conditional jumps that can never occur (such as jump-on-zero with a nonzero register contents), jumps to the immediately succeeding location, and subroutine calls to return instructions (the vacuous subroutine) are all proven and useful time-wasters. These delays are useful over the 10 to 100 ms range. Longer intervals usually require the use of time-delay loops if timing is software controlled.

A one-bit output from a microprocessor can be used to form a stable repetitive marker or a one-shot strobe pulse. A pulse of some particular width can be repetitively generated. However, the pulse jitter may be relatively large, depending on other pieces of software that may be executed.

In general, software controlled timing is performed by executing program loops (Figure 8.7). The instructions in the loop have a (hopefully) known execution time. Usually, the loop has an associated counter that is incremented or decremented until zero is achieved. The time spent in delay is approximately equal to the average execution time multiplied by the number of times the loop is executed. The execution time of the delay subroutine is the sum of the following:

1. The calling and set-up overhead
2. The count-body time multiplied by the initial count
3. The clean-up and return time

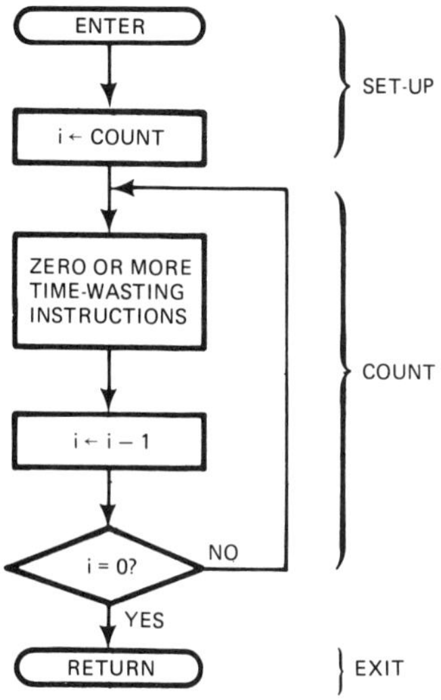

Figure 8.7 Simple software timing.

The count can be easily supplied to the delay procedure as an argument (typically in one or more of the CPU registers).

To strobe a particular output line for 1 ms, the delay subroutine is repeatedly called (Figure 8.8). We assume that the delay time is exactly 100 ms per loop interation. Ideally, in this example the delay from A to B should be 1 ms. Nevertheless,

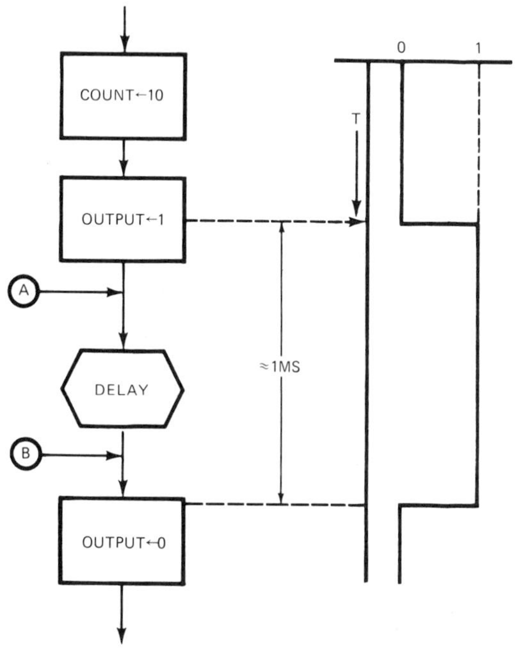

Figure 8.8 Generating known pulse widths from software.

there will nearly always be some timing error. The example will take more than 1 ms if the subroutine is adjusted to occupy precisely 100 ms because additional time will be consumed in calling and returning from the subroutine.

More precise timing can be accomplished by making the delay loop shorter and increasing the count. In some cases, the delay loop requires only a few microseconds; then the initial count can be adjusted to compensate for the call-return time so that the total time delay is precise. In many programs a gross delay uses a fine delay subroutine.

Many of the digital functions that you are used to performing with one-shots and counters can now be replaced by software. When sending data to a teletypewriter, for example, bits must be presented serially about 9 ms apart. Designers have for years used 9-ms oscillators; lately, use of the Universal Asynchronous Receiver/Transmitter (UART) with 9-ms oscillators has become popular. However, if your processor is only lightly loaded by the software, you need not build any of these extra clips into the product. The processor can be programmed to be a "software UART."

The program begins by issuing a one-bit out on some port; this is the start-bit After a 9-ms delay, the least-significant bit of the data word is put out to the data port; after another 9 ms, the next bit is put out there and so on until all eight bits are out. Finally, the program sets the selected output bit to zero and delays about 18 ms to create the two stop-bits. The advantages are manifold: You can change speeds, data formats, and codes with ease because the details are in software. You can also allow for different speeds dependent on some input bit; certain terminals can be connected with this bit set high and others can be connected with the bit set low. If the output software subroutine interrogates this bit before setting up the delay loop count, then two different speeds can be easily accommodated.

Input from the teletypewriter is slightly more difficult because the software must cope with noise along with the signal. However, the software UART can actually be made significantly more noise tolerant than the hardware version.

If software of this complexity sounds forbidding, it is only because you haven't done it yet. A typical software UART takes less than 120 bytes of code. Furthermore, the control of time, synchronization, and time delays are so basic to many microprocessor interfaces that these elements must become familiar tools to you.

Many applications can't use software clockery. Critically timed external events, for example, may need to be sensed precisely. At the same time, it may not be acceptable to tie up the processor in waiting loops. In the software UART, for example, the processor is committed to that one function for 100 ms at a time. In these cases, it is important to know about external clock circuits that can relieve the software.

There are two classes of clocks that can be connected to a microcomputer. The simplest clock is a pulse generator that the computer constantly checks (through input or interrupt operations) for each "tick." More elaborate clocks use an external counter between the computer and the pulse generator. The counter is primed from software and then counted down; when it gets to zero, the computer is notified that the specified time period has elapsed. The simpler approach is far more popular with microcomputer-designers because of its lack of external hardware.

The easiest way to implement a real-time clock is to connect the pulse generator to an interrupt input. Each time the clock "ticks" the interrupt service program increments a counter maintained in read-write storage. All other programs refer to this counter to find out (relative) time. If you need to resolve only relatively long time intervals (say, longer than 100 ms), then this is easy to do. If the timer needs better resolution, you have to compute the impact on the overall execution time: Multiply the number of pulses per second from the clock by the number of microseconds of execution time needed to service each clock interrupt; the resulting number is the number of microseconds per second spent in that one small routine. If the number is above about 10 ms total, you probably ought to look to another alternative.

Clocks the software must scan should come true when the time period elapses; the latch that holds the "tick" should be cleared only by the input instruction that reads it or the interrupt acknowledge signal. If the clock is read in by interrupt, then the maximum jitter of the clock will be dependent on how long the computer is operated with the clock interrupt disabled. If the clock is read in by an input instruction, then the jitter will be a function of how frequently that input bit is sampled. In either of these systems, care must be taken to avoid missing pulses if timing is critical.

It is not uncommon to have two clocks in a system, especially when the clock is read in with an input instruction. One bit represents a "fine" clock; it generally invokes some special short-but-fast routines. Another bit represents a "coarse" clock; it is used to test to be certain that no "fine" clock pulses have been lost and to invoke some infrequent and perhaps slow running routines. Whenever the clock input is nonzero, the "fine" clock has been sensed. At that time the other bit can be examined; if true, the "coarse" clock has been sensed simultaneously.

Clocks that use external counters generally drive interrupts. A counter that can be "broadside" loaded from an output instruction is clocked from a isochronous pulse source. The clock counter is preloaded and incremented (or decremented) until zero; when the counter's content is zero, an interrupt is generated. The width of the counter, of course, depends on the maximum time delay and clock's resolution. Generally, if the counter is wider than the microprocessor word size, you will have clock priming problems (or a lot of extra circuitry). If the counter is two words wide, for instance, you will have to send out part of the counter's contents first and the second part later. If you are not careful, you will create an interrupt between these two events, even though you don't want it. That means that the counter can't be allowed to interrupt until it is entirely primed.

This kind of clock circuitry also needs to have provisions for the counter's value to be read back into the microprocessor. Once a time delay has been imposed, it may be necessary to interpose a shorter delay. This can be done by reading the counter's contents back into the registers, deciding which of the two events should occur next, and retaining the *difference* of the two delays as the time delay to introduce after the next interrupt to schedule the second event.

Programming for Real-time

Real-time programming is like any other programming, only more difficult. It is imperative that the real-time component of the software be isolated, carefully understood, and reduced to an absolutely minimum size. As a guiding rule, remember to "take the real-time out of it." If at all possible, for example, service an interrupt by marking the fact that the interrupt occurred and then let the Supervisor handle the dispatching of some subroutine to deal with the reported condition. In some cases, of course, this marking can take place in a counter. In extreme cases, the interrupt service routine must be lengthy and complex; such cases should be rare and looked upon with suspicion. In most microprocessor applications the software can be divided into the real-time part, the scheduling part, and the actual "worker" part. If the real-time part is much more than a few percent of the actual code, you should seek to pare it back. The scheduler and Supervisor are software components that decide which "worker" subroutine to execute next; they may be small or large, depending on the design and intent of the system. In most cases, less than 5% of the code will be devoted to this part of the program.

The reason for keeping the real-time (and semi-real-time supervisor) software so short is to avoid degrading reliability. The more software there is, the more there is to go wrong. Furthermore, the larger it is, the more components (subroutines, etc.) there are likely to be and the more interfaces to be debugged. Even major operating systems on large computers have only a few thousand bytes of code in the real-time segment.

An example of a real-time servicing program might be a time-of-day clock. In many applications the actual time of day is required so that a data logging printer can record the time of events. Although an expensive independent clock can be purchased and interfaced, it seems more practical to use the microprocessor (since it is already in the system anyway). Our clock will be based on minimum hardware (Figure 8.9, a or b). If these clock sources are too jittery for you, you could use

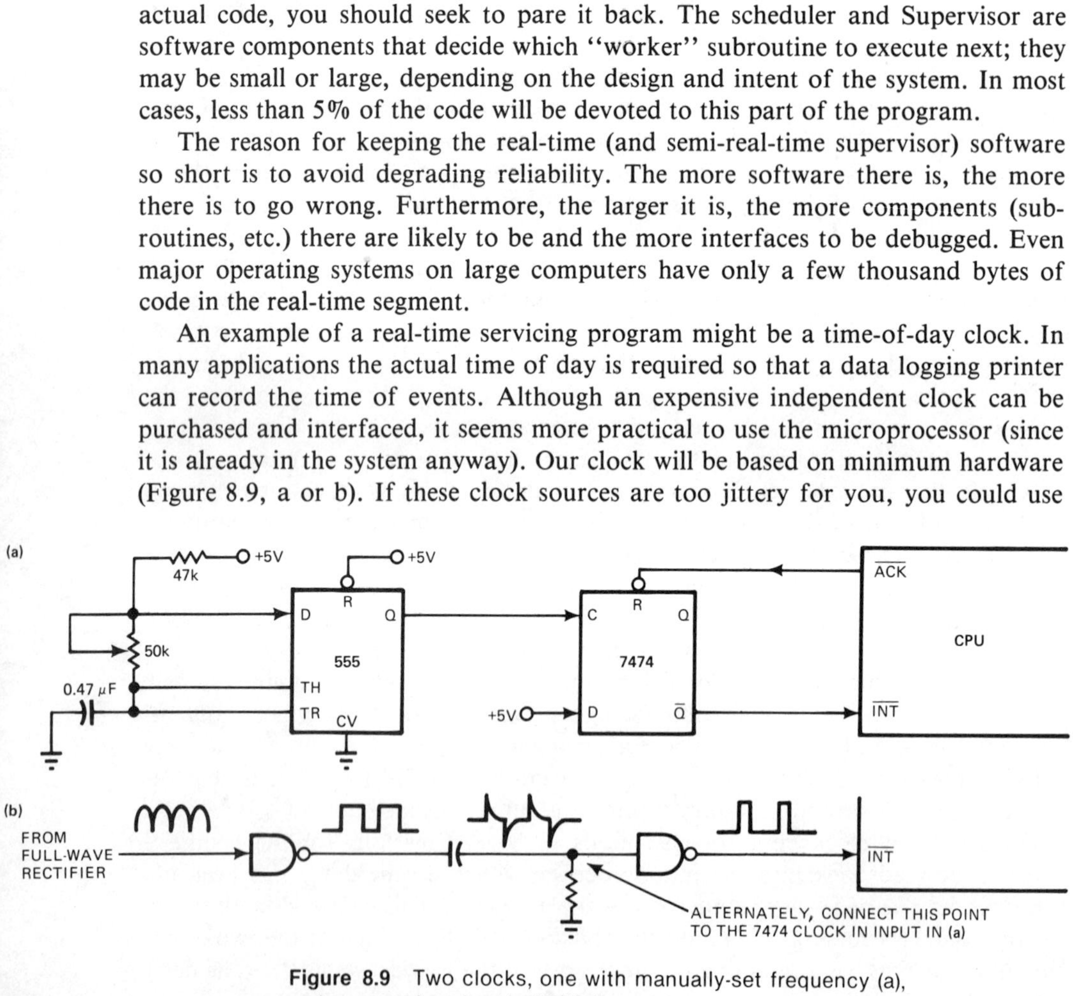

Figure 8.9 Two clocks, one with manually-set frequency (a), and one synchronized to 60 Hc (b).

the master CPU clock and divide it down to some reasonable period. The clock frequency will be selected to provide resolution of the necessary time intervals, yet prevent overloading the processor with too many interrupts. For the purposes of this example, we elect to interrupt once every 16.67 ms; this could also be derived from the 60-Hz power source in an AC-powered system.

The simplest possible software imaginable is shown in Figure 8.10. All the interrupt service routine does is acknowledge the interrupt (which may be done in hardware automatically, depending on the processor), increment a counter in a known location, and resume the interrupted program. In an eight-bit processor, this code may require only ten or so bytes. Certainly, this code is not subject to much potential error and helps contribute to the overall reliability of the program.

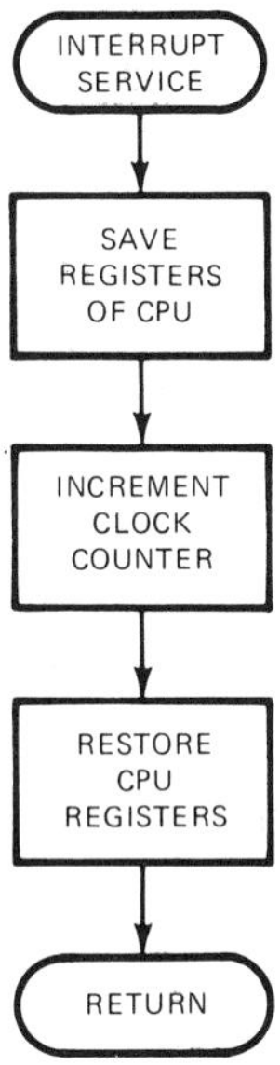

Figure 8.10 Simple interrupt service routine.

Now, some software must be invoked frequently enough to avoid the counter's being incremented past its limit. If the counter is only eight-bits wide, the supervisor will be required to activate the clock-updating subroutines less frequently than (16.67 ms $\times$ 256) once every 4.2667 s. This should produce no undue burden on the supervisor.

The clock-updating routine should be written as a separate and distinct closed subroutine. The inputs to the routine are the timer counter and the area in memory where the most recently updated times are to be found. The outputs will be a cleared counter and an updated time back in the original area. The updating routine is written as a subroutine so that it can be called periodically from the Supervisor; it may also be called from any other subroutine such as the one that prints out, illustrated in Figure 8.11. Note that this subroutine is nearly completely outside the real-time world. It will also be easy to test and debug.

Controlling Testing

Each program is made up of one or more paths, each of which may be populated by bugs. To ensure confidence in the program, it is important that you test each "leg" of the program and the conditions that select between the legs. Each binary decision may double the number of paths you must test. Typical microprocessor programs may have 100 or more paths to be checked.

By studying the program you can derive a good testing strategy. First, select the "main thread"—the sequence in the program that represents the most frequently traversed set of instructions and has the minimum number of decisions. This path should be tested first. To keep track of the debugging process, you may wish to mark a vertical line (most programmers use a colored pencil) alongside the group of instructions that has been tested and is tentatively accepted as correct.

Next, select the "error conditions"—the parts of the program that are invoked when some extraordinary input condition arises. These error conditions should be stimulated and debugged. Now that the main thread and the extreme cases are done, you will find that only a small percentage of the remainder of the program remains to be tested. You should select test cases to gain entry into and to test the sections of your program listing that are still unmarked.

Once your listing is completely marked, you can have some assurances that your program is probably operating correctly. However, you should now engage in "functional" testing, that is, you should try to create sequences of inputs that might be logical (and illogical) to be certain that a design flaw has not crept into the software.

Testing and debugging are expensive activities. They require intense involvement and lots of time. And, if you discover a hardware/software interface problem, you may have your hands full for a long time trying to correct the problem. The testing and debugging effort may be minimized by engaging in adequate and detailed design. The more you correct design flaws at design time, the less trouble you will have during the testing phase close to the delivery deadline.

Nevertheless, there may still be a fly in the ointment. This subroutine is not completely outside the real-time domain since it makes reference to a data variable that is accessed from the real-time domain. Imagine the following worst-case: When the updating subroutine is about to use and then clear the timer's counter, interrupt may occur. In other words, the counter's value is fetched into the accumulator, an interrupt strikes, and the counter is incremented. When the interrupted updating subroutine is resumed, the counter is cleared. You will have lost one clock count. Now the probability of this happening is, unfortunately, predict-

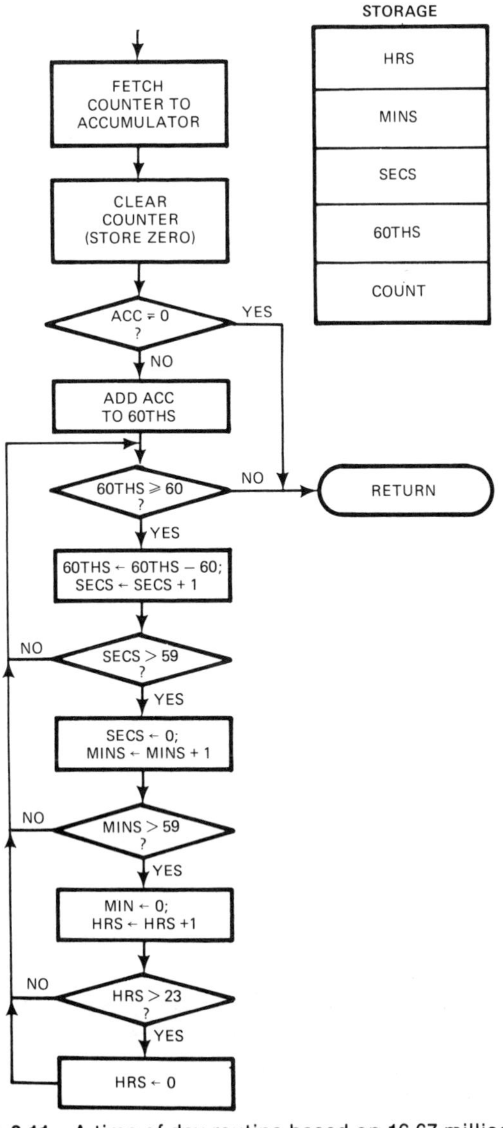

Figure 8.11 A time-of-day routine based on 16.67 millisecond interrupts.

able: It will happen just often enough to be troublesome, but not often enough to be caught.

The solution to this problem is simple enough: Don't allow interrupts to occur during the time between fetching and clearing the data. What is more important and fundamental, though, is knowing that such care must be taken. Interrupts must be used sparingly.

Testing Real-time Software

Assuming that you have followed good design practice, designed using finite-state machines, carefully limited the size of the real-time component of the software, and meticulously desk-checked your code for correctness, you will still have to test your program. And real-time software is not easy to test.

The first rule to remember is that although you may be able to test individual components of most software, in real-time software the interactions between elements of software may be the critical problem. Simply connecting external devices to the microprocessor to exercise the software is not enough; insufficient test cases will be generated and they will not be predictable enough to serve as good tests. To test real-time software, you need a source of repeatable interrupts and input signals that are precisely synchronized. If you detect a software fault, you need the repeatable set of circumstances that causes that problem so that you can isolate the bug. And, after you have found the problem and corrected it, how can you test the software again to be sure that everything works anew unless you can generate the same set of conditions.

The digital inputs and outputs of a microprocessor-based system can often be *stimulated* and compared. Stimulation of the input ports can be under the control of a digital function generator, or even another computer or microprocessor. If programmed, the stimulated inputs can be as complex as necessary to be certain that all the paths of the program are traversed during the testing process.

Imagine that you have a real-time program that has a known bug. The microprocessor has just exhibited some unusual behavior and you have stopped the CPU. Now, will you care about the likely future behavior of this program? Probably not, for in the absence of other bugs, the behavior of this program should be very predictable. Will you be interested in the current behavior? No, because you already know that it is errant. What do you need to know? You need to know the past behavior of this program so that you can reconstruct the path by which the program arrived at this erroneous state. But the data variables in RAM only reflect the current state of the software.

For simplified debugging, you should keep a history of the program's performance. If there is an error, you can then reconstruct the major path followed by the software. Usually, that will exhibit some obvious error in the sequence; just prior to that sequence is invariably where the software bug will be found. Fortunately, the FSM history approach of Chapter 6 can be used to create that history of execution.

9

Hardware/Software Trade Off

It is only after you get thoroughly into the use and application of microprocessors that you discover the real underlying appeal: Hardware and software are essentially interchangeable. This fact can be used to bias the economics in favor of whatever objective you have established.

Software is generally more expensive to implement than hardware, but it is less expensive to duplicate. Because of the inherently sequential nature of computer programs, they are at least an order of magnitude (decimal!) more difficult to design, test, and debug than conventional electronics. However, once software has been correctly implemented, the cost of replicating it is very low in comparison with the equivalent amount of electronics. It is not uncommon to see a TTL-based design of from 150 to 200 IC's replaced by a five-chip microcomputer with less than 1,000 bytes of memory. In these applications even the software design and implementation costs are lower than the engineering costs for the TTL-based equivalent.

As a general rule, however, if you are trying to minimize development costs (because production volumes are not large enough to warrant the additional expenditure to achieve production cost savings), then a generalized microcomputer with simple software is often the best choice. When production volumes warrant, however, you must look carefully at the hardware/software trade off to minimize unit replication costs. This usually means more software and less hardware.

By the same token, initial hardware design may be so dependent on software that 150% of the microprocessor's capacity is needed. In these cases, it is important to know that some external hardware can always be added to ''bail out'' the software timing.

Microcomputer design economics is driven by the objective of minimizing the sum of development and production costs:

$$D + nP$$

If *n*, the number of production units, is small, then development costs will nearly always dominate the computation. If *n* is large, it may be worth spending more development dollars (*D*) to achieve modest savings in production costs (*P*). Theoretically, at least, D/n dollars can be spent to achieve a savings of *P* dollars. In practice, we seldom price things so closely. Usually, if *n* is less than 100, we tend to bias toward minimization of development costs. Certainly, if production volumes are above 1,000, the leverage on additional development expenditures will be justified by reduced production costs per unit.

Virtually anything that can be done in software can be done in hardware, but the opposite case is not always true. There are, however, some practical limitations, like time, that get in the way of generally applying the principle of hardware/software exchange. Almost any digital system that has a clock period of less than 100 kHz can be implemented in either hardware or software. Fortunately, that is where most applications are to be found. However, even systems that have very high data rates generally have a low-speed control subsystem that can often benefit from the application of microprocessors. Correct decisions about the proper dividing line between external electronics and internal software cannot be made without some careful study. Good design requires successive trial designs, each of which is compared to the other alternatives to achieve minimum cost; this is what tends to drive the development costs up.

A Typical Trade Off Example

At some point virtually every microcomputer designer is forced to interface a serial data terminal or a teletypewriter to the processor. Even if the applications don't demand it, the interface is necessary just so that the terminal can be used as a debugging tool during software development. When the circuitry is added to a prototype for debugging purposes, it can be removed before delivery or production engineering.

Serial data terminals operate at various speeds and with various interfacing conventions, but the essential structures are very similar to one another. One of the important properties of data terminals is the code to which they respond. One terminal may print the letter "A" when presented with the bit pattern 010000, but another terminal may print the space character. The American Standard Code for Information Interchange (ASCII, Figure 9.1) has been designed to provide equipment designers with one standard language for terminals and their related equipment. There is nothing magical about the code; it is merely an internationally agreed upon set of assignments of graphic representations to bit patterns.

Today, most computer terminals and data communications equipment are designed to cope with and take advantage of ASCII (except for a few recalcitrant hold-

b_7	b_6	b_5	b_4	b_3	b_2	b_1

b_4 b_3 b_2 b_1	$b_7 \rightarrow$ 0 $b_6 \rightarrow$ 0 $b_5 \rightarrow$ 0	0 0 1	0 1 0	0 1 1	1 0 0	1 0 1	1 1 0	1 1 1
0 0 0 0	NUL	DLE	SPACE	0	@	P		p
0 0 0 1	SOH	DC1	!	1	A	Q	a	q
0 0 1 0	STX	DC2	"	2	B	R	b	r
0 0 1 1	ETX	DC3	#	3	C	S	c	s
0 1 0 0	EOT	DC4	$	4	D	T	d	t
0 1 0 1	ENQ	NAK	%	5	E	U	e	u
0 1 1 0	ACK	SYN	&	6	F	V	f	v
0 1 1 1	BEL	ETB	'	7	G	W	g	w
1 0 0 0	BS	CAN	(	8	H	X	h	x
1 0 0 1	HT	EM	)	9	I	Y	i	y
1 0 1 0	LF	SUB	*	:	J	Z	j	z
1 0 1 1	VT	ESC	+	;	K	[	k	{
1 1 0 0	FF	FS	,	<	L	\	l	¦
1 1 0 1	CR	GS	-	=	M	]	m	}
1 1 1 0	SO	RS	.	>	N	^	n	~
1 1 1 1	SI	US	/	?	O	—	o	DEL

☐ PRINTABLE CHARACTER ▨ AUXILIARY DEVICE CONTROL CHARACTER

░ PRINTER CONTROL CHARACTER

Figure 9.1 The seven-bit ASCII encoding system.

outs, like IBM). ASCII makes generalized hardware/software design simple, because the number of bits in each character is well-defined and the interpretations on the bit patterns are universally understood.

Most data terminals are designed to be connected to computers over telephone lines. Because of the design requirements to utilize what is essentially a voice network, almost all significant data transmission over telephone lines is done one bit at a time. The American National Standards Institute (ANSI) has promulgated, in addition to the ASCII standard, standards for transmission speeds (such as 110, 300, 600, 1,200 and 2,400 bits per second) and for transmission order (in sending parallel data in bit-serial form, both sender and receiver must agree upon whether the most-significant data bit is sent first or last). Because these standards are generally accepted, standard interface circuits have been designed for connecting data terminals to other digital equipment (including microcomputers). These circuits are called UART's (Universal Asynchronous Receiver-Transmitter, Figure 9.2).

Basically, a UART is a parallel-to-serial converter in the transmit direction and a serial-to-parallel converter in the receive direction. Because all timing is controlled by an external clock, almost any data speed can be accommodated. In addition to the pure serialization function, the UART provides for several control and status reporting functions.

If you are designing a single, low-speed interface between a microprocessor and a common data terminal, the UART is a good design choice. As will be shown, it is easy to interface to the address and data bus. Therefore, development costs are low enough that if a terminal is interfaced solely for program debugging

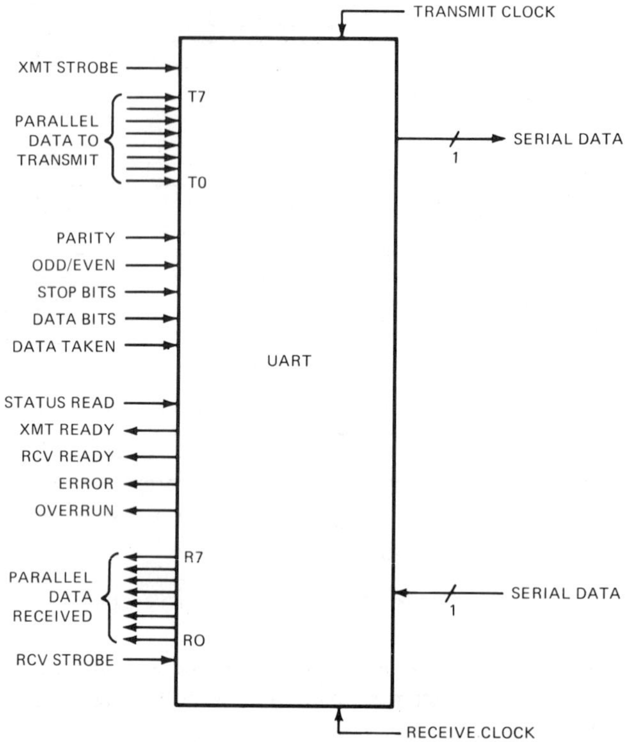

Figure 9.2 A typical universal asynchronous receiver-transmitter.

TABLE 9.1 Definitions of the UART's Control Pins.

PARITY	Set to specify whether parity is to be computed and/or checked by UART
ODD/EVEN	If parity is computed and/or checked, this signal specifies whether parity may be odd or even
STOP-BIT	Specifies whether one or two extra stop-bits are appended to each character
DATA BITS	Specifies whether five- or eight-bit data is to be sent and received
DATA TAKEN	Used after received data is taken from UART to rearm the RCV READY status signal
XMT READY	Signals that the transmitter is ready to accept the next output character
RCV READY	Signals that a character has been received and may be read (is reset by DATA TAKEN)
ERROR	Signals that character received has incorrect parity
OVERRUN	Signals that a second character was received before the preceding character was taken from the UART
XMT STROBE	The timing signal that causes data to be latched into the UART
RCV STROBE	The timing signal that causes received data to be placed on UART's output
STATUS READ	The timing signal that causes the status signals to be presented at the UART's output

purposes, only a small amount of time will be required. In fact, many microprocessor makers (like Intel and Motorola) provide UART's that interface directly with their own microprocessors. However, for our purposes, we will assume the use of one of the popular generalized UART's and will create our own interface circuitry.

The UART can be conceived of as being made up of four registers (remember the register-transfer models of Chapter 1?). There is an output data register into which is placed an eight-bit word for transmission, an input data register from which the eight-bit word most recently received can be obtained, a control register into which can be set some control bits to affect UART performance, and a status register from which can be obtained the current operational status of the device. These four registers are accessed by assigning four discrete device selection codes. In most designs two addresses are used: One address refers to the data register (input or output) and the other address refers to the control/status register. The selection between register pairs, then, is established with the direction bit for the bidirectional data bus [MEMR (to read) and MEMW (to write).] A typical arrangement of control signals for port control is shown in Figure 9.3. Since the output data register is normally a clocked latch, no additional output data latch is

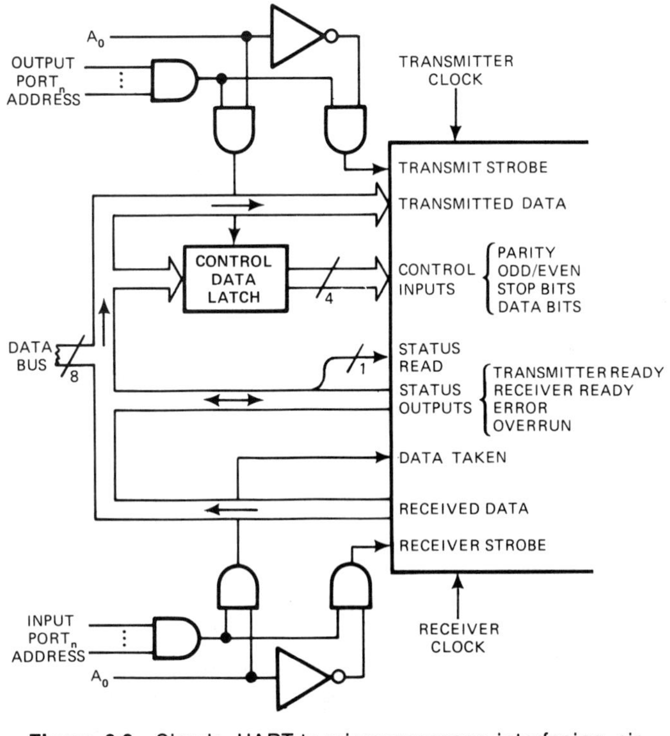

Figure 9.3 Simple UART-to-microprocessor interfacing circuitry.

required. Since, however, the control inputs to the UART are generally level-sensitive, an output data latch is required on the control port in order to be able to hold the latest control signals for the UART. Since the data and status from the UART are often three-state buffered, all that is necessary is to decode the appropriate address-select signals and apply them to the UART control pins.

The serial input and output signals of the UART are usually TTL levels. The data terminals conform to one or the other of two common standards known as the EIA RS-232 interface and Teletype Corporation's 20 ma current loop convention. Some level shifting is necessary to create the proper format signals; the circuitry necessary is shown in Figure 9.4, without comment.

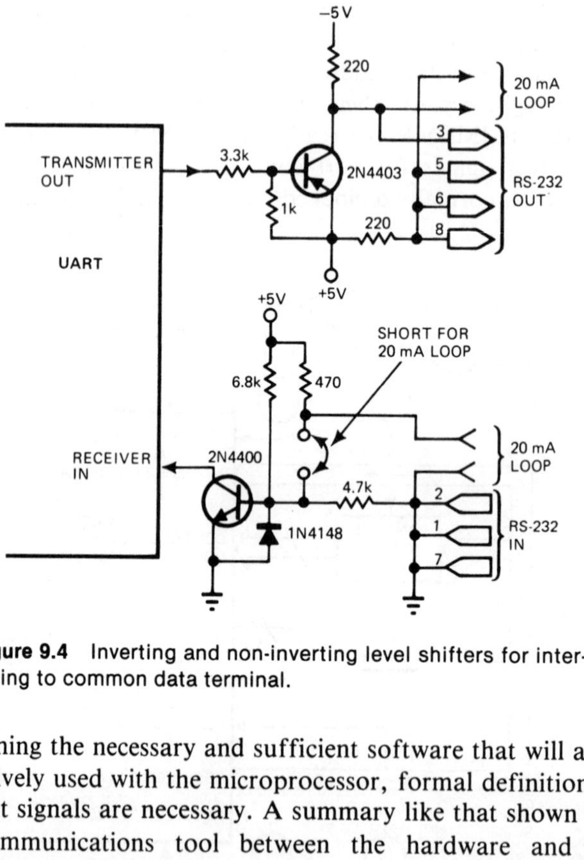

Figure 9.4 Inverting and non-inverting level shifters for interfacing to common data terminal.

Before designing the necessary and sufficient software that will allow the terminal to be effectively used with the microprocessor, formal definitions of all of the input and output signals are necessary. A summary like that shown in Table 9.2 is a necessary communications tool between the hardware and the software designers. Another way to represent the detailed control and status formats is shown in Figure 9.5.

With this design documentation in hand, you may now draft the software needed to make the interface really usable. As explained in Chapter 6, the first thing you should do is to create a description of what you want to do. There are two functions that the software should provide for:

Table 9.2 A typical description of input/output interface conventions.

DATA TERMINAL INTERFACE

ADDRESSING

1. INTERFACE IS BASED ON ADDRESSING BY MEMORY ADDRESSES. ALL I/O DEVICES ARE ADDRESSED IN THE FORM 80xx (HEX).
2. INPUT DATA AND STATUS PORT ASSIGNMENTS ARE:
INPUT DATA: 8030
STATUS READ: 8031
3. OUTPUT DATA AND CONTROL PORT ASSIGNMENTS ARE:
OUTPUT DATA: 8030
CONTROL LATCH: 8031
4. TRANSMIT AND RECEIVE CLOCKS ARE PRESENTLY SET FOR 300 BPS OPERATION (ED. NOTE: NOT ESPECIALLY RELEVANT FOR THE PROGRAMMER, BUT USEFUL INFORMATION)

DATA FORMAT

1. ALL DATA CONFORMS TO 7-BIT ASCII CODE. THE LEAST SIGNIFICANT BIT OF ASCII WILL BE EXPECTED ON THE LEAST SIGNIFICANT BIT OF THE DATA BUS.
2. THE MOST SIGNIFICANT BIT OF AN 8-BIT DATA BUS WILL BE IGNORED ON TRANSMISSION; IT WILL BE SET ACCORDING TO INCOMING DATA ON RECEIVE.

CONTROL FORMAT

1. BITS ARE NUMBERED FROM THE LEAST TO MOST SIGNIFICANT, FROM ZERO.
2. BIT ASSIGNMENTS ARE AS FOLLOWS:
   - 0: DATA TAKEN (ACTIVE HIGH)
   - 1: DATA BITS (0=8-BIT DATA, 1=5-BIT DATA)
   - 2: STOP BITS (0=TWO BITS, 1=ONE BIT)
   - 3: PARITY (0=IGNORE, 1=SET/CHECK)
   - 4: ODD/EVEN (0=ODD PARITY, 1=EVEN PARITY)
   - 5-7:NOT USED (SHOULD BE ZERO)

STATUS FORMAT

1. BITS ARE NUMBERED FROM THE LEAST TO MOST SIGNIFICANT, FROM ZERO.
2. BIT ASSIGNMENTS ARE AS FOLLOWS:
   - 0: TRANSMITTER READY (ACTIVE HIGH)
   - 1: RECEIVER READY (ACTIVE HIGH)
   - 2: ERROR (ACTIVE HIGH)
   - 3: OVERRUN (ACTIVE HIGH)
   - 4-7:(ALL SET HIGH BY DEFAULT; UNUSED)

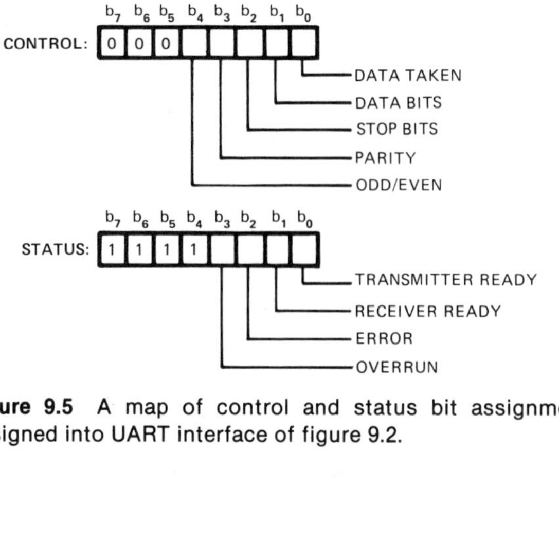

Figure 9.5 A map of control and status bit assignments designed into UART interface of figure 9.2.

1. Read a character into a register from the UART.
2. Write a character from a register to the UART.

But there are many variations on these simple basics. It is important to isolate them early and dispose of the potential problems. For example, what should the software do if there is nothing to read from the UART? In that routine alone there are two (or more) design choices:

1. Stay in the read-character subroutine until a character arrives.
2. Return to the calling program with a signal that specifies that the UART was empty.

For the sake of generality, assume the second case. It is a better choice because the calling program can be written to sit in a loop and wait for a character anyway, thus providing the "wait for a character" function. Fortunately, ASCII has been designed so that the all-zeros character is designed to stand for the absence of a character. Therefore, the read-character routine should return whatever character the UART yields or an all-zeros character if the UART is empty. The relevant finite-state diagrams are shown in Figure 9.6.

Once the requirements are settled, it is time to write the code for a specific microprocessor. In our case, we choose to use the 8080. We elect to communicate

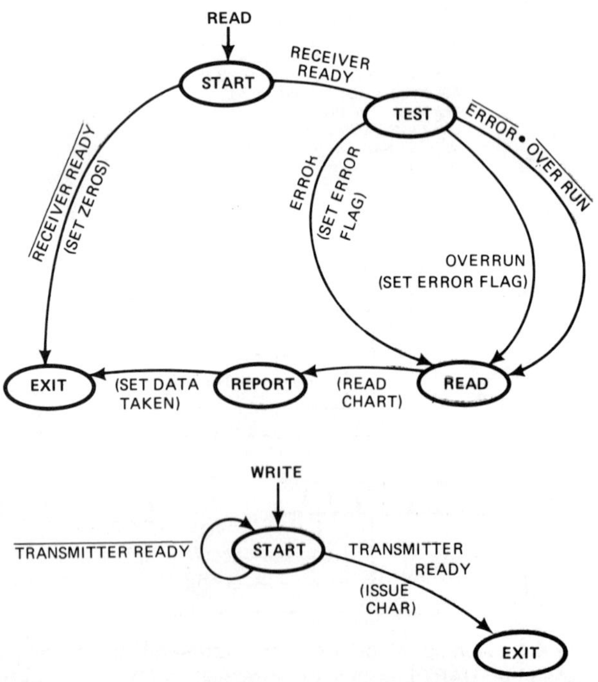

Figure 9.6 Read/write state diagrams.

the character to be written or read in the A-register. The Z-flag will be set when the ASCII null character is set into the A-register; the carry bit (C-flag) will be cleared for normal received data and set for errors or overrun conditions. The flags are not used to communicate anything to the output subroutine. The assembly-language programs are shown in Figure 9.7. Note that because of the design decision made earlier about adopting memory-mapped I/O, all I/O actions are done with load-A (LDA) and store-A (STA) instructions instead of IN and OUT.

```
DATA      EQU   8030H          ; ADDRESS FOR DATA PORTS
CNTL      EQU   8031H          ; CONTROL PORT
STATUS    EQU   8031H          ; STATUS PORT
;
; READ A CHARACTER FROM THE TERMINAL INTO (A)
;
READ:     LDA   STATUS         ; IS THERE ANYTHING READY TO READ?
          ANI   2
          RZ                   ; IF NOTHING, RETURN ZERO
          LDA   STATUS
          ANI   ØCØH           ; ISOLATE ERROR/OVERRUN BITS
          JZ    $+4            ;   NO ERRORS
          STC                  ;   SET CARRY TO NOTE ERRORS
          LDA   DATA           ; READ IN THE WORD FROM UART
          PUSH  PSW            ; SAVE (A) AND (CARRY)
          MVI   A, 1
          STA   CNTL           ; SET DATA-TAKEN HIGH
          XRA   A              ; (A) = 0
          STA   CNTL           ; SET IT BACK LOW
          POP   PSW            ; RESTORE (A) AND (CARRY)
          RET
;
; WRITE CHARACTER IN (A) OUT TO TERMINAL
;
WRITE:    PUSH  PSW            ; SAVE DATA TO BE WRITTEN OUT
          LDA   STATUS         ; FIND OUT IF XMTR READY YET
          RAR
          JNC   WRITE + 1      ; NOT YET READY. WAIT.
          POP   PSW
          STA   DATA           ; WRITE OUT THE WORD TO SEND
          RET
```

Figure 9.7 Terminal input/output driver programs for UART connected to an 8080.

In most practical applications for terminals the ability to send and receive one character at a time is relatively primitive. More often, the need exists to be able to send and receive entire multicharacter messages. Subroutines that send and receive messages make use of the lower-level software and hardware to accomplish this larger task. The primitive hardware-related software is called the *physical* input/output interface software. The subroutines that allow transmission and reception of entire messages is called the *logical* I/O system.

In the logical I/O system some means of communicating an end-of-message is important, unless all messages are of a predetermined and fixed size. Most commonly, a *delimiter* is used to mark the end of the message string. In the outbound direction we may choose to mark the end of a string of characters to be sent with a zero byte. In the inbound direction our design prohibits that because the READ subroutine may return a zero byte in the absence of other data. Therefore, we assume that the terminal operator has been instructed to terminate the message with a carriage return. We must also make the assumption (for simplicity in this chapter only) that when we want to read a message from the terminal, nothing else will happen until that message is completely received. The basic flow charts for the logical I/O described and the code for the 8080 are shown in Figure 9.8.

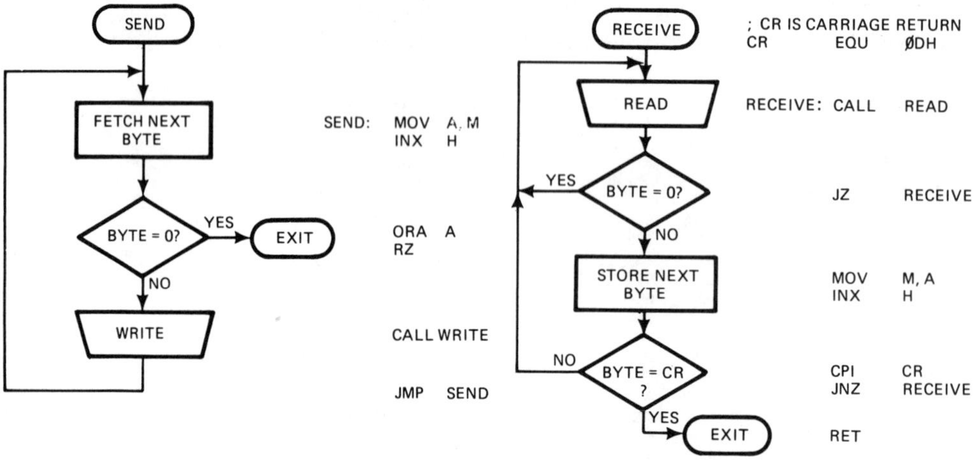

Figure 9.8 Logical I/O for reading and writing entire messages into and out of memory via the UART.

Why Change?

Under what conditions would you ever want to design a different interface with a different hardware/software trade off? Well, many times economics has a large impact. For example, for high-volume production runs, you may wish to avoid the cost of the UART chip and would prefer to handle all the UART functions in software. Or the data transmission speeds may have to be very flexible; since software is more "parameterizable" than hardware, less hardware and more software would seem appropriate. Or you may have to transfer data in and out of the microprocessor very rapidly, say, at a speed beyond the software's ability to cope; here you might want to add more hardware so that you can buffer the differences between the data transfer rates.

There are many reasons for choosing a different hardware/software trade off level, only some of which are purely economic. In some cases, design may require that power consumption be minimized; this will tend to deemphasize hardware and cause greater reliance on software. You may be execution-time limited in your microprocessor and need to add hardware just to make the design practical. Finally, you may elect to use a specific hardware/software combination because it "feels comfortable."

All too often novice designers look at another's work and exclaim, "That's not the way to do it!" If it works, it *is* one way to do it, though. And, given the same conditions, the second designer might emulate the first designer's work. The point is this: There is no *one* way to interface anything. There are economical ways, reliable ways, easy to modify ways, and modular ways (among others). Only you will know if your interface design is "best."

Using More Hardware

Imagine a transmission channel that has been designed for serial data operating at 1 MHz; obviously, no common MOS microprocessor can accept input data at that rate. The first impulse is to slow the data rate down and the most obvious place to do this is at the source. But you may be interfacing to some instrument that has a fixed and committed data rate. To interface at all, you would have to add some hardware to slow the data down. A simple FIFO can be added to the input and output lines that interface the microprocessor to the UART (Figure 9.9). The output data is transferred from the microprocessor

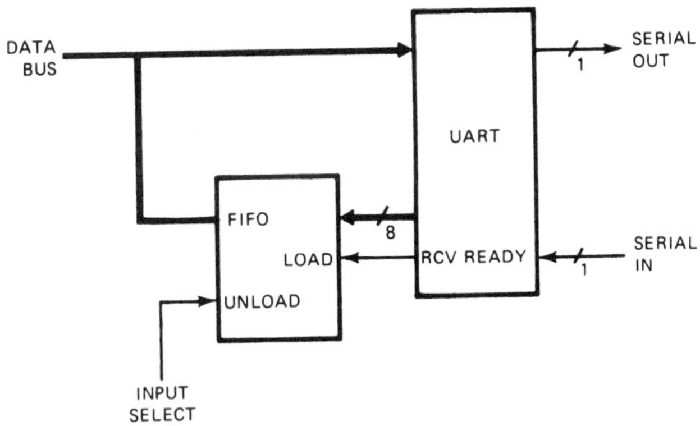

Figure 9.9 Adding a FIFO to the UART can slow the incoming data down to an acceptable rate.

directly to the UART. Since the data channel is asynchronous, you can send data at any rate you want, so long as the bits are clocked at 1 MHz. A FIFO memory is inserted at the input to the microprocessor. Incoming data from the UART is clocked into that FIFO (at approximately 100 kilocharacters per second); that data can be extracted from the FIFO at any rate at the microprocessor's leisure. The depth of the FIFO is a function of message lengths and the ratio between the speed of the microprocessor and the incoming data. In most cases, the FIFO will be rather short. The maximum depth can be computed based on the worst-case message length and how long the data may have to be held.

In this particular hardware addition, there is no net change in the software. However, the addition of the FIFO has prevented the addition of a significant amount of new software that might have to be written instead.

What if the data rate is so high that even a FIFO can't cope with it? In some video displays, for example, it is necessary to continuously resend the same data from memory over and over in order to constantly refresh the displayed image. In this case, there may be a demand for 60,000 characters per second *all the time!* If each character to be transmitted requires about 60 us worth of instruction execution time (Figures 9.7 and 9.8), there isn't enough computer time in each second to do the job. A faster (and, therefore, more hardware-dependent) solution must be found. Since the processor must be bypassed and data must be fetched directly from memory, the Direct memory Access capability of the processor can be used. This hardware modification will also require significant changes in software.

A basic DMA controller that requires no software intervention is shown in skeletal form in Figure 9.10. An initial address is loaded into a counter at the very start of every raster scan of the CRT. Each time that a new character is required, the address is sent to the memory via the DMA circuitry; the fetched data is then displayed and the address is incremented. At the end of the scan the counter is again reprimed to the starting address. During every new raster scan this circuit will fetch the same storage locations over and over again. The contents of these locations can easily be changed under software control. The WRITE subroutine becomes nothing more than a sequence of instructions that copy characters from memory to memory.

An even more generalized hardware system can be formulated on this model. For example, in Figure 9.10 we have assumed fixed allocations of memory address

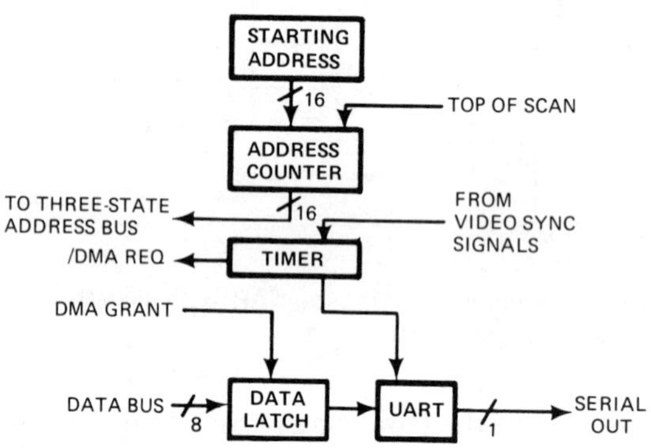

Figure 9.10 A DMA controller for a fast UART application.

for refresh data storage, as well as a fixed number of characters on the CRT itself. In some applications we may wish to treat the starting address of the DMA circuitry as an output port that can be loaded under software control. Similarly, instead of relying solely on the video retrace signal to generate a reset to the starting address, we might wish to have an ending address that can be set into latches under software control. All of these special hardware additions, however, will require additional software to activate their features.

As you can now see, addition of hardware tends to make the resulting product capable of better performance but at a price in generality. To regain the generality that could have been afforded by software, the hardware costs will rise dramatically.

Using More Software

In many designs, particularly those that have anticipated high production volumes, minimizing the parts count is important to the engineer. It may be possible to remove the UART from the interface described earlier and control the serial input/output lines from software without parts penalty. If the data rate is low enough, software can be written to actually read in data from the serial data line directly and assemble the bits into recognizable characters. Each character is sent in a form like that shown in Figure 9.11.

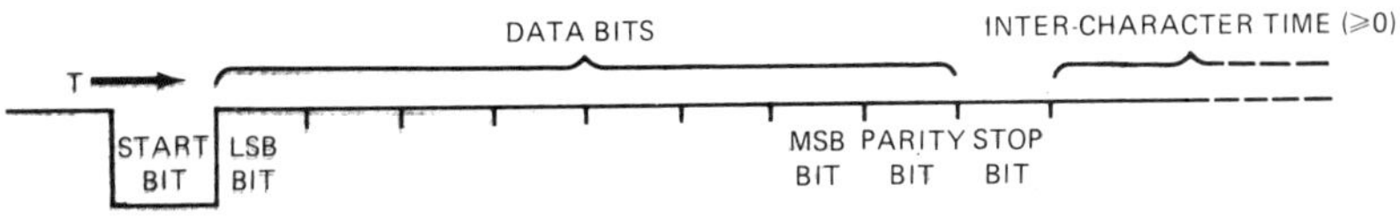

Figure 9.11 Shape of serial ASCII data.

Each character announces its own arrival at the receiving site with a high-to-low transition (or low-to-high, depending on the logic convention of the terminal). This is called the *Start Bit* of the character. After one bit time, the first data bit arrives. After eight data bits are received, the normal intercharacter state (logical low in this example) is held for one or two bit times (again, depending on the conventions of the terminal); these are called the *Stop Bits.* Collectively, Start and Stop Bits are called *Framing Bits.* In asynchronous data transmission the bits themselves are isochronous (that is, nominally all of the same time period). In a terminal with one Stop Bit, one Start Bit, and eight data bits, each bit will endure for one-tenth of the character period. The character period is the reciprocal of the speed of the terminal as measured in characters per second (cps). A 30-cps terminal will receive one character every 33.3 ms; each bit is 3.33 ms long.

The hardware interface without the UART is simplicity itself. The TTL output port is fed directly into the level shifters shown earlier in Figure 9.4. We have arbitrarily chosen to connect the circuitry to the most-significant bit of the output port; any other port could have been chosen as well.

The software to WRITE a character out is, of course, significantly changed. There is no longer a need to wait to see if the buffers in the UART are ready to accept a character because there is no UART. The software that will write out to the serial port is shown in Figure 9.12.

Of course, the analogous process can also be interfaced and programmed for reading data from a terminal. In this case, a half-bit delay is introduced in the software just after detecting the start bit so that subsequent bits are all read near the middle of their time periods for utmost reliability.

Why should you engage in all this software detail at all? Well, in addition to the hardware savings described earlier, this software can be significantly more generalized and easier to modify. If a new character set or speed requirement is levied, only the software has to be changed. Changing the value of the DELAY constant (either at assembly time or during execution of some other program) is

```
DATA    EQU   8030H       ; ESTABLISH THE PORT ADDRESS

WRITE:  PUSH  D           ; FREE-UP (D, E) FOR WORK SPACE
        MOV   D, A        ; SAVE THE CHARACTER WHILE WE
                          ;   ISSUE THE START BIT
        XRA   A           ; SET MSB LOW, ISSUE START BIT
        STA   DATA
        CALL  WAIT        ; WAIT FOR ONE BIT TIME TO PASS
        MOV   A, D        ; RESTORE CHARACTER TO SEND
        STC               ; SET UP A STOPPER BIT TO CAUSE
                          ;   TERMINATION AFTER EIGHT BITS
LOOP:   RAR               ; PUT FIRST BIT TO SEND INTO CARRY
        MOV   D, A        ; SAVE REST OF CHARACTER
        RAR               ; PUT BIT TO SEND INTO MSB POSITION
        STA   DATA        ; EMIT IT OUT TO THE SERIAL PORT
        CALL  WAIT        ; WAIT FOR ONE BIT TIME TO PASS
        MOV   A, D
        CPI   1           ; IS ONLY THING LEFT THE STOPPER BIT?
        JNZ   LOOP        ; NO. GO DO NEXT BIT.
        RAR
        STA   DATA        ; SEND OUT MSB = 1 AS STOP BIT
        CALL  WAIT        ; SEND ONE STOP BIT
        POP   D
        RET
;
; THIS IS THE DELAY SUBROUTINE. THIS DELAY TAKES ADVANTAGE OF AN
;   8080 RUNNING WITH 2 MHZ CLOCK: THE LOOP REQUIRES 28 USEC TO
;   EXECUTE.
DELAY   EQU   118         ; FOR 300 BPS TERMINAL AND 2 MHZ CLOCK
WAIT:   MVI   E, DELAY    ; SET UP DELAY
MORE:   DCR   E           ; (5) COUNT DOWN
        RZ                ; (5) RETURN IF DONE
        XTHL              ; (18) WASTE TIME
        XTHL              ; (18)
        JMP   MORE        ; (10) TRY AGAIN
                          ; (56) CYCLES @ 500 NSEC = 28 USEC
```

Figure 9.12 Software UART for writing out data to a 30 character-per-second terminal that rests high between characters.

easier than changing the timing from a clock countdown chain. If the logical sense of the terminal is inverted, for instance, the software can be easily modified to invert the data before transmission whenever that kind of terminal is connected.

Software can even be written that will automatically determine the speed of the terminal and adjust itself for code, speed, logical sense, and number of Stop Bits. This program is too long and complicated to be shown here, but it depends on requiring the user to send the first character that the software analyzes through high-speed sampling.

In short, so long as the speeds are reasonably low, software offers total generality. That fact can often be harnessed to provide unique and new features or to minimize hardware by more completely loading the microprocessor.

Making the Trade Off

In your own system design you will be faced with many design trade off opportunities. The way you can most easily understand the "best" choice under the circumstances is to first know the circumstances. Make up a project objectives list and outline the points you feel are important. It is not necessary to assign absolute weighting points to each item, but it is essential to place them in an ordered priority. If lowered manufacturing cost is more important than on-time delivery of the prototype, state this in your list. Ideally, you should state each project objective in quantifiable terms (for example, "The design and implementation schedule may slip if substantial savings in manufacturing cost can be shown to result" or "Manufacturing cost reductions may delay the schedule by 5 days for each $10,000 anticipated savings"). Your final list of objectives should contain between ten and twenty items.

With the objective list in hand, examine each interface. If your development costs are to be minimized, what interfaces already exist that would cost little to interface? If manufacturing cost reduction is the goal, what can be done in software that would have little impact on the product's performance? There is a continuum of possible designs ranging from pure hardware and simple software to simple hardware and complex and lengthy software. The choice should be guided by your project goals, not necessarily by how comfortable you may feel with a particular interface point.

10

Programming Software

Programmers very quickly learn to use the computer as a tool to make programming easier. The outgrowth of their early experimentation is a range of software from the simplicity of a program loader to the complexity of an entire operating system. Microprocessors and microcomputers seem to follow the historical trends laid down by earlier maxicomputer and minicomputer generations. Today's software state is primitive, but it is improving. Just what some of the tools are and how they are used will be the subject of this chapter.

Monitors and Operating Systems

The most primitive software level that can be included in a microprocessor offering is a *monitor.* Sometimes called a *debug program,* it is designed to assist you in interacting with your own program. A monitor program coexists in the computer (at a different address, naturally) with your program. Either of these programs (yours or the monitor) may be activated at one time. The monitor always provides a way for you to transfer control from the monitor to your program. It usually provides a way for your program to be modified so that it can return control to the monitor.

Most often the monitor communicates with you, the operator, through a computer terminal or teletypewriter. You type one letter of the alphabet to specify what you want to do (say, **G** to specify that you want to GO to your program from the monitor) and some parameters that specify precise details (such as 1234 to represent the address to which you want to transfer control). Operation of a typical monitor was described in Chapter 3.

When complex peripherals are connected to the microcomputer development system, the manufacturer usually provides an expanded monitor, which is sometimes called an *operating system.* Unlike the despised behemoth operating systems of larger computers, these systems provide a few more features that can ease your work load. The assembler is usually invoked as a monitor command, for example, instead of requiring much manual interaction to get the assembler loaded. Of course, this feature depends on having the assembler in memory or on some peripheral storage medium to which the operating system has recourse.

An effective operating system allows the experienced user to sit at a terminal and edit, assemble, and load a program into storage for execution. The monitor is used to interact with that running program. Some operating systems are better than others (like all products), but since there is usually only one system available from the vendor, your choices will be limited. Once you pick your microprocessor, you are probably committed to that vendor's operating system, whether you like it or not. New vendors, especially the small high-technology firms that support the most popular microprocessors, are adding new systems to their offerings.

The major problem with contemporary operating systems appears to be correctness. Many of these systems are hastily designed and suffer from the lack of attention to detail. You may find that some apparently valid command sequences may cause total corruption of your program in memory. These problems will smooth out in time, but their very existence is evidence of the fact that semiconductor firms will not likely be considered first-rate software houses.

Programming Languages

Learning to work with microprocessors and microcomputers is definitely a process of applying a new vocabulary to old truths. Like hardware design, programming has its tools, its testing strategies, its tricks, and its lore of tried and proven answers. Sometimes it is tempting to ignore these vast mysteries and just plod along putting bits into memory with switches. However, this process is terribly slow and incredibly expensive. Trying to get along in microprocessor applications without an assembler or compiler is like trying to debug new digital hardware without using an oscilloscope: Possible, but painful.

In the earliest computers the programmer had to introduce the program by manually entering the bits one-by-one. Even when paper tape and card readers were added, programmers were still obliged to punch each individual hole to store the program. At best, that tedious and migraine-producing chore was error-prone. When the program was originally conceived, the programmer might write down the steps on paper in an abbreviated form like *octal* or *hexadecimal,* but the form submitted to the computer nearly always had to be binary.

By coding programs directly in the computer's own binary (or octal or hexadecimal) form, the programmer completely avoids the costs of translation. However, when tests fail, the problem of finding the errors becomes incredibly difficult. The binary program in Figure 10.1 was supposed to add two numbers in an

HAND-CODED BINARY		*EQUIVALENT ASSEMBLY CODE*	

01111000
10010001
01111010
	→	MOV A, B
		SUB C
		MOV A, D
			HAND-CODED

INTENDED ASSEMBLY CODE		*CORRECT ASSEMBLED BINARY*	

MOV A, B
ADD C
MOV D, A
	→	01111000
		10000001
		01010111
			ASSEMBLED

Figure 10.1 Hand-coded programs are harder to read and more error-prone.

Intel 8080, but it contains two errors. Can you find them? By way of example, consider the assembly-language version of that same program (still with the errors). The errors should be obvious—a subtract operation instead of an add. The result is destroyed by a load from the destination instead of a load into the destination. The intended program fetches the contents of register 2 into the accumulator, adds the contents of register 3, and then places the result into register 4. The actual program fetches the contents of register 2 okay, but then it *subtracts* the contents of register 3 and then *fetches* the contents of register 4 into the accumulator, thus destroying the result.

When the programmer writes down code, the code is written in a *language.* In programming we use *machine* language, *assembler* languages, and *compiler* languages. When programs are coded in a form acceptable directly into memory, they are said to have been coded in machine language. When the programmer can write down simple sequences of statements as in the example above, we say that an assembler language is being used. When the programmer is allowed to write down statements like the following:

$$X = A + B$$

we say that a compiler language is being used.

Languages and Translators The process of translating a computer program from one language into another is called *compilation* or *assembly,* depending on the language that the programmer is allowed to write. Through the use of some kind of available program, the programmer's original symbolic statements are read into a computer and translated into machine language. The result of the act of translation is always a program (called the *object* program) that is functionally identical to the programmer's specified intent as described in the input (called the *source* program).

The language in which the programmer may write is defined as the acceptable input to the language translator. There are grammatical rules that must be adhered to, and for each valid statement or sentence in the language there is some predictable kind of machine language that results. The source program, then, has a set of rules of *syntax;* if the source program deviates from those rules, then the language translator should pinpoint the spot and notify the programmer of the obvious error. However, many programmer statements are syntactically valid but semantically erroneous or meaningless. When the programmer specifies the subtraction operation instead of addition, that is a *semantic* error; the translation process will blindly produce absolutely correct code for the *subtract* operation. Language translators can't read programmer's minds.

Kinds of Programming Languages There are many different classes of programming languages. The complexity ranges from simple machine-language binary code through sophisticated problem-oriented languages that accept static problem definitions and produce final sequential code sequences. For microcomputer and microprocessor programming there are four practical alternatives:

1. *Machine* languages are forms directly executable by the computer. These are almost always expressed in numeric form, usually in binary, octal, or hexadecimal.
2. *Assembly* languages are human-oriented varieties of machine languages; precisely the same final program code can be produced from an assembler as by handcoding machine language. However, assembly languages are more convenient for people than the numeric-only machine languages.
3. *Compiler* languages (also called high-level languages) are much more people-oriented than assembly languages are. Because they are people-oriented, few details of the particular computer for which the program is intended are evident to the programmer. These languages are easy to read and write, and they provide programs that can be easily moved from computer model to computer model.
4. *Systems implementation* languages are essentially compilers that have assembler-like features. These languages allow the programmer to take advantage of compiler-level languages, but they revert to assembler languages when necessary.

Unless only machine language programming is done, language translators are necessary programs in the software tool kit. The translators for assembly language (called, oddly enough, *assemblers*) are relatively simple programs that make few important decisions about the programs they process. Compiler and systems languages are considerably more complicated.

The best way to discriminate among the three alternatives of translators is to determine which one is responsible for the allocation of resources of the destination computer. The primary resources are:

1. CPU registers
2. Memory locations
3. Time

Because most microcomputers and microprocessors have limited numbers of accumulators, general-purpose and index registers, intelligent planning of their contents during program execution can mean the difference between tight and sloppy programs. Inefficient register allocation can cause the size of a program to be as much as five times as large as necessary. It is also desirable to position the data to be operated on in specific selected memory locations with patterned addresses. It is not uncommon in microprocessor applications to select memory locations to hold data that can have their addresses directly computed from other data. Finally, in real-time applications (as most microprocessor applications are), time is a precious commodity that cannot be squandered. A program can be implemented in an infinite number of different ways; some take more time than others. In order to get best time efficiency, the programmer may have to plan very carefully to take full advantage of his computer.

If the programmer is responsible for all resource allocation, the language is clearly an assembly language. If the programmer is denied the ability to perform any detailed resource allocation, the language is clearly a compiler language. If the programmer has control over whether the translator or the programmer does resource allocation at specific points in the program, the language is a systems implementation language.

Most of the microprocessors on the market today are supported by one or more assemblers. There has also been widespread interest in the Intel PL/M compiler; that translator can produce code for the Intel 8008 and 8080 microprocessors. Other PLM compilers have been introduced for the 6800, National's PACE, and the Signetics 2650. Because the assembler versus compiler choice must be faced repeatedly by people who use micros, it is important to know enough about each to make an intelligent choice.

Use of Binary Code Machine language programming is necessary whenever the costs of translation become prohibitively expensive. That can occur with a very small program or with a larger program to which only a few minor changes need be made. Many times in the course of microprocessor system development special diagnostic programs are needed to demonstrate that the computer works. The easiest way to provide a diagnostic tool is to insert a jump instruction into memory. The jump is inserted at the first location to which control is transferred at power-up, and it contains a jump to that same location. The effect of the one-instruction program is to produce a repetitive set of 'scope patterns that can be used to diagnose the hardware. It is not necessary to use an assembler in this simple case; a glance at the programmer's reference manual for the processor will show clearly how to write down the binary digits of that instruction.

Assembler Features

Programmers of the earliest vacuum tube computers very quickly became dissatisfied with programming in binary. Somebody (nobody remembers who, but it was probably an engineer) decided to write a short computer program that would accept words that stand for instructions and automatically write out the equivalent binary form. These words, called *operation codes,* were short sequences of letters that stood for a brief description of the object instruction they represented. The addition operation, then, instead of being written "10000011" could be written "ADD 3." Since it is easier to remember the word instead of the digits, these are called *mnemonic* (literally, memory-evoking) codes. Throughout this chapter you can safely avoid trying to understand the meanings of these codes; become aware of the general form.

Now, instead of working with groups of binary digits that were difficult to read and understand, it was possible to read the sequence of operations to be performed. However, computers do not live by procedures alone; there must be data to process. These data are referred to by addresses, usually given as numbers. However, it is seldom true that the programmer needs to know the precise address of each and every data in a program. It is enough to know that when some variable (perhaps named "CLOCK") is referred to by its name, the same memory location is always referred to. There, the simple assembler was extended to allow the programmer to introduce his own symbols (see Figure 10.2). Each of these symbols stands for one or more registers or memory locations. The spelling of each symbol is left up to the programmer so that words with mnemonic value can be chosen. It is common to label a small counter "COUNT" and a clock input "CLOCK." It is not considered good practice to name things arbitrarily, like "XLPZ43."

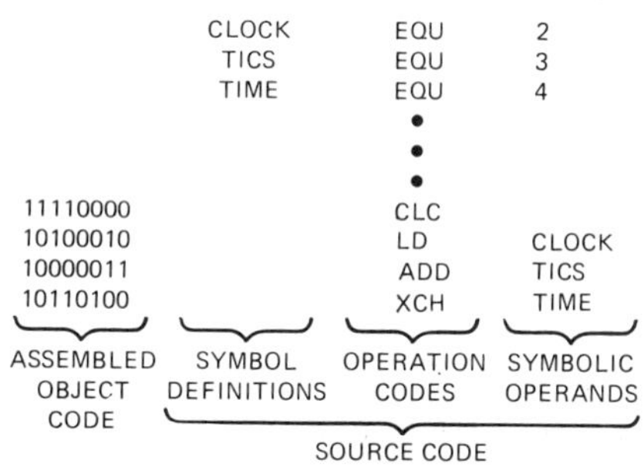

Figure 10.2 From the source code, an assembler automatically produces the object code that is equivalent.

The assembler handles two different kinds of symbols: Mnemonic operation codes are predefined symbols in a static table that stand for the instructions of the machine; symbolic addresses are arbitrary names in a dynamic table established by the user to represent memory locations where data is stored. The mnemonic operation codes are nearly always predefined; if the codes are spelled incorrectly, the assembler is forced to reject them (unless, of course, that spelling is acceptable as a different instruction). The assembly language for operation codes is predefined by the author of the assembler. The symbolic addresses are seldom limited and can spell out any word, subject to a practical limit on the number of letters and digits (usually six). Incidentally, assemblers and compilers aren't censors: Prudes wouldn't dare read some highly successful programs!

Pseudo-ops There are some conveniences offered to the programmer by an assembler that don't represent instructions to be generated in the object program. An example is the declaration of data. Most assemblers have special mnemonic operation codes that cause the generation of data without any corresponding instruction. An example is a special code spelled "ASCII." This mnemonic code doesn't stand for any object machine language instruction. Instead, it instructs the assembler to translate the characters that appear among the operands into binary equivalents according to the popular ASCII code standard. Thus, instead of writing out groups of eight bits for each character (and transcribing them wrong), the user can write the required characters down and expect the assembler to do the job right (Figure 10.3). In this particular example (from the National IMP–16 assembler), the message to be sent out to the teletypewriter is stored as two bytes in each sixteen-bit word. The text is presented to the assembler as an operand of the ".ASCII" special code in National's assemblers. All of these codes start with the period character to distinguish them from instructions of the computer. The fourteen characters of the message (between the special apostrophes) occupy seven words of an IMP–16's memory. Another code word, ".WORD" is used to mark a statement that is to cause a sixteen-bit word containing the value given in the operand; zero in this case. The zero is used to signal the end of the variable-length text string the program is to print on the terminal.

```
          LD      3,MSG          ;REGISTER 3 POINTS TO 'MSG'
LOOP:     LD      0,(3)          ;GET TWO BYTES INTO REG. 0
          BOC     1,QUIT         ;IF ZERO WORD, FINISHED
          •
          •
          •
          JUMP    LOOP
QUIT:     •
          •
          •
MSG:      .ASCII  'ARE YOU READY?'
          .WORD   0              ;MESSAGE STOPPER
```

Figure 10.3 The operation codes .ASCII and .WORD are really just instructions to the assembler and are not executed by the computer.

Operation codes that aren't really operation codes are called *pseudo-operations.* They can be best understood as orders the programmer issues to the assembler. Other pseudo-ops control the address at which program segments or data are generated (ORG or ORIGIN pseudo-ops), numeric data descriptions (DATA pseudo-ops), or data and buffer area arrays (BSS or DS pseudo-ops). Each individual assembler has its own set of unique spellings for these common functions; the programmer should study them carefully to ascertain what power they contain.

Almost all assemblers have these basic features. An experienced systems programmer can produce a simple assembler like this for any computer in just a few working days. More sophisticated assemblers have many other features of value to the programmer; the quality and utility of an assembler are usually inversely proportional to the wealth of pseudo-ops provided. Another important feature that can be added to any language translator is a *micro* ability.

Macro Assemblers A macro assembler allows the designer of a program to introduce a convenient "shorthand" notation to simplify work. A sequence of one or more instructions is given a name; any time the name is written it is automatically replaced with the instructions. The assembler remembers the shorthand definition and expands it out as necessary. Macros are to programmers what MSI chips are to engineers.

Macros can be used to define common sequences of code that are likely to appear frequently in a program, but these kinds of macros are more often replaced by calls to subroutines. The most powerful use of macros is in the definition of input/output control routines. The original author can define the appropriate instruction sequences for controlling the input and output equipment. Then, the macro definition is copied into each program that requires it. When the programmer wants to use the input/output facility, the macro is invoked and it becomes expanded and assembled into machine language code.

Some pseudo-ops are almost always introduced along with macro ability. These are called *conditional assembly pseudo-ops* and they allow the programmer to predefine large sequences of instructions, only some of which are actually assembled into the final program. This means that a single macro can be defined with a wide variety of different options; the unused options don't cause extraneous object machine language code to be produced and this means that more efficient programs can result. Typically, a conditional assembly pseudo-op evaluates some Boolean expression and then causes the succeeding statements to be assembled or skipped, depending on whether the outcome of the evaluation is true or false.

In the example of Figure 10.4 a macro named INDEX is defined in the macro language for Intel's 8080. The macro performs the calculation of an index to an array in storage in the H–L registers. The H–L contents, however, are not destroyed by the indexing process. The second argument specifies whether the B-C or D–E pair is the index register. The third argument calls for (if zero) a one-byte fetch into the A-register or (if nonzero) a two byte fetch into the B–C pair.

Assembler Operation Almost all assemblers operate in basically the same way: There are two different phases and each phase must read the source program (Figure 10.5). In the first pass each operation code and pseudo-op is read and partially assembled—enough to determine what the starting and ending address of each instruction sequence will be. At the same time, each symbol that is used by the programmer is placed into memory along with the corresponding starting address. In the second pass the entire program is read again. Now, however, the symbol definitions are generally ignored; each operation code and pseudo-op is read and completely assembled. The appropriate object program bits are fetched from tables inside the assembler and combined with the values of symbols specified by the programmer. Each symbol (like "COUNT") is looked up in the dy-

```
INDEX       MACRO   BASE, REG, NR
            PUSH    H               ; SAVE (H, L)
            LXI     H,BASE
            DAD     REG             ; ADD IN THE INDEX
            IF      NOT (NR AND 1)

            MOV     A, M            ; LOAD BYTE DATA

            ENDIF
            IF      NR

            MOV     B, M            ; LOAD ADDRESS DATA
            INX     H
            MOV     C, M

            ENDIF
            POP     H               ; RESTORE (H, L)
            ENDM
            •
            •
            •
            INDEX   ARRAY, B, 0     ; LOAD BYTE FROM ARRAY (B)
; MACRO EXPANDS TO THE FOLLOWING EQUIVALENT CODE FOR ASSEMBLY:
            PUSH    H
            LXI     H, ARRAY        ; (NOTE SUBSTITUTION)
            DAD     B               ; ( . . . AND HERE, TOO)
            MOV     A, M
            POP     H
            •
            •
            •
            INDEX   ARRAY, D, 1     ; LOAD AN ADDRESS
; EQUIVALENT CODE GENERATED:
            PUSH    H
            LXI     H, ARRAY
            DAD     D
            MOV     B, M
            INX     H
            MOV     C, M
            POP     H
```

Figure 10.4 Definition and two different invocations of a typical macro for the 8080.

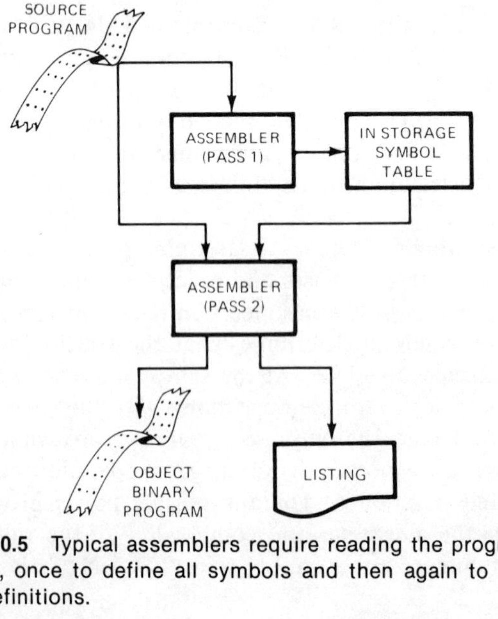

Figure 10.5 Typical assemblers require reading the program in twice, once to define all symbols and then again to use those definitions.

namic symbol table to determine its numeric value; this value is assembled into the object code. If the named symbol cannot be found in the dynamic table, the assembler reports an error to the programmer. While this assembly is being accomplished, the source and object programs are printed out and the final object code is written out onto some storage medium (like paper tape) so that it can be loaded into the microcomputer's memory at a later time.

Because each symbol introduced by the programmer requires space in the memory area, limited memory space in the translating computer limits the number of symbols the programmer may introduce. This is especially important with the development systems that are microcomputer based. If a symbol can be made up of as many as six characters and an address occupies two bytes, then each symbol introduced by the programmer will require another eight bytes of RAM during the assembly process (it will *not* require that additional space during program execution, only during translation). If the assembler reports a diagnostic message like "SYMBOL TABLE FULL," it will be necessary to change some of the symbols into constants. Another way out is to buy more memory for the symbol table to occupy.

When a macro assembler is used, there is an extra input process in the first pass that expands all of the macro invocations into assembly language. The macro expansion is incorporated into the first pass of the assembler, but the user can conceive of macro expansion as a separate and distinct "front-end" process. During the first pass of a macro assembler the source program is read in and each time a new macro is defined its list of instructions is read into memory and stored. The macro's name is added to the operation code table inside the assembler. Each statement read in that is *not* a macro definition is looked up in the operation code table; if the operation code is the name of a macro, macro expansion takes place. Otherwise, the source code is simply copied over. The output of the entire macro expansion process is a program in assembly language that can be handled by a conventional two-pass assembler.

To expand a macro into assembly language, the macro processor software goes to the place in memory where the macro's definition was stored. The characters there are copied out one by one until the macro prototype has been exhausted. Then, the normal external input medium is used for the next input sequence.

The use of macros causes more assembler-environment memory bytes to be used up. The macro "model" must be stored in memory, one character per byte. Since the space used is often within the symbol table area, that macro use may further limit the number of symbols that can be defined. Even worse, macro expansions may involve the use of more symbols to allow references within the expanded code; these symbols that are local to the macro still occupy memory space. Macros are generally used sparingly on microcomputers. If a larger computer is used for translation (like a minicomputer), then macros can be a significant programming aid.

There are special assemblers that are especially attractive for debugging use. These fast translators are called *one-pass assemblers.* By reading in the source program only once and generating the final object code directly into memory, these assemblers can act just like very sophisticated program loaders. "Forward references" cause problems to one-pass assemblers. A *forward reference* is the use of a symbolic name that has not yet been defined (i.e., it appears later in the program). This most frequently occurs because of a jump to a place a few more lines down in the program. Since the destination symbol's value has not yet been determined, it is impossible to immediately generate final object code for this instruction. Instead, the needed address is left at zero and the undefined symbol is added to the symbol table; instead of a value, however, the symbol table holds the address of the location in memory where this symbol's value is needed. When the symbol is finally defined by appearing in the input stream, that old reference is "fixed up" by the assembler and the new value is placed into the table for all future references.

A one-pass assembler may be of the "load-and-go" or deferred execution type. A load-and-go assembler produces the object code directly in the memory of the computer; after the assembly is finished, the program is ready to be executed. In a deferred execution one-pass assembler, the object code is written out to a storage medium for later reloading into the computer's memory. Because some of the "fix-up" code may be generated out of sequence, it is necessary to be able to load the entire program into memory at one time, and the loader must be able to deal with noncontiguous memory locations.

A load-and-go assembler is fast, but the programs that can be assembled must be limited in size because the assembler and the final object program must be able to coexist in the same memory during the assembly process. When an external storage medium is used, program sizes are limited only by the requirement that the entire program must be able to fit into the target computer's memory at one time. Since reloading takes place after the assembly has been completed, the assembler's space can be occupied by the final program. A reasonable one-pass assembler will let the user select which kind of output is to be produced.

Assembler Environments Assemblers can operate on the computer for which they produce object machine code, or the assembler may exist on a different computer. A *native* assembler operates on and generates code for the particular microcomputer. A *cross-assembler* is a program that operates on a (generally larger and) different computer to produce code for the desired machine.

Native assemblers are nearly always simple and are written in their own language. Some of these assemblers have macro capabilities while others do not. Almost all of them are designed to operate in very small configurations of a computer; typical requirements are 4,000 bytes of read-write memory and a teletypewriter with paper tape for input-output. Because of the small sizes and limited input-output capability, these assemblers almost always require considerable manual intervention to read in the source program as many times as required.

A native assembler can be either *resident* or *nonresident.* A resident assembler is one that exists in read-only memory and does not have to be loaded into the microcomputer each time it is required. In microcomputers with small storage capabilities the resident assembler may exist alternately with other storage facilities; the flick of a switch brings up the assembler. Few microprocessor applications require above about 10,000 bytes of storage capacity; therefore, a resident assembler that occupies 4,000 out of 65,000 bytes of addressable space impacts the development environment insignificantly. A nonresident assembler generally exists on paper tape, magnetic tape (or cassette), or disc. When required it is read into memory. Only the most expensive configurations have more than slow paper tape or cassette. In simple systems, hours of tape-reading time may be saved by putting the assembler in a reserved area of memory and leaving it there in ROM.

Cross-assemblers operate on minicomputers or large-scale computers, or they can be accessed through popular time-sharing systems. Because these assemblers are designed to be portable so that they can be used with a variety of different host computers, they are most often written in FORTRAN. FORTRAN, of course, is a compiler language. When the assemblers are written in FORTRAN, advertising and promotional releases often refer to FORTRAN assembler, and this may lead the unsuspecting engineer to believe that a *compiler* for FORTRAN is being offered. The subtle wording should be noted: A FORTRAN assembler is an assembler written in the FORTRAN language; A FORTRAN compiler is a translator for the FORTAN language; it may or may not be written in FORTRAN.

Highly portable assemblers are generally very inefficient on a particular computer; in order to gain portability some efficiency has to be sacrificed. Often, a proficient FORTRAN programmer can improve the assembler's efficiency in only a couple of days.

Running the assembler on a minicomputer often requires the use of a teletypewriter, just like with a micro. However, if the minicomputer is large enough to compile and execute FORTRAN programs, it probably has a significantly larger main memory and perhaps some other peripheral devices that can speed the process of assembly.

When a large- or medium-scale computer is used for programming support, additional peripheral equipment may be required. Since most of these computers don't have the kinds of inexpensive peripherals (like paper tape) that microcomputers use, you may have to invest in a magnetic tape drive or punched card reader in order to communicate object programs from the assembling computer to the target computer.

Time-sharing systems are accessed via teletypewriter terminals connected through telephone lines to central large-scale computers. The same terminal used with the time-sharing system is used with the microcomputer so that a common medium is assured. The time-sharing environment offers the user more potential services than minicomputers. They usually have highly sophisticated text editors, for example, that permit rapid modification of stored and preserved programs.

Comparing the various alternatives available to the engineer/programmer is not simple. However, some measure of relative costs might be useful to newcomers to the software world. There are a few basic factors the user should be concerned with:

1. *Turnaround Time.* How long it will take to assemble a program, exclusive of the time it takes to print out the programmer's updated listing
2. *Printing Time.* How long it will take to print out the programmer's listing, regardless of turnaround time (these are not always separable, but they are assumed to be for the purposes of this illustration)
3. *Edit Time.* How long it will take to read through the source program, make a minor change, and save the modified program in a form suitable for the assembler.

These four different environments can be compared as shown in Table 10.1. The microcomputer and minicomputer options assume that the equipment is leased (or purchased and amortized over 12 months). For all these examples we assume an average of one assembly each working day; that is typical for a medium-sized microcomputer program. The *monthly cost* is the fixed part of the cost; it includes basic equipment and terminal expenses. The *cost per assembly* is the variable cost factor.

Table 10.1 A comparison of some alternative edit-and-assemble environments.

	MICROCOMPUTER	MINICOMPUTER	BATCH	TIME-SHARING
TURNAROUND TIME (MINS)	45	10	90	3
PRINTING TIME (MINS)	30	30	–	30
EDITING TIME (MINS)	20	10	–	5
MONTHLY COST (FIXED)	\$475	\$900	\$150	\$400
COST PER TRANSLATION	–	–	\$15	\$32
TOTAL MONTHLY COST	\$475	\$900	\$450	\$1040
AVERAGE TRANSLATION COST	\$24	\$45	\$23	\$52

The microcomputer is roughly comparable to the batch computer alternative. Given the disadvantages of turnaround time and the media incompatibilities, the microcomputer is probably a wise investment. Note that if the number of projects increases so that the microcomputer is used more than once per day for assemblies, the costs will drop dramatically for each of those assemblies. Similarly, the minicomputer and time-sharing alternatives are closely matched in price. If the minicomputer has a good text editor (and, perhaps, a disc storage unit for programs), then it is very comparable to time-sharing systems. Again, if usage exceeds an average of one assembly per day, the minicomputer will turn out to be more economical than the time-sharing service. The casual programmer of microprocessor should investigate the time-sharing services that offer microprocessor support software.

Compiler Features

Compilers for microprocessors and microcomputers are rare and new. The most significant language being considered by users today is Intel's PL/M language. There is some industry talk of FORTRAN being implemented, and some limited versions of the BASIC language have been implemented on micros. However, since the vast majority of programs written for micros are created by engineers who have little programming experience, the virtues of these popular languages may remain concealed for some time to come. A new language for microcomputers, FORTH, has been announced for the 8080 and RCA's COSMAC.

The major advantage of higher-level languages is the ability to express complex programs in simple statements instead of having to resort to arcane assemble language. It will almost always be easier to understand a PL/M program than its assembly-language counterpart, particularly if the PL/M is written with the reader in mind. Since the language in which the program is written (see the example of Figure 10.6) is closer to the original language in which the problem was stated, there are fewer chances for transcription and coding errors, and it is almost always easier to detect errors in the program when they do exist.

```
/*      PRINT OUT THE "N" BYTES AT "LOC" */
PRINT:          PROCEDURE (N, LOC);
                    DECLARE N   BYTE,
                            LOC ADDRESS;

                    DECLARE PTR ADDRESS,
                            I   BYTE,
                            WORD BASED PTR BYTE;

                    PTR  =  LOC;
                    DOI  =  1 TO N
                            OUTPUT (2) = WORD;
                            PTR = PTR + 1;
                    END;
                END PRINT;
```

Figure 10.6 A very small PL/M example.

Compiler Operation There are few compilers that can be executed on microcomputers. Since all PL/M compilers to date have been written in FORTAN a larger computer is required to compile and execute the PL/M compiler itself. This means that some additional support services will be required to use PLM. The FORTH system has been designed to compile and execute in its native environment, and BASIC has been implemented on several micros.

A compiler can operate in two passes just the way an assembler does. In the first pass the source language statements are converted into an internal and coded form and all of the symbols defined by the programmer are installed in symbol tables. Since the compiler is responsible for more resource allocation than an assembler, much more information is retained about each symbol than just the address.

In the scond pass the symbol table and the intermediate program are read in together and the necessary code is generated. The object code produced can be efficient or inefficient, depending on the cleverness of the compiler writer. The more clever the compiler, the more complicated and expensive it will be. Typical commercial compilers produce programs that are about 15% larger than good assembly language equivalents; similarly, the speed of a compiler-produced program may be somewhat slower than a good assembly-language version of the same functional program.

Evaluation

There are two major language options available to the microcomputer designer: Assemblers make machine-oriented programming easier and compilers make application-dependent programming easier. Although assembly language permits the programmer to control the discrete execution of individual instructions more carefully, it also forces you to repeatedly program little tasks like calculating addresses and returning accumulator results to proper storage locations. A compiler can relieve most of this tedium, but it forces you to relinquish nearly all control over resource allocation.

Proponents of compilers extravagantly claim (sometimes) that their translators can produce better code than an individual programmer: That is bunk. There is no computer program that can outdo a proficient and dedicated programmer. The compiler can only be as clever as was its original author; the human programmer may take advantage of conditions in the environment or data to produce a significantly better program, but the programmer will take a longer time and spend more money. In general, compilers are about as good as a low-level novice programmer at quality code production. So long as that performance level is satisfactory (for example, when producing only a few copies of the program), you should be satisfied. If, however, you must fit as much as possible into a small program space, you can *always* find a way to beat a compiler by using an assembler.

No matter what programming language you choose, you will inevitably be dissatisfied in some respects. Programming in PL/M or other languages will certainly save some programming time and get your project running sooner, but the resulting design is bound to be both slower and larger than strictly necessary. Up to production volumes of about 100 units (total) these penalties are probably negligible, but above about 250 manufactured units these penalties can represent substantial dollar amounts that could have been better spent in handwriting the code in the first place.

11

Project Control

Now that you have completed the first ten chapters, you are ready to embark on your own design. Before you do so, however, it might be worthwhile to take one last look at the entire project process to see what you are in for. Implementing systems with microprocessors isn't difficult, only different. It will take some getting used to, especially the software part.

First, pick a small job. Ideally, the first job you tackle will be much like the design you just completed. If you are attacking a new application and a new technology simultaneously, you can expect to compound your problems.

Second, carefully study and understand *all* the manufacturer's literature on your selected micro. If possible, get some sample designs and make sure that you understand them before you begin.

Third, invest in good tools. The microcomputer development systems are important; you should look into the new logic state analyzers and other special microprocessor test gear now being introduced. Working without adequate test equipment is bound to get you into trouble.

Fourth, plan your work carefully. Many engineers like to plan projects by using a critical path chart, like the one shown in Figure 11.1. This sample chart for a typical small job shows what has to be done and in what order it has to be done. You will notice that there are four major pathways through the chart, for example:

1. Hardware, CPU, memory, etc.
2. I/O interface circuitry
3. Software
4. Testing

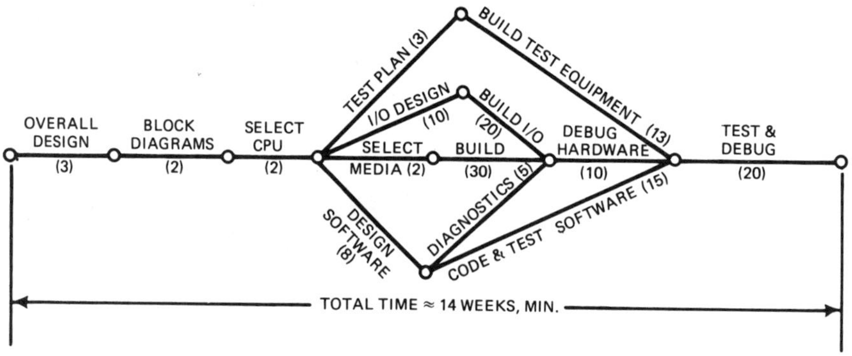

NOTE: (n) = WORKING DAYS TO COMPLETE INDICATED TASK

Figure 11.1 Plan of attack for a small project.

This example assumes that the task is small enough to be accomplished by one engineer. We estimate that it will require about 14 elapsed weeks. Shorter times have been heard of but only from experts who have had lots of experience and who have had everything available at their fingertips.

Team Organizations

When a project is large enough to warrant a team of experts, you will have to be especially careful to avoid friction. There seems to be an almost natural competitive spirit between hardware and software designers. Without cooperation at the outset, these two forces can only be set on a collision course.

The hardware designer must, at the outset, be prepared to value the software expert's opinions about required features and desirable attributes of the computer. Similarly, the software designer must be prepared to have some items in the "wish list" denied because of excessive cost or infeasibility. When battles break out over these kinds of questions, the project will suffer. There will be enough natural finger pointing near the end of the project as emotions run high. It is not necessary, however, to have this tension throughout the life of the project.

Start early by making the key designers co-equals in the project. These (preferably two) people will be responsible for the architecture of the system. If possible, place them in the same office and away from the rest of the team. This provides less opportunity for each side to cower and prepare defensive positions.

In this project plan we have established the need to understand what the system is supposed to do before programming or hardware design begins. Notice that the system is designed *before* the processor is selected, not after. The pacing item in this small project is the time spent awaiting parts ordered; we assume in this small example that the engineer has opted for premanufactured cards. While we're waiting for the cards we can design and fabricate the necessary application-dependent input/output hardware and establish a test plan. While the technician is fabricating the hardware the engineer can be writing the programs.

When the computer and memory boards arrive, a two-stage testing phase can be entered. In the first stage some small helpful diagnostic programs are loaded into the computer so that the new special input-output hardware can be debugged. Once the entire configuration is working, the actual applications software is put in and combined with the special test equipment so that the whole system can be tested.

Special Test Equipment

If you wait until all the software is written before trying to debug it, critical scheduling situations develop. The software that is written last often depends on the accuracy and performance of software written earlier. If that earlier software hasn't been tested and measured, the later software may be depending on characteristics that don't exist. Suppose, for example, that a primitive function is designed to work in 100 μs and other parts of the software depend on that timing. You may discover that after that function is debugged it takes one ms: It happens very frequently. Now, if we know about it soon enough, we can compensate for it in the rest of the design. But if we don't discover that change in the performance early on, we will write all of the rest of the software wrong. This can only be wasted effort, doomed to be torn down and replaced at significant additional cost in both schedule and money.

A software development system (SDS) is a breadboard that gives the software team the tools it needs. If the project is small, the hardware and software design may be handled by the same individual. In that case, the SDS may be nothing more than the prototype itself augmented with some additional hardware and software to make debugging easier. If the project is large enough to warrant separate people for the hardware and software tasks, a separate SDS built out of available components is absolutely required for orderly project completion.

In a medium-scale project you should plan to implement the SDS on a prototyping system. The special input/output facilities necessary for the application are constructed and connected (perhaps through special interface logic because the bus structure differs from the prototyping system). The external devices that are to be connected to the microcomputer are simulated or duplicated and connected to the SDS. With this additional hardware, and the software and hardware tools inherently provided by the prototyping system, the application program can be developed and checked out.

In a small-scale project it isn't generally acceptable to have two different systems being built at once. In these cases, the prototype will also be the SDS. This can be done, but some removable hardware and software must be designed into the prototype so that the system can be debugged. Certainly, if the application involves the use of ROM, there ought to be an external circuit board that uses RAM but plugs into the prototype. Then the programs can be read into the computer and executed without having to "burn" ROM's each time a change is required. Even if the application doesn't have a requirement for a teletypewriter, the prototype must have some provisions for interfacing one (perhaps on a removable printed circuit card). Similarly, the finished product will probably not need a programmer's panel that allows the CPU to be stopped and displays bus contents and the status of the system. However, these facilities need to be designed into the original prototype. Lack of these capabilities means needless weeks spent in trying to debug without the essential tools. Would you debug new hardware without test equipment? Remember, these lamps and switches and the teletypewriter are the software equivalents of hardware test points and they are just as essential.

Hardware Design

When you set out to design and implement your own microcomputer, there are logical steps to follow. The step that is almost always taken first—because it is the most exciting—is the design of the CPU module. This is logical because the CPU can then be used to check out other hardware subsystems.

The design of the CPU usually starts with the clock. A good place to look for hints is in the semiconductor manufacturer's own application notes or schematics of boards he sells. However, some of these clock circuits are designed for bench "diddling," not production line assembly. Some of them even violate the manufacturer's own specs! Note the characteristics that the specs call for and design the clock to operate for those. Be sure to check it under a dynamic load.

Once the clock is in operation, the CPU itself can be fired up. You may have to implement some outboard logic to buffer things; again, you might start with the vendor's literature, but use it as a guide, not a cookbook.

If the product is made up of more than a few integrated circuits and you expect to have a moderate size program, you will have to design and implement some kind of manual operator's panel. The packaging of the system will determine what shape your panel takes on. If your system is being made up of individual modular cards, the panel ought to be an independent card. If the entire application is to be built on a small set of densely packed cards, then leave some socket space on those cards that an external, cable-connected panel can plug into.

The operator's panel should display the contents of address and data buses; if available, the other important signals at the CPU chip's edge should also be brought up to LED's. Some switches to control stop, go, and single-step ought to be provided; single-step operation means that the CPU executes exactly one instruction each time the single-step switch is pressed. The panel should also provide some way of specifying an instruction from the panel itself, preferably from switches, and depositing that instruction into memory.

The operator's panel is used only during hardware and software debugging. However, in the latter stages of testing it will prove invaluable. The lack of an operator's panel on even a small project will cost you at least one man-month in unnecessary wheel-spinning; it takes only a day or two to build.

Diagnostic Software

The first diagnostic program that you write should probably be one to write all ones or all zeros to memory and then compare to ensure operation. Of course, you don't want to write to that part of memory that holds the program itself. Write one diagnostic program that resides in the bytes lowest in memory and checks all the rest of the bytes. Next, write a diagnostic program that resides in a verified part of memory and checks the part previously occupied by the first program.

When you design and implement the RAM and ROM parts of the microcomputer, be sure to leave plenty of room for expansion. If you design for a fixed number of ROM's, for example, you may find that the software becomes larger than you can accommodate. That might happen through poor program size estimating or if expanded services are demanded by the customer. It is almost a certainty that after the first production is underway, somebody will want to add a new feature for a new product. This, of course, will require more storage capacity.

The first input/output facility on your budding microcomputer ought to be a simple UART-based interface to a terminal. Many of the microprocessors now being marketed have or will have UART-like chips in the family. Once you have a terminal interfaced, pirate the ROM-based monitor that your manufacturer provides in his prototyping system and plug it into your own microcomputer. Now you can easily insert programs into RAM from the terminal and debug those programs with on-line tools.

With the combination of CPU and operator's panel, RAM, ROM (with the monitor installed), and a UART-based interface to a terminal, you have a complete and useful microcomputer system. You can now actively engage in software development and hardware input/out device expansion. The software monitor installed in ROM is the real key to the operation of this system.

One of the easiest ways to check out hardware is to use the microprocessor as a testing aid. You write special programs that are developed solely to set up known operating conditions; some of these programs can actually diagnose some faults and report them automatically.

Programs to test RAM are well-known. There have been dozens of schemes published, although most of them are devoted to testing semiconductor chips themselves. We are not generally interested in pattern sensitivity and other sophisticated tests; these are used in the characterization of the semiconductor RAM's. By writing (and then reading) all ones, all zeros, and checkerboards (alternating zeros and ones) we can usually determine whether the memory is working or not.

Diagnostic programs are most useful when testing new input/output equipment. For input ports, the diagnostics expect some present external conditions; the data present at a port is compared with stored patterns or is printed out on the terminal for inspection. If the incoming data rate is rapid and uncontrolled, a diagnostic can be designed to "dump" the input data into RAM so that the terminal can be used to print out selected portions. Output devices are stimulated into action by programs that use known patterns of data or input from a teletypewriter to control the port. Some observable phenomena must be watched for to ensure output port operation. You should get used to writing these little diagnostic programs at the drop of a hat. Without software, the hardware is lifeless.

Once the diagnostic routines are operating and the hardware has been tested, all of the diagnostics ought to be combined together and put where they will be reachable from the debugging monitor. One entry point into the diagnostic package should cause it to run through all of the nondestructive tests (for example, read from RAM several times to ensure repetitiveness, but don't write into RAM). Other entry points should allow testing of specific input/output ports and equipment. This on-line diagnostic tool will be invaluable in deciding whether the hardware or software is at fault in certain instances. If an input/output port is suspected of faulted operation, the diagnostic program can be invoked to check it out before continuing. The overall system test can be run daily before any debugging begins to ensure that the system is still there.

Any diagnostic routine must be able to run in a loop with a fairly short execution time. The loop mode allows an oscilloscope or digital analyzer to be used to detect anamolies in operation.

The existence and use of these diagnostic programs makes a significant but perhaps unobvious contribution to the design project schedule: They serve as a check, fairly early in the proceedings, that the characteristics of each interface are understood by both the hardware and software builders. This gets some common misunderstandings or oversights out of the way long before integration of the total system.

Software Design

Meanwhile, software is being designed. In a small project the hardware and software are designed together by the same system architect. In larger projects the hardware and software designers are different people who must work together easily. In either event, software must be *designed.*

It is amazing to see that engineers who wouldn't think of starting a project by rushing to the bench are the same people who try to begin the software task by writing down assembly-language instructions. That isn't design; it is disaster.

Most applications are characterized by an inexact problem definition. Although the major features of the desired product may be well-known, handling of error cases and special phenomena has not usually been well though out. Software doesn't know the difference between normal cases and special cases; all of

Using Programmers

In general, computer programmers are spectacularly unsuccessful at programming microprocessors. That is not to indict all programmers—merely most. The vast majority of people who are called programmers don't understand electronics, computer architecture, input/output programming, or small computers. There are many excellent programmers who do superb jobs in their fields, but they will not be of use in applying a microprocessor.

Ideally, engineers should be able to design both the hardware and software for microprocessor applications. However, that is not always practical. So, if a programmer is inevitable (or forced upon you by management fiat), choose carefully. Be sure that when you discuss the internal functioning of a component like a UART or a decoder the programmer understands what these parts do. Experience with a minicomputer (the smaller the better) is a good sign. A programmer who has vast experience solely in COBOL or FORTRAN or PL/I or exclusively in data processing on large computers will be worse than useless—he will be a definite hindrance in most cases.

On the other hand, don't shy away from the programming people. If you find someone who can take an interest in your project, you may find some valuable experience to tap. It is becoming a popular practice for programmers to read one another's code; have a qualified programmer read yours and critique it. You may be reinventing the software wheel and a qualified software expert can help show you easier and better ways to do the same job.

them have to be programmed and all of them have to be handled correctly. It is imperative that all of the requirements of the job be understood at the outset.

Suffice it to say that software development is just as difficult as hardware development. It is not easier and it is not more difficult. By understanding and following the same basic rules you apply to hardware in the design and implementation of software, you won't go wrong. Paper designs are inexpensive and easy to change. As with hardware, there is an almost infinite variety of ways to design software; choosing the right one is usually an exercise in economics.

How long software takes to write is virtually anybody's guess. There are measures of programmer productivity likes bytes per day, but these are all misleading. It is a lot easier to write a 6,000-byte program to do a particular job than to write a program for the same job in less than 2,000 bytes. There is continuing effort among computer scientists to identify and quantify the important variables in software production costs, but there has been little progress. We can categorically state that programming costs correlate well with the inherent job complexity, the number of people involved in the project, the inexperience of the programmers, and the instability of new and developing hardware. In today's microprocessor applications we tend to be constructing systems of moderate complexity with few people, but the programmers are inexperienced (or totally devoid of experience) and the hardware is in a state of flux during software development. It is not uncommon to spend several man-months in developing a moderately complex microprocessor program, especially if the entire microcomputer is being designed from the chips up.

If you total up the costs of programming man-power and computer time and the costs associated with a software development system, you can estimate that the software will cost about as much as the hardware, and perhaps a little more. If the project includes the design and fabrication of a unique microcomputer, the software costs will about equal the hardware development costs. If the project is developed on a stock microcomputer bought from a vendor, software costs will far exceed the hardware costs. For rough estimating, you can use a cost of about $5 per byte of code. However, remember that the actual costs may range from $1 to $20, depending on complexity, skill, and other important factors.

Test Plans

Before the design is too firm, it is a good idea to establish some plan of attack on the problem of verifying operation of the eventual system. Sometimes the designers get too close to the design and lose sight of the original intent of the product so that the test plan suffers. Furthermore, as the project progresses and the deadline looms near there is pressure to shortcut the testing procedures. If they are written down that is more difficult to do.

Computer-based products are inherently more complex and more difficult to test than common digital logic systems. Because nearly everything is sequential, all of the combinations of inputs are multiplied by the time scale; the potential number of discrete things to test becomes astronomical. Software people have a bad reputation for inadequate testing, and the effect of this bad reputation has been felt by many people. However, because of the nature of most programs' environments, once the problem is detected, it can be easily corrected by changing the program. With microprocessors this is no longer true. If a subtle program bug with catastrophic effects is discovered after several thousand models are delivered with mask-programmed ROM's, the cost of correcting the bug becomes astronomical. Thorough testing of the system after it is "working" is the best insurance available.

A good test plan calls for initial software testing and debugging to be performed with the program stored in RAM. Later, as some parts of the software become trustworthy they are graduated into PROM. Finally, the whole program is placed into PROM for initial field trials. After this phase has been passed the program can be released for production use of mask-programmed ROM's.

The test plan must be designed from two different viewpoints: the end user's and the designer's. The first tests should be planned before the product is completely designed; these tests are related to the normal and abnormal things that might happen in the field. Both usual and unusual input combinations should be tried. Remember: A debugged program is one for which the inputs that will make it fail have not yet been supplied. Try to use test circumstances that will make the program fail. This is the crux of the testing issue: The programmer and engineer trying to debug an imperfect system try to develop test cases that will make the system *work*. A test plan must aim at making the system fail.

The second part of the test plan should concern itself with testing the design as it was finalized. The weakest points in the design should be probed so that the boundary conditions of performance are well understood. A classic example of the difference between user-oriented and design-oriented tests is in data rates. The application is probably designed for some nominal incoming data rate. In the user-oriented tests, extremely fast data rates should be tried to determine the effects on the hardware and software. If the design data rate can be exceeded only slightly before the system goes wild, then the design is not very robust; this is the time to correct it, not after several more months of experience.

System Integration

There comes a time in every microprocessor project when the hardware and software converge on the critical path of the schedule and they have to work together. Here is where most projects appear to fail; actually, the failures have occurred earlier but they weren't noticed. If each of the hardware and software components has been subjected to some kind of unit test and passed, then the only remaining errors should be misinterpreted interfaces. If adequate unit tests have been conducted, system integration will be painless, perhaps marred by one or two minor problems that might take a day or two to iron out. If the hardware designer is depending on correct software to test against and the software designer has been waiting for debugged hardware, then integration can take months. It is a good idea to leave plenty of slack in this part of the schedule because the exact nature of the potential problems is impossible to predict. But this slack shouldn't be considered a cushion to be absorbed by slippage in earlier critical path items. If all the time isn't needed, more elaborate tests can be devised to ensure a more reliable end-product.

Index